God and Man According to Tolstoy

GOD AND MAN ACCORDING TO TOLSTOY

Alexander Boot

GOD AND MAN ACCORDING TO TOLSTOY
Copyright © Alexander Boot, 2009.

First published in 2009 by PALGRAVE MACMILLAN® in the
United States - a division of St. Martin's Press LLC, 175 Fifth Avenue,
New York, NY 10010.

Where this book is distributed in the UK, Europe and the rest of
the world, this is by Palgrave Macmillan, a division of Macmillan
Publishers Limited, registered in England, company number 785998,
of Houndmills, Basingstoke, Hampshire RG21 6XS.

Palgrave Macmillan is the global academic imprint of the above
companies and has companies and representatives throughout the world.

Palgrave® and Macmillan® are registered trademarks in the United
States, the United Kingdom, Europe and other countries.

ISBN-13: 978–0–230–61586–1
ISBN-10: 0–230–61586–4

Library of Congress Cataloging-in-Publication Data is available from the
Library of Congress.

A catalogue record of the book is available from the British Library.

Design by Integra Software Services

First edition: June 2009

10 9 8 7 6 5 4 3 2 1

Printed in the United States of America

For Naum Grubert, who unwittingly inspired this book.

For false Christs and false prophets shall rise, and shall shew signs and wonders, to seduce, if it were possible, even the elect.

(Mark 14:22)

Contents

CHAPTER 1

INTRODUCTION

Not so long ago I reread Malcolm Muggeridge's book *Jesus Rediscovered*. This is a moving account of one man's search for something he once had but has since lost: faith. Faith not in an abstract deity, not in the force behind nature, not in a metaphysical or philosophical concept, not in the Good, not even in the Creator—at least not just any of those. It was faith in Jesus Christ, fully a man but also fully God.

The book rang true, partly because the writer had built a capital of trust with me. For Muggeridge, then a young reporter for the *Manchester Guardian*, was one of many Western writers who visited Stalin's Russia during the murderous famine organized by the bolsheviks in the early 1930s. He also was one of the few to tell the truth about it. Western coverage of that mass murder was at the time dominated by the likes of the Webbs, G.B. Shaw, Walter Duranty, and Romain Rolland, who either denied the famine or saw nothing wrong with it. Muggeridge went to the Ukraine without authorization, saw the piled corpses and wrote a three-part report, a watered-down version of which was published without attribution. As that kind of writing ran against the grain of both the paper's policy and its genetic code, Muggeridge was soon fired and had to take his chances writing novels.

The way one responds to a personal message largely depends on how one feels about the person. So, reading *Jesus Rediscovered*, I was predisposed to believe every word. And by and large I did—until the writer began to list his spiritual influences. First among those was Tolstoy, whom Muggeridge believed to be not only one of the greatest writers of all time, but also one of the greatest Christians of all time.

I had no quibble with the first part of the accolade, but the second jarred instantly. There must be some mistake, I thought. Having read most of Tolstoy, and much about him, I knew he was not one of the greatest Christians of all time. He was not a Christian at all. To say otherwise could only mean to me that a perceptive man who was not taken in by Stalin was taken in by Tolstoy. Or else Muggeridge's definition of Christianity was different from mine.

To be kind to Muggeridge, I do not think he studied Tolstoy's non-fiction in great detail (*A Confession* is the only source he quotes). Few have—more than half of the 90 volumes Tolstoy left behind are works of theology, philosophy, journalism and polemic, most of them recondite and barely readable. To be even kinder to Muggeridge, he is in good company. For many specialists who have studied Tolstoy's non-fiction in great detail also have been taken in. It is thanks to them that Tolstoy still sports the halo of a kindly, omniscient secular saint who showed us all, to use the title of his posthumous book, *The Way of Life*.

The artist of genius speaks in such a thunderous voice that many otherwise alert people have been rendered deaf to the false notes Tolstoy strikes all over his non-artistic work. For example, Marcel Proust described Tolstoy as a "serene God" although he manifestly was neither. Bernard Shaw, Virginia Woolf and other Fabians regarded Tolstoy as a prophet, although it is hard to see what it was exactly that he prophesied. Albert Camus got his idea of an ethic wholly based on reason from Tolstoy, and had his portrait hanging above his desk, as did Sartre. Wittgenstein was hugely influenced by Tolstoy, especially by *The Gospel In Brief* and *A Confession*. And both Mahatma Gandhi and Martin Luther King cited Tolstoy as their inspiration.

That is not to say there have been no critics. There have been, some quite scathing. Collectively, every contemporaneous Russian philosopher[1] of note tore apart every thought Tolstoy ever uttered. But the weight of his authority was such that, having mocked his pet ideas, and shown the paucity of his thinking, most of them had to add a laudatory afterthought, along the lines of I.S. Turgenev's comment made on *A Confession* in a letter: "It is built on wrong premises—and in the end leads to the most macabre negation of any normal human life . . . This too is a kind of nihilism . . . And still Tolstoy is hardly not the most remarkable man in Russia!" The philosophers too, having brushed Tolstoy's ideas aside, had to add an incongruous afterthought "but of course Tolstoy was a great thinker nonetheless." (Soloviov, Leontiev, and Merezhkovsky are exceptions. Though admirers of Tolstoy's art, they did not rate his mind. Thus Merezhkovsky in *Tolstoy and Dostoyevsky*: "He is insufficiently intelligent for his genius, or else too much of a genius for his intelligence.")

I beg to differ. If one defines a great thinker as someone who uses a systematic process to come up with great thoughts, then Tolstoy was not a great thinker. He was not even an average one. His philosophy was equally weak on first principles and last things; his conclusions equally lacking in logic and plausibility. There were no great thoughts. All he had were countless embryos of scattered ideas, but whenever he tried to gestate them to cohesive maturity they all came out still-born. That is not to say he was not intelligent. He was, very much so. But general intelligence relates to philosophical ability the way musicality relates to musicianship. The first is just aptitude; the second is aptitude plus craft. There is an intricate technique to systematic thinking, just as there is one to musicianship. Without it, what will come out at the other end will be incoherent sounds, and Tolstoy's work provides ample proof of this.

But one can understand how hard it must have been for a Russian to be uncompromising about Russia's pride, a man of whom E.M. Forster wrote with self-deprecating truthfulness that no English novelist has given so complete a picture of man's life. If Tolstoy had such an effect on an Englishman, you can imagine the feelings of people who grew up with the writer the way one grows up with one's own parents, who lived with his characters as if they were their own siblings, who trod the same soil, breathed the same air, longed for the same absolutist Russian truth. For such people it was impossible to treat Tolstoy without at least some piety. I used to be a Russian myself, so I know.

Understandably, foreign critics who are not weighed down by the same emotional baggage do not always evince the same piety. Thus the Norwegian writer Knut Hamsun was certain that one couldn't find a philosophy punier than Tolstoy's, Paul Johnson gave Tolstoy an expert—and well deserved—thrashing in *Intellectuals*,[2] and more recently A.N. Wilson dismissed Tolstoy's politics as "silly." I agree, but with one proviso.

Tolstoy's philosophy may indeed be puny and his politics silly. But he himself was a giant, arguably the best novelist who has ever lived, one of half a dozen best writers in history. Moreover, at the age of 50, still bursting with creative energy and physical strength, he declared he was giving up his art to teach the world a lesson in how to live. And he was almost as good as his word. Although even in his last 30 years he could not refrain from coming up with the odd masterpiece (such as

The Death of Ivan Ilyich or *Hadji Murat*), most of his output during that period consisted of books and articles of polemic, religion and philosophy. And no matter how sharply we disagree with Tolstoy's religion and philosophy, or how resolutely we reject his answers, at least he did pose what Heine called "the accursed questions." That alone cannot fail to command some, however limited, respect.

Tolstoy's lesson was weak, but the man himself was not—and his influence even less so. In the last quarter of the nineteenth century and until his death in 1910, he was perhaps the best-known personality in the world, the universal proto-guru. People from four continents, ordinary readers, politicians, writers, philosophers, went on a pilgrimage to his estate, hoping their lives would change. For many, they did change.

More important, Tolstoy has changed all our lives since then, though we may not know the origin of the change. Even those who never have read a single word of any of his books subsist every day on the fruits of his labor. For—quite apart from his unmatched impact on modern literature—Tolstoy made a formative contribution to our anomic, pacifist, nihilist, touchy-feely counterculture with its philosophical leaning away from our Western roots and toward Oriental agnosticism.

Such important modern movements as theosophy and many other occult practices, politicized vegetarianism, militant environmentalism, animal rights, anarchism, anti-capitalism, anti-colonialism, back-to-nature populism have all been directly, and some decisively, influenced by Tolstoy. But for him, modern gurus spreading Zen and other Asian philosophies in the West would have a much harder time. His rabid propaganda of anticlericalism against the background of vicious attacks on the state in general and the Russian state in particular played into the bolsheviks' hand, contributing to their victory. That is why Lenin and his culture vulture A.V. Lunacharsky canonized Tolstoy in Soviet Russia. And they did this in spite of his sermon of non-violence, which they neither welcomed nor heeded, and his incessant references to God, which they deplored.[3]

Gandhi based his life's work, the dismemberment of the British Empire, to a large extent on Tolstoy's philosophy. And with Gandhi as the intermediate link, Tolstoy exerted a powerful influence on Martin Luther King's version of the civil rights movement. The oxymoronic Christian socialists owe him an important debt. Even the Nazis, though hardly proponents of Tolstoyan non-violence, made good use of Tolstoy-like nationalistic blood-and-soil self-simplification accompanied by anti-capitalist, anti-West and anti-church invective.

Elsewhere, I have described Russia as the trailblazer of nihilist modernity[4] Of course it never was merely that. Just as the Russian national character tends to swing between extremes, so has the country's contribution to the world. At one extreme, during Tolstoy's lifetime, Russia went through an upsurge in arts and philosophy. In concentrated intensity this was fully comparable to Athens at the time of Pericles, Paris at the time of Aquinas, and England at the time of Shakespeare. In the nineteenth century and the first couple of decades of the twentieth, Russian literature was unmatched in the world, her music second only to that of Germany and Austria, her painting not far behind and her religious philosophy perhaps the most interesting of the time. And even Russian science was coming up in the world, through Mendeleyev and Lobachevsky, Pavlov and Korsakov—and practically the whole staff of the Pasteur Institute, apart from its founder.

Alas, side by side with those achievements festered the kind of nihilism that eventually brought the country down. In fact the very word "nihilist," though Latin in form, was coined by Ivan Turgenev in his 1862 novel *Fathers and Sons*, which contemporaries read practically as reportage. Apart from originating the word, the Russians either invented or else perfected much of what we today identify with various manifestations of nihilism.

The political use and tactics of modern terrorism were pioneered in Russia. Modern anti-Semitism uses the Russian forgery *Protocols of the Elders of Zion* as its scripture. Hitler was directly influenced in that respect (not that it took a lot of influencing) by Russian émigrés and refugee Balts from Russia, such as Alfred Rosenberg. Though the Russians did not invent anarchism, they were the ones who turned it into a worldwide political movement, courtesy of Bakunin and Kropotkin. The same goes for Marxism, with the Russians having realized, though not yet fully, its murderous potential and spread it all over the globe. Various occult practices were either invented by Russians (Blavatsky, Gurdjiev, Uspensky) or turned by them into worldwide phenomena. Avant-garde art, the artistic expression of nihilism, first made a big splash in Russia (Kandinsky, Malevich) as did avant-garde ballet (Diaghilev, Nijinsky) and avant-garde theatre (Meyerhold, Tairov).

All those movements were nihilistic in that they were expressions of latent, or not so latent, rejection of the West—either its Judeo-Christian, God-king-and-country rural tradition or its liberal, industrializing urban modernity, or sometimes both. The list of such movements inspired by Russia can go on and on, as can the list of the Russians who did the actual inspiring. But however long it gets, Tolstoy's name will remain near the top.

His attacks on the West (and things Western in Russia) were not unique in their specific targets: traditional Christianity with its history and culture, the Western state in general and parliamentarism in particular, urbanism, capitalism, individualism, wealth, landed property, hedonism, immorality. But those attacks were original in the platform from which they were launched: quasi-Asian agrarian primitivism. This was linked to a vaguely Oriental rationalism married to a kind of religion without God and Christianity without Christ. That particular tree has produced much poisonous fruit in the West, and it is still as fecund as ever.

Another contribution Tolstoy made to modernity was his pioneering use of barely nascent mass media. Not for him the contemplative solitude of a Kant or a Nietzsche. Tolstoy consciously built up his public personality as an important part of his message to mankind,[5] to a point where the personality became most of the message. The first color photograph taken in Russia was of him. His was the crackling voice on the first Russian phonograph record. His disheveled visage, deliberately modeled on the crude public perception of God's appearance, flashed through the first Russian newsreels and countless films to follow.

Tolstoy's disciples Chertkov and Biryukov presaged modern PR techniques by keeping the world's press informed of every new twist in the great man's life, while Tolstoy himself never turned down a media opportunity. And the world was already sufficiently corrupt not to sense the incongruity of a back-to-nature prophet ostensibly rejecting modernity, while at the same time chasing publicity wherever he could find it. Nor could the world see that great artistic talent, or indeed expertise in any area, does not automatically make its possessor an authority on everything else. Today this credulity has been pushed to its extreme. We no longer cringe when a popular actor pontificates on the global ramifications of warm weather or when a tattooed footballer with a useful left foot tells us we "shouldn't of went" into Iraq. Such people are of course entitled to their opinions. But only these days do they feel entitled to an audience.

Naturally, Tolstoy cannot be solely blamed for every facet of modernity that has used some aspects of Tolstoyism. It goes without saying that individuals, no matter how powerful and well publicized, only affect collective consciousness in complex, often indirect ways. But it is equally clear that they do affect it. Therefore, whenever a public figure has an opportunity, and the necessary qualities, to exert an influence on his time, he acquires tremendous power. It is up to him to use that power responsibly because his lack of restraint can divert the course of history toward an undesirable destination.

For, contrary to what Marx and Tolstoy preached, the earthly history of mankind is not predetermined. It is not a pawn in the hands of some invisible forces only the chosen few can understand and none can resist. Things happen not because they were bound to happen but largely because driven, not to say possessed, individuals turbo-charge the coughing engine of history with their charismatic appeal.

Granted, it was not just barbarian attacks that brought Rome down, but her own fatigue. But without Alaric, she might have been able to hang on until she found a second spiritual wind. Similarly, there were conditions in place for Napoleon to appear. But without Napoleon, France would not have conquered most of Europe. The bolsheviks destroyed a consumptive Russian state, but without Lenin they would not have destroyed it. Nazism would not have become a powerful evil force without Hitler: the evil was in the air but the powerful force came from him.

By the same token, few public figures have as much claim as Tolstoy to be considered the midwives of modern counterculture. It might possibly have been delivered without him, but it would not be so robust, shrill and pervasive as it has become. So, regardless of whether we ill-advisedly love the counterculture or laudably loathe it, we must take a closer look at what Tolstoy himself saw as the worthiest part of his heritage. He earned the right to have his thoughts weighed in the balance before they are found wanting. This book proposes to do just that.

But why bother arguing with a thinker long since dead and not much read? The answer is that flogging a horse is only useless when the animal is certifiably deceased. However, Tolstoy's teaching, with all its multifarious offshoots, is alive and kicking. Anyhow, written works of the past do not have to continue to be read to remain influential. *Das Kapital*, for example, does not these days appear on many best-seller lists outside North Korea. But its influence is still as pervasive as it is pernicious. In Tolstoy's case too, though his non-fiction is no longer read widely, its echoes are still reverberating in the hollow spaces of counterculture throughout the world. Confronting his thought and faith is thus largely tantamount to confronting today's counterculture, and that, in my view, is not done often enough or forcefully enough.

Modern counterculture includes as its inevitable constituent variously strident attacks on God, Christianity and the church, coming from the likes of Peter Singer, Richard Dawkins, or Christopher

Hitchens (I am using Anglophone examples, but foreign readers could easily replace them with others closer to home). These people are different from Tolstoy in many ways, literary talent being the most salient, but their attacks receive as much public acclaim today as Tolstoy's did in his time. However, one thing in their favor is that they honestly and proudly admit to being militant atheists. Tolstoy, on the other hand, claimed to be a different and better kind of Christian.

That is why any criticism of him, especially if it sets out to prove, among other things, that Tolstoy was neither a Christian nor any kind of believer, would be impotent if it did not proceed from what the critic sees as a sound Christian position. After all, if one claims someone is wrong, then, for the sake of credibility if nothing else, one had better counter with what one considers to be right.

Thus this book represents what I see as the Christian—or Judeo-Christian, if you would rather—response to Tolstoy and everything he stands for. Built into that, of necessity, are some elements of theodicy, defense of God. That too is sorely needed, for these days attacks on God, similar to those launched by Tolstoy, vastly outgun—or at least outshout—the counter-attacks. In launching my counter-offensive I shall have to be guided at least to some extent by my own understanding of religion. And as one man's understanding is always bound to be imperfect, I am sure there will be some Christians who will disagree with some of the things I say. But even they will probably concede that my understanding of Christianity is not dramatically different from theirs in principle, much as it may differ in certain details.

A rigorous logician may argue against the validity of defending Christianity by using its own terms. And that pedantic individual would be right if theodicy were the primary, not the secondary, aim of this book. The primary aim is to show up the metaphysical folly of Tolstoy for what it was; and he himself chose Christian metaphysics as his battleground. Since he attempted to operate within the system of Christian concepts, one feels justified in turning those very concepts against him.

However, there is an admission I have to make at the start, lest I should be accused of impartiality. While I am second to none in my admiration for Tolstoy the artist, none is second to me in my rejection of his message. Since this book is all about the message,[6] its tone will be polemical and at times ironical. You will have to decide whether this is called for, and I for my part shall try to put my case down as persuasively as I can.

Chapter 2

Uncovering the Secret

Vengeance is mine; I will repay.

Leo Tolstoy

All mediocre writers are alike; every great writer is great in his own way. Everything about Tolstoy's life was confusion:

- Proud heir to his rolling acres, about 4,000 of them, complete with 330 serfs, he renounced landed property.
- "Aristocrat to his bone marrow," to use his brother-in-law's phrase, he tried to impersonate a poor peasant, complete with folk garb, a plough, bad teeth and no baths.
- The highest-paid and hardest-working writer in Russia, he spoke in favor of nothing but menial labor for one's daily bread.
- Champion of celibacy, he spent his youth in brothels and the rest of his life producing 13 legitimate children (and at least as many illegitimate ones), forcing on his exhausted wife what he described to Chekhov as his "insatiable"[1] sexual appetite.
- Sadistically cruel to animals, he became a militant, self-righteous vegetarian.
- Having written immortal pages on love and family, he turned his back on both, not to mention on the immortal pages.
- Champion of reason, he denied that science had any value.
- Philosopher of history, he denied history.

- One of the greatest literary artists of all time, he mocked every kind of art.
- Having preached, at the age of 50, that it is impossible to live without faith, he proceeded for the next 30-odd years to do just that.
- Calling himself a believer, he denied God.
- Calling himself a Christian, he denied Christ.
- Preaching Christ's Gospel, he found himself in conflict with the church and was excommunicated.
- Preaching a faith of universal love and tolerance, he attacked other people's faith with venomous, offensive rudeness.
- Having based his philosophy on non-resistance and resignation, he was in fact a rebel.
- While most people's rebellion mellows with age, his became more strident.

We have all heard of contradictory personalities, but this is ridiculous. Even accepting that all geniuses are a bit off-center,[2] we have to admit that on the face of it much about Tolstoy simply does not add up. That would be a fair admission—unless, of course, we succeed in identifying the frightful demons tearing him apart, those he tried to slay his whole life and that ended up slaying him—unless, in other words, we uncover the secret of this unique man.

And there was a secret, for nothing about Tolstoy is straightforward. In that, he resembles his own characters, few of whom are what they seem to be on the surface. This resemblance is not coincidental. Like no other writer, Tolstoy was able to climb under the skin of his protagonists the way he would climb under his wife's blanket. And there they were in their psychological nudity, every hidden crevice revealed.

If Flaubert, the lesser artist, thought he was being paradoxical when declaring "Madame Bovary, c'est moi," then Tolstoy had every right to say the same thing about all his protagonists. And, by forcing his own vices on them, he used his creations to exorcise the demons that kept tearing at his soul, gnawing at it piece by piece.

Later in life he used his moral preaching for the same purpose. The greater his own vice, the more he would extol its opposite virtue. His sadistic cruelty to animals became the sermon of militant vegetarianism. His priapism screamed for celibacy. His propensity for violence fizzled out into non-resistance. His inability to love anybody clamored for the *ukase* to love everybody. Tolstoy's virtues were his

vices with the opposite sign; his characters were his vices external-
ized. Having created them, he would then take a step back and judge
his protagonists, which is to say aspects of himself, pronouncing his
verdicts, meting out either punishment or mercy.

Thus Tolstoy spared Natasha Rostova who, though engaged to
Prince Andrei, first betrayed him with another man, then married
yet another but a few months after her fiancé's death. He spared
Natasha's brother Nikolai who savagely beat up the same peasants
Tolstoy loved so much. He spared Steva Oblonsky for his petty infi-
delities. He even spared Dolokhov, the beastly cad. But he made the
altruistic, self-sacrificing Sonia, Nikolai's jilted fiancée, live a life of
lonely, unrewarding misery. And he forced Anna Karenina[3] to throw
herself under a train.

To Tolstoy, Anna's sin was unforgivable: she loved for the sake of
loving, not just for the sake of spawning little Karenins. Christ showed
mercy to the woman taken in adultery; Tolstoy could not. "Vengeance
is mine; I will repay, saith the Lord," he quotes in the epigraph to
the novel. Of course, in accordance with the legal principle in the
Old Testament, a woman taken in adultery must be stoned to death.
Tolstoy develops this theme with sublime power, only replacing the
old-fashioned stones with the technologically advanced locomotive
that takes Anna's life. The locomotive thus acts as an instrument of
divine retribution so beloved of Kant—and so alien to Christ who
treated adultery not with wrathful vengeance but with divine mercy.

Neither does God rely on people killing themselves to take his
vengeance—he himself is perfectly capable of smiting the sinner. And
few sins are graver than suicide, the only one that the sinner cannot
repent. It is not for nothing that many theologians regard Judas's suicide as a worse crime than his betrayal, and that suicides are denied
Christian burial, though murderers and traitors are not. So God here
acts as merely one of Tolstoy's characters; it is not God's vengeance
that strikes Anna down but Tolstoy's own. Just like Lyovin's or Vronsky's inner monologues, God's words are used merely to express
Tolstoy's own views.

This is how the careful reader first stumbles upon the great secret of
Count Lev Nikolayevich Tolstoy.[4] It is really quite simple: He wished
to be more than a novelist, even one of genius. He wished to be more
than a seer or a soothsayer, although that would have been a good
start. He wished to be God.

Just as he created the world of the Bolkonskys, the Rostovs, the
Lyovins, the Bezuhovs and the Oblonskys, so did he yearn to recreate
the real world. He wanted to correct God's mistakes in having allowed

the world to become imperfect and sinful. He, Count Tolstoy, called by Turgenev "the great writer of Russia's land," set out to usurp God's job. But the job was already taken, and the deity stubbornly hung on to it. Therefore Tolstoy declared war on God and fought it with every means at his disposal. Alas, though he tried many lines of attack, each disguised by the camouflage of pseudo-Christian verbiage, Tolstoy came off a poor second. By way of revenge, he came, in effect, to deny God the Father, ignore God the Son and dismiss God the Holy Spirit. No one, not even God, was allowed to defeat Tolstoy and get away with it.

There we have it. The secret is out—the formal charge of self-deification has been filed. But no jury would convict on the strength of such scanty evidence; they would demand proof beyond reasonable doubt; they would want the prosecution to make a watertight case. Acting for the prosecution, I shall attempt to do this.

But, like any defendant, Tolstoy ought to be allowed to make his own case. And he will get his chance, for I shall quote him as profusely as space will permit and your patience can stand. In doing so I shall only provide exact references when they are essential. For, contrary to the widely held view, Tolstoy's ideas changed little throughout his life, or from one work to the next. He expressed much the same thoughts in his eighties as he did in his twenties. For example, in 1852 Tolstoy wrote *The Morning of a Wealthy Landowner*, which shares the same principal character (Prince Nekhliudov, one of Tolstoy's many doppelgängers) and exactly the same moral message as his last major novel, *Resurrection* (1899). The content was the same; only the form differed.

CHAPTER 3

WHAT KIND OF MAN WOULD TAKE ON GOD?

And who are the judges?

Alexander Griboyedov

1

Trying to answer the baffling "accursed" questions, even an intelligent man can go off on a tangent. Philosophy is like any other science in that one first comes up with a hypothesis, then tests it against available evidence, and then, depending on how the test turns out, either accepts the hypothesis or not. Philosophy is unlike any other science in that there are no instruments whose flashing displays and flailing cursors can tell the thinker to turn around and backtrack to his starting point. The thinker acts as his own testing equipment: his mind says the ostensibly promising idea does not really work, his integrity accepts the disappointment, his inner strength forces him to do an about-face, however painful such a reversal may be.

This means that, when a manifestly intelligent man persists in making manifestly silly pronouncements on just about every subject, it is not his brain that is to blame. And nor is it just his lack of skill in wielding philosophical methodology—this is only necessary to come up with great thoughts, not to avoid uttering silly ones. The real culprit is his character. In our case, Tolstoy's intelligence is in no doubt: producing time after time "a complete picture of man's life" would have been impossible without a first-rate mind. That is why, since Tolstoy's ideas mostly came not just out of the left field but out of the stadium's parking lot, we must start our case by examining his character—before we examine the ideas.

Tolstoy himself always gave his protagonists two lives: one unfolding out in the open, and the other hidden beneath the surface, visible only to the writer's piercing eye. I propose to turn the tables in this chapter and try the same trick on him. As I cannot lay claim to even a fraction of his artistic talent, I shall have to stay in the realm of facts, some well-known, some more arcane. In this endeavor I shall rely not only on Tolstoy's device but also on his own work, for no other author has ever written so much about himself. I shall also draw on the work of others, for no other author has ever had so much written about him. His close family and friends, his contemporaries, rivals, admirers, hagiographers, critics, not to mention a regiment of scholarly biographers the world over, have created a corpus of work that one would be foolish to ignore.

Let us start with the official biography, more or less as it is taught to schoolchildren in Russia and university students in the West:

Leo Tolstoy was born in 1828 to one of the noblest families in Russia. His mother was Princess Volkonsky, and the streams feeding his family barrel came from the Miloslavskys, the Trubetskoys, the Gorchakovs, the Obolenskys, the Odoyevskys, the Ostermans, and so on. In fact, if a Russian Who's Who existed, you could open it on just about any page at random and not go wrong. Suffice it to say that, when writing to a Romanov tsar, Tolstoy addressed him as "brother," and he meant that in the dynastic, not just Christian, sense. The family has produced statesmen, scholars, diplomats, military leaders, and several other notable writers, such as the novelist and poet A.K. Tolstoy in Leo's own generation, the novelist A.N. Tolstoy in the next one, and the British historian Nikolai Tolstoy in our own. None of these is Leo's next of kin; they are all distant cousins far removed.

Orphaned early (he lost his mother at two and his father at nine), Tolstoy was brought up by various aunts, ending up in Kazan where in due course he entered the local university. He thus became one of the two most illustrious students in the history of that institution, Lenin being the other. Neither man got his degree: Lenin was dismissed for troublemaking, Tolstoy for academic failure,[1] with his professors describing him as "neither willing nor able to learn." In *A Confession* he only mentions with uncharacteristic reticence that he "left the university," not the reason for leaving.

In general, just as most of Tolstoy's fiction is largely autobiographical, most of his autobiographies are largely fictional. Even when ostensibly self-flagellating, they tend to be self-serving, and as you read on you will find plenty of evidence to support this observation.

At the age of 21, Tolstoy settled in the Tula province south of Moscow, at his family's estate in Yasnaya Poliana,[2] amid his 4,000 acres and 300-odd serfs. Even such a large arable area proved insufficient for sowing his wild oats, and Tolstoy moved to Moscow where he plunged headlong into a life of wine, women, and song. Actually, it was light on the song but heavy on gambling debts.

In 1851 Tolstoy went to serve with an artillery unit in Chechnya, a province that by all accounts always has had a large potential for young men with martial glory on their minds. While there, he wrote his first—autobiographical—novel *Childhood*, which made him an instant celebrity. But he was not quite finished as a military man. Commissioned in 1854, Tolstoy saw heavy action in the defense of Sebastopol during the Crimean War. From then on all his experiences would be distilled into literature, which he proved by writing *The Sebastopol Stories* published during the siege. There he first tried a narrative based on inner monologue, presaging the "stream of consciousness" of the next century and setting a literary standard Joyce and Proust struggled to emulate. Soon after the war Tolstoy left the army and spent the next five years traveling both in Russia and in Europe.

When in Paris, he witnessed the execution of a murderer, which had a traumatic effect on him, or so he claimed. As a result, he denounced judicial killing, later denying the state's right to judge, to punish, or indeed to exist.

Like Dostoyevsky some years later, Tolstoy was appalled by the West with its soulless materialism and suffocating legalism. He reflected those feelings in the story *Lucerne*, featuring the same hardworking Prince Nekhliudov who also did duty in several of his other works. With deafening echoes of his idol Rousseau, Tolstoy contrasted the delicate beauty of the alpine landscape with the moral ugliness of the rich tourists, most of them English. The beastly Brits enjoyed the performance by a Tyrolean busker while ignoring his repeated pleas for a few coins: "Again, not one of those exquisitely dressed scores of people standing to listen to him threw him a penny. The crowd laughed heartlessly," wrote Tolstoy.

To his credit, *Lucerne* condemned the philistine West[3] more subtly than Dostoyevsky did in his *Diaries of a Writer*. "I'd rather live my whole life as a nomad in a Kirghiz tent than worship the German way of amassing wealth.... They all work like oxen and save money like

Yids. . . .[4] Really, I don't know what's worse, Russian swinishness or the German way of saving through honest work." For what it is worth, one could opine that on balance industry and thrift are preferable to swinishness—but *de gustibus* . . . , and all that.

When in Moscow or St Petersburg, Tolstoy lived the life of the literary world—and hated it. That scene was dominated by the intelligentsia, much of it born to the clergy. Tolstoy detested both groups, mostly for social reasons. As his brother-in-law recalled, "He himself admitted his pride and vanity. He was an aristocrat to his bone marrow, and though he always liked common folk, he liked aristocrats more. The middle ground between those two extremes didn't appeal to him."[5] The two groups Tolstoy loathed fell precisely into that middle ground. Those wretches even traveled in second-class carriages, whereas Tolstoy never did: as a matter of principle he always chose either the patrician first or the plebeian third.

Having had enough of that middle-ground intelligentsia, Tolstoy fled to Yasnaya Poliana and the peasants whom he adored with a passion. This passion was not wholly moral or aesthetic: he loved kissing peasant men on the lips, burying his face in their bushy beards, smelling their "spring-like aroma." We do not know whether he went beyond foreplay with the men, but he definitely did with the women, driving his *droit de seigneur* home with unquenchable thirst in the surrounding woods. At that time he was intermittently suffering from bouts of V.D., which neither stopped him from having profligate sex nor encouraged him to forewarn his partners. In the process Tolstoy densely populated his estate with illegitimate children (12 by the most modest count; twice as many at the other extreme) and fell in love with Aksinia, the married mother of one of them.

Remorse followed, accompanied by a flare-up of social conscience. A repentant aristocrat, the quintessential Russian type, Tolstoy felt guilty about the plight of the serfs who made up about 90 percent of the population. That feeling was not wholly misplaced—peasants were being sold like cattle, flogged and imprisoned for the slightest transgression (such as not taking their hats off fast enough when espying the master), lost at cards, taken advantage of sexually—and Tolstoy himself had done all those things.

To assuage the guilt, Tolstoy, having learned about "free" education in the West, started a school for peasant children. The founding principle was best expressed by his (and Freud's) Scottish follower A.S. Neill who wrote that "The function of a child is to live his own life—not the life his anxious parents think he should live, nor a life according to the purpose of the educator who thinks he knows what is best."

Tolstoy believed that pupils must never be coerced into learning, and their instincts must not be repressed. They themselves should choose what, how, and when to learn. In any case, it was not saintly peasants who needed to learn from the decadent intelligentsia, but rather the other way around. Tolstoy then enlarged upon his newly acquired pedagogic insights in the magazine *Yasnaya Poliana*, which he published. The insights may have been good, but the results were not. Left to their own devices, the children chose to learn their favorite subject: nothing. In a few months the magazine folded, and Tolstoy lost interest in the school.

But at least the children of his school did not have to suffer the dire effects of traditional education, which at that time included as a compulsory subject the study of Tolstoy's lifelong nemesis, God. As he wrote later in *The Way of Life*:

Of all the ways of spreading a false faith, the cruelest one is indoctrinating children in the false faith. The way this works is that, when a child asks his elders who have lived longer and have had the time to learn about the wisdom of other people, life and the relationship between the two, the elders don't reply according to what they think and know, but according to what was said by people who lived thousands of years ago, something that none of the grown-ups believes or can believe. Instead of the necessary spiritual food the child is asking for, he is given a poison killing his spiritual health, to which the only possible antidote is great efforts and suffering.

As was usually the case with Tolstoy, once he became interested in education it took him at most only a few weeks to regard himself as the only authority on the subject. In general, he ascribed to himself the ability to acquire instant expertise in anything he turned his mind to, however briefly. Once he gave the matter the slightest of thoughts he felt with the impudence of a megalomaniac autodidact that some truths were revealed to him that had been hidden from the experts. Thus, never having studied those subjects in depth, he felt qualified to argue violently with world authorities on education, history, economics, biblical scholarship, music, medicine—not to mention religion.

Chekhov noticed this tendency, commenting in his letter to Gorky upon:

the audacity with which Tolstoy holds forth about what he doesn't know and is too obstinate to learn. Thus his statements about syphilis, foundling hospitals, the aversion of women to sexual relations and so on, are not merely debatable, but show him up as an ignoramus who has not, during his long life, taken the trouble to read two or three books written by experts.

If Tolstoy ever did turn to the experts, it was not for knowledge but for confirmation, as was the case with his views on education. Thus he went to Germany to meet the famous pedagogue Friedrich Froebel but was bitterly disappointed: in spite of being "just a Jew" who ought to have known his place, the old man dared to have ideas on his subject that were different from Tolstoy's.

In 1862 he married Sophia Andreyevna Behrs, Sonia—a plain and impressionable girl half his age. On the eve of the marriage, Tolstoy, who mistakenly believed in total honesty between spouses, made his virginal bride read his diary describing in graphic detail dalliances with serf girls, gypsies, and prostitutes, and also his homosexual cravings. When Leo then gave her the full benefit of the experience thus gathered, Sonia was shocked. Barely a fortnight after the wedding she wrote in her own diary, "Physical manifestations are disgusting." Nonetheless she went on to produce 13 children, of whom ten survived childhood. Tolstoy's wife had the intelligence to appreciate his genius, the taste to offer good suggestions, and the dedication to help him with editing, proofreading, and copying. The story has it that she copied out *War and Peace* seven times. Those few of us who ever have scribbled 12,000 book pages longhand will probably appreciate Sophia Andreyevna's devotion.

War and Peace (1865–69) and *Anna Karenina* (1877–78) placed Tolstoy for ever into the first rank of literature. But shortly after the publication of *Anna Karenina* he experienced the crisis he describes, eloquently if not always truthfully, in *A Confession*, a pamphlet loosely patterned on similar works by St Augustine and Rousseau. There Tolstoy talks about his lifelong search for God and the meaning of life, resulting in the realization that life is its own meaning.

Art in general and literature in particular are frivolous pursuits. Only moral self-perfection can save the world. One cannot live without faith, though Tolstoy is vague on the kind of faith one cannot live without. He himself, he writes, has tried several, including Christianity.[6] All had something wrong with them, especially Christianity. God cannot save us if we do not save ourselves by creating God's kingdom on earth. Love and non-resistance will save the world or, if the world proves unworthy, destroy it—in that case, good riddance. Formal learning is despicable. Atheists in general are better people than believers, unless the believers are peasants. Only Russian peasants have virtue—a hard view to accept for anyone with first-hand experience of that social group, but there we have it.

A Confession is widely regarded as the watershed of Tolstoy's life. After it came out he was no longer a mere novelist. He became a prophet in the eyes of the world. And Yasnaya Poliana was no longer a mere baronial estate. It became a latter-day Ferney or perhaps Santiago di Compostella, if not quite Jerusalem.

Disciples streamed in; new sects were formed; existing sects, such as the Dukhobors, put Tolstoy on their icons. His disciple Vladimir Chertkov founded Tolstoyan communes in Russia; his disciple Mahatma Gandhi did the same in South Africa, calling Tolstoy "the greatest apostle of non-violence that the present age has produced." Anarchists welcomed Tolstoy as one of their own. So did, with reservations, the oxymoronic "God-seeking communists," such as A. Lunacharsky and A. Bogdanov. Even Lenin, while rebuking Tolstoy as "the landlord obsessed with Christ," praised him as "the mirror of the Russian revolution."[7]

Though most of Tolstoy's non-fiction was censored in Russia, his worldwide fame prevented the government from taking the kind of action a lesser man would have suffered. For example, Dostoyevsky, already an established though not yet internationally known author, had been sentenced to death for the heinous crime of reading Fourier's utopian fantasies. After a nerve-shattering mock execution his sentence was commuted to penal servitude. But, given Tolstoy's virulent animadversions, his might not have been, had the government felt free to go after him. Luckily for him, the police kept a blind eye. The church, however, had to act: it was not so much that Tolstoy kept attacking it savagely as that he claimed at the same time to be the sole practitioner of true Christianity. The church disagreed, and in 1901 the Holy Synod excommunicated the writer. He protested by writing an open reply in which he accused the Holy Synod of lies and libel (we shall soon see who was right).

Most of Tolstoy's family, especially his wife and sons, neither shared his views nor approved of his actions. They rather hoped, sagely yet forlornly, that he would abandon all that nonsense and "return to literature," as Turgenev beseeched him to do. (Few commentators realize that this was a tacit rebuke: Turgenev clearly did not think much of Tolstoy's extra-literary activities.) They also hoped he would not give away all his property, as he threatened to do.

"Charity begins at home," they pleaded, and, the pleas failing, came up with counter-threats of their own, such as committing him to an institution. Grudgingly Tolstoy assigned the copyright of his great pre-1881 works to his family, though bequeathing his later output to the people, and to Chertkov as their proxy. That did little to relax the tensions at home, and finally, in 1910, Tolstoy could not take it any longer. Accompanied by his youngest daughter Alexandra and his doctor, he left home for an unknown destination. Along the way Tolstoy caught pneumonia and died at Astapovo, a remote whistle-stop on the Moscow-Yelets line.

2

Proust may have described Tolstoy as "serene God," but even the official biography makes the adjective as hard to accept as the noun. Even harder is it to see how people who have actually read Tolstoy can persist in contrasting his spiritual health with Dostoyevsky's sickness.

So much more interesting it is then to read the accounts of psychiatrists who analyzed Tolstoy's personality from a professional point of view. The best known of them is Prof. A.M. Yevlakhov, and in this chapter I shall be drawing on his clinical analysis, first published in 1930.[8] The author denied Tolstoy's "spiritual health." Having analyzed thousands of pages written by and about Tolstoy, Prof. Yevlakhov came up with a diagnosis—epilepsy, the same "holy disease" from which Dostoyevsky had suffered. But before we immerse ourselves in Yevlakhov's analysis, some disclaimers are in order.

Only a professional psychiatrist can judge the clinical validity of his diagnosis. But even a rank amateur will suspect that, considering the advances made in medicine since 1930, some, though certainly not all, symptoms mentioned by Yevlakhov may be attributable not to epilepsy but to a different abnormality. Nevertheless an abnormality it probably was, and his analysis cannot fail to convince the reader that Tolstoy was hardly the paragon of mental health. Mentally, he was no healthier than Dostoyevsky.

If a modern psychiatrist were presented with a patient showing Tolstoy's symptoms, as described by Yevlakhov, he may diagnose not only epilepsy but also severe personality disorder. The Diagnostic and Statistical Manual of the American Psychiatric Association (fourth edition) defines this condition as: "An enduring pattern of inner experience and behavior that deviates markedly from the expectation of the individual's culture, is pervasive and inflexible, has an onset in adolescence or early adulthood, is stable over time, and leads to distress or impairment."

Specifically, Tolstoy showed clear symptoms of narcissistic personality disorder, characterized, according to the same source, by:

1. An exaggerated sense of self-importance (e.g., exaggerates achievements and talents, expects to be recognized as superior without commensurate achievements). 2. Preoccupation with fantasies of unlimited success, power,

brilliance, beauty, or ideal love. 3. Belief he is "special" and can only be understood by, or should associate with, other special or high-status people (or institutions). 4. Need for excessive admiration. 5. A sense of entitlement. 6. Selfish, taking advantage of others to achieve his own ends. 7. Lack of empathy. 8. Envy of others or belief that others are envious of him. 9. Arrogant, haughty, patronizing, or contemptuous behaviors or attitudes.

It is interesting to compare this clinical picture with that drawn by Yevlakhov and his contemporaneous colleagues. We shall look at the symptoms they describe and see whether they fit epilepsy or severe personality disorder—or both. One way or the other, they definitely fit no reasonable idea of a normal person, which it is the aim of this chapter to demonstrate. What is significant is that professionals regarded Tolstoy's mental health as worth analyzing. That the results of their analysis are less well known than similar data on Dostoyevsky can be put down to Tolstoyan propaganda dating back to his own lifetime and still ongoing.

Tolstoy's epilepsy was first brought to light by the Russian psychiatrist G.V. Segalin. In his paper *On the Pathography of Leo Tolstoy* (*O patografiyi L'va Tolstova*) he described the writer's epileptic seizures complete with fainting, delirium, hallucinations, and ensuing amnesia. Prof. Segalin concluded that Tolstoy suffered from so-called "affective epilepsy," in the form first isolated by Bratz. His younger colleague, Prof. Yevlakhov, later concentrated on how the disease affected Tolstoy's personality, work, and ideas. Both physicians believed that Tolstoy's heredity was conducive to psychopathology:

- His paternal grandfather—a fanatic gambler and, according to Tolstoy himself, "mentally limited"—evidently killed himself.
- His grandmother, a sadist who tormented both her family and servants, suffered from optical and aural hallucinations (for example, she saw and had dialogues with her late son).
- Tolstoy's grandfather and father gambled away most of the family fortune.
- His father's younger brother was a hunchback who died in infancy.
- One of Leo's sisters was an insane mystic while another, also a mystic, retired to a convent but refused the last rites on her deathbed.
- At the age of 16, Tolstoy's father suffered from a psychiatric disorder which his family hoped to cure by mating him with a serf girl. She produced a mentally retarded son who grew up to be a street beggar.
- Tolstoy's mother died of a brain disease.

- One of Tolstoy's brothers, Nikolai, was an alcoholic; another, Sergei, was a taciturn schizoid who would spend months locked in his room; the third, Dmitry, an even odder man, combined religiosity with extreme cruelty. He also habitually walked the streets wearing nothing but an overcoat over his naked body.

Before Tolstoy developed full-blown "*grand mal*" epilepsy toward the end of his life, he had suffered from "epilepsy equivalents," which Prof. Yevlakhov traces as far back as 1867. These days, psychiatrists are likely to regard some of Tolstoy's episodes, especially those involving a trembling lip and eyes transfixed on one point, as actual epileptic fits, rather than just their "equivalents." But at no time would any professional dismiss his symptoms as insignificant. One of them was frequent outbreaks of uncontrollable rage, usually directed at his nearest and dearest.

Tolstoy's sister-in-law describes one episode when he took exception to Mrs Tolstoy's sitting on the floor. "Get up at once!" he screamed and rushed into his study. When his wife followed him there, he yelled, "Get out! Out!" He then grabbed the tray with the coffee service and violently hurled it against the wall. Not satisfied with the destruction, he tore the thermometer off the wall and smashed it. When his sister-in-law peeked in, "Sonia wasn't there. The smashed dishes and thermometer were on the floor. L.N. was standing in the middle of the room, pale, *his lip trembling*. His eyes were transfixed on one point. I pitied and feared him—I'd never seen him that way."

This is how Mrs Tolstoy herself describes her husband's mood in her diary a few years later:

He had fixed, strange eyes, as if he was no longer of this world.... What then happened had happened many times before: Lyovochka became nervous and depressed. Once I was writing, he came in, his face awful.... 'I've come to tell you that I want to divorce you, I can't live this way any longer, I'm leaving for Paris or America'.... What happened, I asked. 'Nothing, but if the carriage is overloaded more and more, the horse will stop'. What he meant by overloading, he didn't say. Then he began to scream, reproach, swear...I saw he was crazy and, when he said, 'The air is poisoned wherever you are,' I began to pack my case.... He begged me to stay. I stayed, but suddenly he began to sob hysterically...to quiver and shake all over.

Biryukov, one of his secretaries, recalls how, having finished his translation of a Victor Hugo story *Un athée*, Tolstoy began to weep and sob hysterically. Then he slowly, slowly sank down on his back. I ran to him, tried to support his back, but was unable to hold him up and he fell on the floor.... We picked him up, he sat down on the floor, muttering incoherently 'Leave me ... I'll fall asleep.... There's a pillow here somewhere'. We laid him down on the sofa. Some five minutes later he came to and could remember nothing of what had happened.... He seemed to have forgotten everything—his relations' names, places he knew well.

Here is another recollection, by a different secretary (V. Bulgakov), supported by other witnesses of this and similar events:

L.N. got terrible convulsions, first in his legs, then in his face and whole body. All of us, several men, tried to hold L.N. down as we feared the convulsions would drive him off the bed onto the floor, but couldn't handle the terrible contractions of his muscles. Such seizures were repeated five times, with calm periods in between ... during which he was delirious.

Yevlakhov comments:

Thus, if one follows the course of Tolstoy's illness, one cannot escape the conclusion that, from January 1867, he showed clear symptoms of epilepsy, though at first in the form of equivalents: his family noted that during his aggressive attacks he had strange, senseless eyes, transfixed ... on one place— the same eyes as he later had *before* his attacks—and also a pale, awful face and trembling lip.... From 1905 sudden 'falls' begin, with subsequent depression, acute amnesia, paramnesia, delirium and hallucinations.

In fact, many observers mention Tolstoy's persistent hallucinations. For example, he often saw his late brother standing next to him, or else heard voices telling him when he would die.

It is important to mention that epilepsy is usually seen not only as a neurological disease but also as a psychiatric disorder, affecting the sufferer's personality in a variety of ways. It is not, however, like schizophrenia in that it does not destroy every link with reality. Nor does it affect the sufferer's mind over the long term. What Yevlakhov pays particular attention to is the effect the disease had on Tolstoy's writing. Here he occasionally finds himself on weaker ground: some of the symptoms he mentions, if far enough advanced, would have made it impossible for Tolstoy to come up with literary masterpieces.

One such symptom is "labyrinthine" (what modern psychiatrists call "sticky") thinking, leading to an inability to express a thought in a concise way. Patients suffering from this condition in its complicated form often find it impossible to finish a simple sentence, which is one accusation that cannot be leveled at Tolstoy. If he had indeed suffered from that particular condition, he must have had it in a mild form. Incidentally, modern psychiatrists would not usually associate "stickiness" with epilepsy, but that may be because these days they hardly ever see untreated epileptics. The disease is now caught early, and such advanced symptoms, though commonplace in the past, are rarely seen in clinical practice.

But, whether or not it was due to epilepsy, the problem of verbosity did exist, and Tolstoy himself was aware of it. Many critics point out his tendency to repeat himself and to write unnecessarily long passages, bulging with extraneous details. Flaubert, for example, having read the first French translation of *War and Peace*, exclaimed, "Il se répète! Il philosophise!" Turgenev mentioned that at times Tolstoy's style resembled "an impassable morass." Sometimes Tolstoy found it hard to end a sentence, instead building more and more clauses, often with confused antecedents, onto the same creaking structure. In fact, Nikolai Nekrasov, his first publisher, told him in no uncertain terms to use full stops much more often.

Tolstoy also tended to develop his thoughts on a lofty scale. That may be why, at the mature age of 23, he realized it would take three volumes to write his autobiography. This precocious feat was not matched in world literature before or since, at least not until the 19-year-old footballer Wayne Rooney undertook to produce a five-volume memoir.

Some critics ascribe the tendency to write long, meandering prose to an innate trait of the Russian character. That is demonstrably untrue, as will become instantly clear to any reader of Pushkin's *Tales of Belkin*, Lermontov's *A Hero of Our Time*, Leskov's prose, Gogol's and Chekhov's stories, or, later, M. Bulgakov's novels. This tendency is not collective but individual, really observable only in Tolstoy and Dostoyevsky, one probably and the other definitely an epileptic. However, Tolstoy in particular usually overcame that weakness by meticulous editing, which may explain those famous seven rewrites of *War and Peace*. But sometimes one finds the odd sentence half a page long even in his great fiction.[9]

According to Yevlakhov, another characteristic trait of an epileptic, also evinced by Tolstoy throughout his work, is the tendency to repeat the same words several times within short passages. Thus, for instance, in *War and Peace*: "Occasionally he'd look at the *familiar* shelf, surrounding him, and again at *his own* legs. Both were equally *his own* and *familiar* to him." Psychiatrists describe this tendency as "perseveration," typical, though not uniquely so, of epileptics who can only think in details.[10]

My favorite example (Yevlakhov would have had a field day with it) of Tolstoy's "labyrinthine," "perseverated" writing comes from his commentary on the Gospels, a work to which we shall return later in a different context:

For those who saw the divinity of Jesus in that he is not like other people, his resurrection could have persuasiveness, i.e. could prove to them that he is not like other people, but only that he is not like other people, and nothing more; but only for those who saw that Jesus died, made sure he died, and then saw that he was alive, and made sure that he was alive.

How could a competent, never mind great, writer produce such a sentence?[11] Tolstoy was probably trying to say that, resurrection or no resurrection, Jesus was only a different kind of man, not God; but none of the Russians I know can make heads or tails of this passage. Though it is of course true that Tolstoy did not edit his non-fiction as fastidiously as his artistic writing, simple carelessness does not quite explain this. So perhaps Yevlakhov had a point after all.

The same tendency can lead to an exaggerated desire for order. In particular, psychiatrists note that epileptics often keep an extremely detailed diary. Tolstoy is an example of this. He started a diary in his youth and persevered more or less his whole life. In fact, his diaries are the starting point of most of his fiction. Characteristically, Tolstoy records everything in order, often assigning rubrics and numbers to statements. For example: "Here are the reasons for most mistakes: (1) indecisiveness, i.e. lack of energy, (2) lying to yourself, (3) haste, (4) *fausse honte*, (5) bad mood, (6) incoherence, (7) imitation, (8) inconstancy, (9) lack of thought."

Or else, in his preface to the moralizing novella *The Romance of a Landowner*: "The main thought of the story: happiness is a virtue. Secondary thoughts: principal drivers of human activity: (1) good: (a) virtue, (b) friendship, (c) love of art; (2) bad: (a) vanity, (b) greed, (c) passions, (a1) women, (b1) cards, (c1) drink." This is published prose, not a preliminary sketch.

Reading Yevlakhov and others, one begins to think that the clinical picture of epilepsy they describe applies to Tolstoy so accurately that it might have been written with him in mind. Various authors cite such typical manifestations as cruelty, miserliness, pettiness, extreme irritability leading to outbursts of rage, depressiveness, unsociability, intolerance, contrariness, impulsiveness. Tolstoy showed all of those symptoms throughout his life, as observed both by others and himself.

Even downright sycophantic biographers of Tolstoy, such as his acolyte Pavel Biryukov, mention that he was already rather odd even as a boy. Once, for example, he cut off all the hair on one half of his head. On another occasion he cut off his bushy eyebrows. Aged eight, he decided he could fly and put that theory to a test by jumping out of a window about nine feet high, injuring his legs and knocking himself out for a few minutes. Unconsciousness became sleep; little Leo slept for 18 hours and woke up in fine health.

As a young man, he, like Pushkin and Dostoyevsky, was a fanatic gambler. Once, on his way to the Caucasus, Tolstoy met another officer at a roadside inn and they played cards through the night. The young count ended up losing all his money and his carriage. He was about to bet his whole estate on one hand when an old major stepped in, took Tolstoy aside, and scolded him. Gorky remembers in his *Reminiscences of Lev Nikolayevich Tolstoy*: "He plays seriously, passionately. And when he picks up his cards his hands become so very nervous, as if he is holding live birds, not inanimate pieces of cardboard." In 1855, at the time he first decided to found a new religion, Tolstoy gambled away the baronial manor at Yasnaya Poliana, which the winner took apart and transported to another province. The count then had to raise his large family in a relatively modest five-up, five-down wing.

His army comrades often mentioned Tolstoy's odd behavior and tendency to vanish into thin air. Sometimes he would disappear for days on end. Later it would turn out that he had either gone on an unauthorized raid or else had been losing his shirt at cards. When after the war he came back to civilization, nothing much changed. Turgenev remembers: "He stayed with me and really went for it: boozing, gypsies[12] and cards all night long; and then he sleeps like a corpse till two o'clock. I tried to reason with him but gave it up."

Already as a young man Tolstoy displayed a tendency to flee places on impulse. In 1857 he suddenly left for Paris, then shortly thereafter wrote in his diary: "Got up early, ill, read for a while and then a simple and reasonable idea came to me—to leave Paris." In mid-January 1861 Turgenev wrote to their mutual friend, the poet Fet, from Paris: "At last Tolstoy's letter arrived from Livorno. He declares his intention to go to Naples but at the same time he wants to be here in February so as to flee to Russia. I've no idea what will come out of that." What came out was that after a few months in Russia Tolstoy suddenly "fell ill, more spiritually than physically, gave everything up and fled to the Bashkirs in the steppe, to breathe fresh air, drink *kumis*[13] and live an animal life." This resuscitating escape "to the Bashkirs" became an almost annual event.

Tolstoy displayed the same impulsive fervor in getting married as in everything else. On 12 September, 1862, he wrote in his diary, "I'm in love, the way I never thought it was possible to love. I'm crazy, I'll shoot myself if this goes on." And the next day: "Tomorrow, when I get up I'll go there and either say everything or shoot myself."

The suicide theme, hardly a sign of spiritual health, is recurrent. For example, this is how 20 years later Tolstoy describes his reaction to his widely publicized spiritual crisis:

And then I, a happy man, took a sash out of the room where I was alone every night, undressing, so as not to hang myself on a rod between two wardrobes; I stopped hunting with a gun not to be tempted by an all too easy way of relieving myself of life.

Incidentally, this passage from *A Confession* repeats almost word for word the thoughts of Lyovin, Tolstoy's *alter ego* in *Anna Karenina*. Tolstoy's autobiographies fed his novels and vice versa.

A few paragraphs down Tolstoy develops this theme: "Nothing prevents us, along with Schopenhauer, from denying life. But then kill yourself—and you won't be thinking about it. . . . You've joined a jolly party, everybody is having fun, they know what they are doing there, while you are bored and disgusted—so leave." The very thought of killing oneself just because one feels "bored and disgusted" would be abhorrent to any believer in any God. Even tepid faith precludes regarding life as merely a party to which one has been invited. Life is a gift that cannot be turned down; it must be treated with gratitude and respect. Such little hints of Tolstoy's atheism are strewn all over his work, no matter how hard he tries to hide them behind the jam jars of theistic verbiage.

Tolstoy's urge to run away did not disappear after marriage. For example, in 1869 he had gone on a business trip to Penza, but veered off on the way, having had a nightmare of death. While on the run, he wrote a letter to his wife (note the repeating words):

How are you and the children? Has something happened? It's two days now that I've been tortured by fear. The other day, at *night*, I was spending the *night* at Arsamas and something extraordinary happened. It was two at *night*, I was terribly tired and sleepy, nothing hurt. Suddenly I *experienced* angst, fear, terror—the kind I'd never *experienced* before. I'll tell you the details of this feeling later, but I've never *experienced* a more painful feeling before and, God willing, no one else will ever *experience* it.

In treating others, the champion of universal love was explosive, intemperate, often malicious. His brother-in-law S.A. Behrs relates the story he heard from his mother who, at the time both she and Tolstoy were nine, was the object of little Leo's affection. When, however, she had the temerity to talk to another boy, Leo pushed her off a balcony (Behrs does not mention the height, but presumably it was the same nine feet that Leo himself had jumped off). As a result, the girl walked with a limp for a long time. One can only guess how she felt 25 years later, when Tolstoy married her daughter.

In his diary Tolstoy himself often mentions things like "got carried away—swore at Yepishka,"[14] "got angry—beat up Alyoshka." When he arrived in St Petersburg in 1855, Tolstoy was involved in several quarrels and duels, most of which he himself had provoked. Many eyewitnesses describe him as "wild." The writer Druzhinin calls him "a vandal"; another writer, Chernyshevsky, "a wild man."

Then he quarreled with Turgenev. That was caused by Tolstoy's insulting remarks about Turgenev's illegitimate daughter, whom, according to some reports, the count had kindly described as a bastard. The difference between the two men was that Turgenev had acknowledged his out-of-wedlock child, which Tolstoy never did for any of his. Turgenev raised and brought the girl up as a young lady of his social circle, while Tolstoy used his son by Aksinia (nothing is known of the others) to do menial jobs around the estate, never even bothering to teach him to read and write. Turgenev, the mildest of men, took exception to Tolstoy's rudeness and was challenged to a duel for his trouble. The tragedy, which could have deprived the world of two major writers, was only averted at the last moment. Following this clash, Turgenev described Tolstoy as "a troglodyte."

In his diaries, Tolstoy himself remembers many episodes that could validate such epithets: "Had dinner at Turgenev's, where, having been stupidly offended by Nekrasov's poem, I told everybody many unpleasant things. Turgenev walked out." "Had dinner at Botkin's. Grigoriev and Ostrovsky, I was trying to insult their convictions. What for? I don't know."

Many observers remark that Tolstoy could not stand being contradicted, which Yevlakhov also ascribed to his epilepsy. In arguments, recalls the writer Grigorovich, "his agitation was so great that it took much effort to quiet him down." This is confirmed by the Italian psychiatrist Lombroso who once visited Tolstoy (the police let him do so only because they thought he could offer the writer professional help, thus reducing their workload): "I saw the total impossibility of talking to him about certain subjects without irritating him." Lombroso then describes "the angry and evil look in Tolstoy's eyes throughout our argument" when "he frowned his awesome eyebrows and cast terrible lightnings at me from his deep-set eyes."

In his diary, Tolstoy talks about himself with palpable sadness: "Why is it that not only people I neither like nor respect . . . but everyone without exception is noticeably uncomfortable in my presence? I must be an unbearable, difficult man." Well spotted.

Years later he again castigates himself with fulsome sincerity:

> I can't recall those years without horror, disgust and heartache. I killed people in the war, challenged them to duels so as to kill them, lost at cards, ate away the labor of my peasants, beat them, fornicated, cheated. . . . There wasn't a crime I didn't commit, and for that I was praised, was considered . . . to be a relatively moral man.

When one hears such admissions shouted through a megaphone at a street corner, one expects to hear next, "And then I woke up one morning and saw a little baby by my bed. It was baby Jesus." However, Tolstoy saw different visions, and he did not need a megaphone to scream *urbi et orbi*.

Like many epileptics, Tolstoy combined sentimentality with cruelty.[15] Again, with his customary ability to look at himself as if from aside, he describes himself in this, seemingly humorous, way: "Patient No. 1. Sanguinely inclined. . . . Mania: the patient thinks it possible to change the lives of others by words. General symptoms: unhappiness about the existing order, denouncing all but himself and irritated verbosity without paying attention to the listeners; frequent transitions from anger and irritability to unnatural, lachrymose sensitivity."

It is true that Tolstoy cried easily and on any provocation, or without one. Thus his 1852 letter to his aunt: "Votre lettre m'a fait pleurer. J'ai toujours été Leo-cry-o."[16] His diary a few days later: "De nouveau je pleure." His 1856 diary: "I was reading Nikolenka's story and burst out crying again." In 1852, having heard a Pushkin poem recited, he "went to Botkin's room and wrote a letter to Turgenev, then sat down on the sofa and burst out sobbing for no reason."

His secretary confirms this proclivity: when dictating an account of his defense of Shabunin, a soldier sentenced to death, "Tolstoy wept three times." And then, "Reading Leskov's thoughts on religion and life, which had much in common with his own, he read another sentence, then suddenly turned around and went off to weep." Again, "After dinner, Kh. recited a Nikitin poem with pathos but without particular inspiration. Everybody liked his recitation. L.N. wept."

Another typical symptom of epilepsy is an exaggerated response to music. Tolstoy's was a combination of his usual lugubriousness and terror. His wife remarks: "I noticed that what he felt about music was accompanied by light pallor and a barely noticeable grimace conveying something that resembled terror." Tolstoy's secretary remembers that, when the violinist Erdenko played to him at Yasnaya Poliana, the writer "wept several times." The pianist Goldenweiser recalls that Tolstoy, who in general "wept easily," did so "not from grief but when recounting, hearing or reading something that touched him." He also "wept often when listening to music." That he did, at the drop of a hat. For example, when Tolstoy's friend, the composer Sergei Taneyev, took him to an organ recital, the writer burst out in tears on hearing the first note.[17]

"In other words," comments Yevlakhov, "his tears were not caused by true grief, real suffering, but by aesthetic, made-up feelings, by that treacly sensitivity, sentimentality that was highly typical of him as an epileptic."

Whether or not his sentimentality was caused by epilepsy, there is no denying that Tolstoy had that quality in spades. And nowhere was it more pronounced than in his militant vegetarianism, yet another part of his heritage that modern counterculture has taken on with alacrity. For in modern times it was Tolstoy who first added legitimacy to vegetarianism, turning it from an amusing quirk into some kind of political statement.

When he grew old, Tolstoy's affection for animals knew no bounds. For example, he could not stand flypaper—he pitied flies so much—and sermonized that one ought to "get rid of them without killing . . . for, having permitted himself to kill insects, a man is ready to permit himself to kill animals or people."

Some may regard this as a bit of an exaggeration unsupported by empirical evidence: we all know many people who kill their fair share of insects, but never animals or people. And speaking of empiricism, exactly how does one get rid of flies without killing them? One could ask them to leave without trouble, like; but what if they say no? Then again, Tolstoy's utopian ideas could never pass the "how?" test, and seldom the "why?" test. However, one does not need to be a psychiatrist, or even a psychoanalyst, to see how such hysterical sentimentality, along with Tolstoy's non-resistance and non-violence, can be a reaction to his own sadistic cruelty. And with him, even Freud could not go far wrong.

Both Tolstoy himself and others cite numerous examples of his cruelty. Once, when his horse was too tired, it would not leave the stables. Tolstoy flew into a rage:

No matter how much I beat him, he wouldn't go.... Angry with the horse, I was beating him as hard as I could with my whip and feet. I was trying to hit the spots where it hurt the most, broke the whip and was hammering the horse on the head with what was left of the whip.

That is cruelty. Then, suddenly, "I took pity on Voronok, and began to kiss its sweaty neck, begging him to forgive me for beating him." That is sentimentality. When the two come together in this fashion, it is hard to tell which is worse.

Looking back on his earlier life, Tolstoy remembers: "I used to be a hunter, I shot hare. I would squash a wounded hare between my knees and slash its throat. And I'd do that without the slightest pity." His son Sergei describes Tolstoy's cruelty in the 1870s, not long before the count's "conversion": "Not only was father not a vegetarian at the time, but when hunting he killed animals mercilessly. Thus, having winged a bird, he'd finish it off by yanking a feather out of its wing and sticking that very feather into its head. He taught us to do the same." Once, having smashed a wolf's skull with a club, Tolstoy admits "experiencing real rapture at the sight of the dying animal's suffering."

Nor was Tolstoy's cruelty reserved for animals only. He was attracted to killing of any kind. For example, this is how he describes his feelings about the mass murders and tortures committed by Peter I: "I was attracted to those monstrosities; when reading, I saw and heard them.... I didn't know what I needed from this, but I ineluctably had to know, see, hear it all."[18] And going off to war he writes to his brother in 1851: "To the best of my ability I shall use my cannon to exterminate truculent Asiatics and other vermin." When people, however objectionable one finds them, are described as "vermin," it is usually a bad sign.

When in 1862 the police searched Tolstoy's house in his absence, he writes: "That police colonel is lucky I wasn't there—I would have killed him." He meant it too; the sermon of non-resistance was still years away. In a letter 10 years later he writes about similar sentiments in a different situation: "Varia,[19] my favorite, is marrying Nagornov and for the first time I felt like the cruel father in comedies. Though there is nothing wrong with the young man, I would kill him if we hunted together." One shivers trying to imagine what Tolstoy's response would have been had he actually found something wrong with Nagornov.

He himself admits that when he witnessed a guillotining in Paris (the same one that, as he later alleged, traumatized him for ever) he was attracted to the execution because of his "stupidity and cruelty." Years later, already in the grip of his non-violence, he says to his secretary: "How can one not be curious? I wouldn't be able to keep myself from attending an execution even now." The secretary also remembers: "In his dream he took an iron staff and went somewhere with it. And a man followed him, telling passers-by, 'Look, there goes Tolstoy! How much damage he has done, the heretic!' Then L.N. turned around and killed the man with the iron staff." Dr Freud, call your office. There is a ghoul on the prowl.

The great Russian psychiatrist S.S. Korsakov writes: "Some [epileptics] manifest extreme hypocrisy, tendency to boast and self-aggrandize; with false humility they point out their superior qualities and high morals, they talk of God and at the same time are extremely cruel to their kin."

Yet again, Tolstoy must have sat for this clinical picture. For he had few rivals in his capacity for moralizing self-aggrandizement, bordering on megalomania. In fact, Tolstoy always was a moralist—both before and after his "conversion." Characteristically, his favorite writers were the didactic moralizers Rousseau, Flaubert, and Dickens (all, incidentally, also believed to have been epileptics). Tolstoy worshipped Rousseau in particular; he even wore his miniature portrait in a locket around his neck, where Russians keep icons.[20] Even his brother found this obsession mildly amusing: "You are asking me to send you the first volume of *La Nouvelle Héloïse*. What for? Judging by your letters . . . you remember it by heart."

Just as characteristically, Tolstoy could not stand Shakespeare, whom he called a "charlatan" mainly for what he described as Shakespeare's "amorality." How anyone could regard the author of *Hamlet*, *Macbeth*, and *Lear* as amoral defies imagination. One assumes that what he meant was that Shakespeare shunned the long moralizing asides so beloved of Tolstoy himself. In a less charitable mood, one could venture a guess that he saw Shakespeare as one of his few real rivals in literature, for which reason he also disliked Dante. Tolstoy did not countenance rivals, whether human or divine. That is why he professed admiration for Flaubert and Dickens whose writing was similar to his own, but not quite so good. Tolstoy did venerate Homer, but mostly because he proclaimed himself, not without justification, to be the Greek's direct heir.

But it is true that his attitude to aesthetics was generally moralistic, and he condoned only the kind of art that preached a moral message overtly, rather than weaving it subtly into the narrative fabric and dialogue, Shakespeare-style. When that was not the case, he would attack the artist savagely and not always in good faith. For example, in his essay *What Is Art?*, wishing to prove the incoherence of modern poetry, Tolstoy merged three of Maeterlinck's poems into one.

Tolstoy had the power of his moralistic convictions and never recoiled from trying to teach others how to live. Thus, when visited by the famous aviator Utochkin, he told him didactically: "You'd do better learning how to live well on the ground than how to fly badly through the air."[21] On another occasion, when entertaining the American feminist Jane Addams, he scolded her for not wearing a folk costume. What did he think the American folk costume would be? Indian feathers? Miss Addams clearly did not know, so she continued to sport her decadent middle-class attire.[22] But Gandhi, who was more receptive and had a ready set of props at his disposal, did begin to wear folk garb under Tolstoy's influence.

Yevlakhov believes that another trait of an epileptic is a rather detached, not to say cynical, approach to morals. Tolstoy himself admits to hypocrisy with his usual double-bluff naivety: "Every time I write my diary honestly I am not so cross with myself for my weaknesses; I feel that if I've confessed them, they are no longer there. Nice."

He filled his diaries with moral rules for himself, then proceeded to break every one, only to itemize the transgressions the next day. As a matter of fact, one characteristic of the diaries is a clean break between Tolstoy's life and his perception of it. The diary often shows him not as he is but as he either imagines or wills himself to be. Tolstoy realized this. On June 11, 1855, he writes: "It's ridiculous to start writing the rules down at age 15 and continuing to write them down at 30, having disbelieved and broken every one of them."

Any reader of *A Confession* will remember the poignant pathos with which Tolstoy describes the devastating effect his brother's death had on him. In fact, he cites this event as one of the key reasons for his "conversion." But he never visited Nikolai throughout his illness, and only witnessed his death because Nikolai himself had staggered into his flat to die. At the time another brother, Dmitry, died, Tolstoy wrote down in his diary (February 2, 1857): "Really, it seems to *me*, to *me*, that the worst thing about his death was that it prevented *me* from taking part in the show at the court." The "me" generation was alive and well in the mid-nineteenth century.

In 1866 he agreed to act as counsel for defense in the case of Vasily Shabunin, a soldier who had committed the capital offence of striking an officer. Tolstoy decided to take part in the trial not because he cared about the young man or justice but because he sought a platform for broadcasting his opposition to capital punishment. He did not prepare the defense properly and failed to engage a professional lawyer, instead screaming his usual platitudes throughout the trial. Shabunin was promptly sentenced to death and shot. Later in life Tolstoy was to claim he had been deeply affected by the case. But the day after Shabunin's death he went on a long hunting trip and, upon his return, hired the same band that had accompanied the execution to play at a ball he threw.

We have already seen that Tolstoy's writing was impregnated with moralizing long before his "conversion." This was by design. Here is what he wrote on December 20, 1853, at the onset of his literary career:

... I wonder how we've lost the idea of the only purpose of literature—moral—to such an extent that should you talk about the need for moralizing in literature, no one would understand you. However, it wouldn't be bad if, like a fable, every work of literature would have a moral attached at the end: its *aim* is.... This is a noble and, for me, realistic *aim*—to publish a magazine whose sole *aim* is to disseminate (morally) useful writings, with submissions only accepted if they contained a moral message.

All morals and no art could make Leo a dull boy, not to mention a sloppy writer.

However, Tolstoy's morality was peculiar. It was for instance able to accommodate defense of prostitution. Here he is writing to his friend, the writer Nikolai Strakhov: "Imagine London without its 70 thousand Magdalenes. What would happen to families? Would many wives or daughters remain pure? What would happen to the moral laws so dear to people? I think this class of women is essential for the family as it now is." A curious thought, that. Do the red-light districts of Hamburg and Amsterdam send moral messages through their windows then? The conventional—and intuitive—reaction would be to regard them as dens of iniquity, but perhaps Russian bordellos, which Tolstoy knew so intimately, were different.

Tolstoy's morals were general, not concrete, springing as they did not from a natural predisposition or innate kindness but from a convoluted philosophy. We shall discuss this aspect of it later, when talking about Tolstoy's theology and moral philosophy. Suffice it to say now that, when morals lose their grounding in everyday behavior, they often become immoral and always hypocritical. Also, people who have too much love for mankind, often have none at all for men. The general subsumes the particular, and the particular disappears—except when it comes to loving themselves. Unable to feel proper love, they replace it with amour-propre.

Tolstoy understood the neighbor that the Bible tells us to love as the whole of mankind. But mankind at large does not really exist, as far as our daily lives are concerned. Our neighbors include our families, friends, an old woman who needs help crossing the street, a cripple begging for a few pennies. These are our concrete neighbors, and, if we are able to love them with all our heart, we have already done well. But the amorphous, impersonal mankind out there cannot be loved with all our heart—we shall never know it well enough to love sincerely. It is only when the abstract becomes concrete, as, say, when a weak person is attacked by a ruffian, that our actions must be guided by love for people we do not know.

The concrete and abstract emotions here are not only dissimilar but indeed antithetical. Thus, it was for the sake of abstract love that Tolstoy destroyed love in his own family.[23] His wife wrote to him in 1885, "It's sad that, when you live with your family, you are further apart from it than when you actually do live apart." And, in her own 1890 diary, "If a man's salvation lies in destroying the life of his family, then Lyovochka has been saved."

Her brother, upon witnessing Tolstoy distributing money among the poor so as to make a moral point, writes: "I found in him a moral change for the worse, i.e. I had fears for his sanity." As to his half-hearted attempts to give up all his property, the concerned family declared that they would have him committed for madness. "Thus," writes Tolstoy's biographer, or rather hagiographer, Biryukov, "he ran the danger of ending up in a mad house, while his property would stay with the family anyway. Only then did he change his mind." Charitable impulses can indeed be most selfish. And, when considering Tolstoy's character, one should never forget that egotism was his main driving force.

When Tolstoy went to Sebastopol it was not to serve his country but "to find glory by whatever means." Only when this did not work did he decide to devote his life to literature, as an alternative route to glory. On October 10, 1855, Tolstoy writes: "I've been lazily-apathetically depressed for a long time . . . my career is literature—to write and to write! As of tomorrow I'll be working my whole life, abandoning all, rules, religion, decency—all." And a few months later: "I am completely ignoring, and wish to ignore for ever, all those postulates and categorical imperatives." This sounds odd coming from a moralist, but not, according to Yevlakhov, from an epileptic.

Nor did Tolstoy practice his abstract approach to morals as a young man only. Here, in 1905, he makes a critical admission:

I have all the vices and to the highest degree: envy, venality, greed, lustfulness, vanity, ambition, pride, malice. No, perhaps not malice, but rage, falsehood, hypocrisy. I've got it all, and to a higher degree than most people. The only salvation is that I know about it and fight against it. That's why they call me a psychologist.... It's good that I can be malicious, and miserly, and disgusting, and know this about myself. Only thanks to that can I (unfortunately only sometimes) meekly forgive, withstand the malice, stupidity, nastiness of others.

Reading his diary, his wife exclaimed in 1890: "My God, what a tone, alien, fault-finding, even mendacious!" And: "His self-adoration is evident in all his diaries." Indeed, "the tendency to boast and self-aggrandize" that Korsakov wrote about was amply present in Tolstoy at every stage of his life.

In his 1852 diary—at the age of 24!—he writes, "I must get used to the idea that no one will ever understand me." Next year he reiterates,

Almost every time I meet someone new I experience a cruel disappointment by imagining him to be like me and applying this yardstick when studying him. I must once and for all get used to the idea that I am an exception, that I am ahead of my age—or else I am one of those asocial, difficult people who are never satisfied. I must use a different standard (lower than my own) to judge people. Then I'd make fewer mistakes. I deceived myself for a long time fancying that I have friends, people who understand me. Nonsense! I have never met a person who would be as good morally as I am, who would believe that there has not been a single moment in my life when I was not pursuing the good and was ready to sacrifice everything for it.

Tolstoy thought he was the most moral of men, whereas in fact he was only the most moralizing. What is astonishing is that he made his claim to moral ascendancy in between visits to brothels, mercury treatments, all-night gambling sessions and repeated attempts to kill people in the duels he himself had provoked. Boy will be boys, and it is possible not to be too bad a person while doing such things, especially if one repents them afterward. It is only the superiority claim that is cringingly bothersome.

By 1855 his native country still had not seen the light: "I wish Russia were always to have such moral writers [as me]." In 1857 came another contortionist pat on his own back, "I am totally happy all the time. I take delight in my moral movement—ahead and ahead." And his unswerving moral progress was essential not only for Tolstoy himself. In 1874 he explains, "At least, whenever I do something, I am always certain . . . that the whole world would perish if I stop." He did and it did not, so there. But then hindsight is always 20–20.

As Tolstoy's moral message had little in common with what he really was, it failed to convince even himself. Like such epileptics as Mohammed, Swedenborg, and Dostoyevsky, he founded his morality wholly on religion, or at least so he claimed. But unlike them, Tolstoy was not in the least devout at any moment of his life, and his morals were not religious in any scriptural or eschatological sense but utilitarian and rationalist, based on Socrates's idea that virtue is knowledge. His own knowledge, that is.

In fact, Tolstoy's religion was as solipsistic as his morals. Gorky's recollection is typical:

In the diary he gave me to read I was struck by the aphorism 'God is my wish'. Today, having returned the diary, I asked what that meant. 'An unfinished thought', he said squinting at the page. 'I must have wanted to say God is my wish to know him . . . No, not that . . .' He laughed, rolled the notebook into a tube and stuck it into the wide pocket of his blouse. He has a very uncertain relationship with God, but sometimes they remind me of two bears in the same den.

This is a telling observation, and we shall come back to it later, when discussing Tolstoy's self-deification in detail. Gorky probably did not know Tolstoy's theology very well; otherwise he would have seen that "God is my wish" followed a distinct pattern. Tolstoy wrote countless passages suggesting, or flatly stating, that either God was but an extension of himself or, at his most modest, the other way around. In that he repeated almost word for word a similar statement of one of his heroes, Kant: "God is not a being outside me, but only my thought."

By the way, throughout this book, I shall be mentioning Kant often—because Tolstoy did. For, when it came to intellectual influences, the count was an equal-opportunity employer: he referred equally often to the figures of both the French and German Enlightenment. Apart from Rousseau, Kant in particular struck a chord with Tolstoy: he had put down many thoughts Tolstoy could (and did) call his own. The Prussian's ideas on rational religion, his detestation of church dogma, his "moral law within me," his epistemology based on separation between knowledge and faith all appealed to Tolstoy because they fit in with his own beliefs. But he treated Kant as selectively as he treated the Scripture: he took out what fit his own ideas and rejected what did not.

Often Tolstoy simply misunderstood the philosopher (it has to be said he was not the only one). He himself admitted as much, as in this diary recollection of his first reading of *The Critique of Pure Reason*: "I read Kant and understood next to nothing." That did not prevent Tolstoy from borrowing many of Kant's thoughts—while referring to some others as "nonsense!" For our purposes, it is equally interesting to see what he welcomed and what he rejected. In either case, Tolstoy was largely driven by hubris: he took equal pride in accepting those of Kant's ideas that were similar to his own and in rejecting those that were not.

In its extreme—Tolstoyan—manifestation, pride is perceiving one's own person above everything and everyone else, including God. A man in possession of such pride lives, consciously or unconsciously, according to a simple guiding principle: only my own reason matters. Actually, Tolstoy expressed this thought in as many words on numerous occasions throughout his life, unaware of how monstrous it sounds: "If there is no higher reason—*and there is none*[24]—then my own reason must be the supreme judge of my life." Therefore, "my own reason" (which Tolstoy equated with common sense) reigns, and I set the rules for others, rules I may not follow myself but will insist that others do. Expressing such sentiments in the context of everyday life is called arrogance. Expressing them in the context of religion is called atheism.

Tolstoy would produce variations on this solipsistic theme throughout his life. The only thing ever changing was the context and the angle. To cite a few examples from *The Way of Life*: "It is impossible to add something irrational to your faith with impunity." Or, "No truth can enter the soul of man other than by reason." Or else, "One ought to use what the ancient sages and saints taught us about the law of life, but we must check their lessons with our own reason: to accept everything that agrees with reason and to discard everything that doesn't." Saints and sages are thus allowed to act in an advisory capacity only—the slightest disagreement between them and Tolstoy's empirical reason, and down into the bin they go. Yet, as he admits in *The Critique of Dogmatic Theology*, even reason played second fiddle to his ideology: "Even if I saw that everything theology tells me is reasonable, clear and proven, even then I'd have no interest in it." Why, pray tell, not? Obviously because it was the existence of a wrong God that would have been "clear and proven."

The "tendency for self-aggrandizement" mentioned by the psychiatrist Korsakov was in Tolstoy a reflection of the sin he himself admitted. Seventh in sequence but, to me, first in importance, pride is the only deadly sin that makes faith impossible. Most of Tolstoy's actions and ideas sprang from it, no matter how many critics may ascribe them to different motives. For example, some may regard Tolstoy's rejection of his art as an heroic act of religious asceticism. But some others may attribute his motives to the pride of a man who, no longer satisfied with the calling of a great artist, wanted to act as a prophet, founder of a new religion. This did not fool the more astute observers.

After Tolstoy produced his version of the Gospel he went to Optina monastery,[25] where he tried to peddle that heretical scribble to Elder Ambrosius (one of the prototypes for Dostoyevsky's Zosima). There Tolstoy ran into the philosopher Konstantin Leontiev who at the time lived at Optina as a lay monk and whom Tolstoy knew well. The two men had a clash, for, true to his nature, Tolstoy mocked Leontiev for believing "all this nonsense," meaning Christianity. In Tolstoyan, words like "nonsense," "stupidity," and "rubbish" stood for whatever he happened to disagree with.

"If you lived here, you'd believe it too," replied the philosopher, recalling the episode in his book *The East, Russia, and Slavdom*. "Of course," jeered Tolstoy, "they lock you up here, so you have to believe willy-nilly."[26] He then spent an hour secluded with Ambrosius. After Tolstoy left, the elder responded to Leontiev's unspoken question by saying, "Too much pride in him. . . . This man is hopeless." Leontiev agreed, as testified by Tolstoy's entry into his diary: "Visited Leontiev. Had a lovely talk. He said, you are hopeless."

Tolstoy did not particularly mind: other people's views were only of interest to him if they agreed with his own. "A man has his own judge—conscience," he writes in *The Way of Life*, "only its verdict must be valued." And later, "Live alone, said a sage. That means you solve the problems of your life by yourself, with the God who lives within you—and not according to the advice or judgment of others." And still later,

Nothing either corrupts people's lives, or deprives them of true virtue, as much and as surely as the habit of living in accordance not with the wisdom of sages or their own conscience, but according to what is approved and regarded as good by the people among whom the man lives.

Clearly, Edmund Burke was not on Tolstoy's reading list, so he could easily ignore inference from the experience of others as part of what constitutes "true virtue." If philosophy was autobiography to Nietzsche, to Tolstoy it was nothing but that. Things either came out of his own experience or they did not exist. Unfortunately, one man's experience is always too limited to form the basis of a philosophy. It is barely sufficient to build a set of prejudices, especially those that do not sound too embarrassing when articulated.

Such was the mind-set of the man who decided to take revenge on God for distracting the world from Tolstoy's sermon.

CHAPTER 4

RELIGION WITHOUT FAITH,
CHRISTIANITY WITHOUT CHRIST

> Tolstoy was alien to Christ's religion as few have been since
> Christ lived; he was devoid of any feeling for the person of
> Christ.
>
> Nikolai Berdiayev

Falling in love with yourself may indeed be the beginning of a lifelong romance, in Oscar Wilde's phrase. It is also the beginning of
lifelong atheism.

For the starting point of faith has to be God, not one's own self.
The contrary belief is an Enlightenment fallacy one can trace back to
Descartes with his "cogito, ergo sum." "I think, therefore I am" is
a reversal of the theist outlook. It is tantamount to saying that man
created God, not the other way around. Relativist modernity all came
out of that Cartesian maxim. So did Tolstoy with his belief that nothing beyond his mind's reach existed, that his own reason was the
beginning and end of everything, the ontological be all and end all.

This is how he expresses the Cartesian idea in his most mystical—
and most Manichean—essay, *On Life*: "If at any moment of my life
I asked my consciousness, What am I? I would reply: 'Something that
thinks and feels', that is something related to the world in a quite special way. Only this and nothing else do I recognize as being my self."
Such self-perception leaves no room for God as either the Creator or
living presence.

On the other hand, "God is, therefore I am" would be an acknowledgement of the Creation. We may have been created in God's image, but created nonetheless. We are secondary; God is primary. Faith then is an attempt to go back to the Creator by humbly placing one's individuality at his feet. It is an act of submission, the self-effacing acknowledgement that our sins are so grave that we cannot save ourselves without God's help, and our minds so small that only by dissolving them in God's endless mind can we hope to use them for the purpose of salvation. We can be blessed only if we are meek.

If faith is an act of self-sacrifice at God's altar, then the mind is perhaps the greatest offering, especially for people with the greatest minds. But giving one's mind to God does not mean the believer becomes mindless as a result. Quite the contrary: God accepts the sacrifice and rewards the donor by giving him his mind back, having first cleansed it of everything extraneous, scoured it of everything dreary. Thus purified, the mind acquires the freedom it never had before, because, just as no content is possible without form, no freedom is possible without discipline. The greater the mind, and the more sincere its original sacrifice, the greater is God's reward, and the higher the mind can soar.

In the absence of such a sacrifice, the mind forever remains shackled to the earth with its mundane concerns—the mind itself remains mundane. Thus prideful refusal to submit one's reason to God's is punished by a diminished power of the reason. For, when looking at the world, the mind can see so much more by rising above quotidian problems than by staying mired in their midst.

How does one arrive at faith? Many roads lead to Rome,[1] and even more to God. But, whatever the route, it takes intuitive predisposition to embark on the journey. In Pascal's view, "You wouldn't be searching for Me if you hadn't already found Me." This is a brilliant aphorism, as Pascal's sayings tend to be. But in a less epigrammatic format one ought to add that the search must be conducted in good faith. The seeker must not set off determined to look only where God is sure not to be found: the traveler's own ego. Once this condition is met, every seeker will find his own way—and his own level.

Intuitive craving for God is a gift like, for example, a talent for literature. It is presented by an outside donor, and its amount varies from recipient to recipient. Not everyone who responds to literature with his heart can be a writer, and not every writer can be a master like Tolstoy. Similarly, not every believer who reaches out to God can be a saint like St Francis of Assisi. It is not a man who chooses God but God who chooses the man. And it is God who decides each time how much of himself to reveal, how much proximity to himself to allow. The way God makes his choice known varies. Some, very few, people have a revelatory experience: Moses on Mount Sinai, Paul on the road to Damascus, Francis falling off his horse. Such people come into direct contact with God, and from that moment on their lives are no longer their own. They become saints.

But most of us are denied a flash of blinding light or a voice booming out of a burning bush. We have merely a hint of an invitation to make the sacrifice I mentioned earlier. And only after we have made it will we receive our reward. But without such a sacrifice there will be no reward—not in this life and not, one fears, in any other.

What we make of the gift, however modest, is to some extent up to us. An honest grafter who works at his art day and night can become a good writer, though he will not become a Leo Tolstoy. And an honest believer who works at his faith day and night can become a good Christian, though he will not become a Francis of Assisi. Much of this work consists in contemplating the revelation given to others, the lucky few, even—especially—if the believer himself has been denied a revelatory experience.

This lyrical aside was necessary in the context of the previous chapter. For we have already seen that Tolstoy possessed a pride as hypertrophied as his talent. He denied any reason higher than his own "common sense." That by itself precludes faith: saying that there is no reason higher than one's own is as clear a statement of atheism as shouting, "There is no God." But Tolstoy was no common-or-garden atheist, for atheism is actually a kind of faith with the minus sign. The only unmistakable signs Tolstoy evinced were those of rampant egotism, but not without nuances.

While devoid of any true religious feeling, Tolstoy was richly endowed with mysticism. He was a mystical rationalist. His mysticism resided not in his intuition but in his mind—he had to think through his life, find a rational justification for it. And he correctly sensed that within uncompromising materialism the question of the meaning of life can never be answered. This realization is often the starting point of a journey to God for someone who is governed by his mind—provided he is ready to sacrifice it by putting it on hold until further notice. Only thus can an inchoate believer later take the step up from mysticism to higher metaphysics.

But even as there are people with perfect pitch who are incapable of grasping the subtleties of music, there exist people with strong rational minds who are incapable of grasping the subtleties of metaphysics. Tolstoy was such a man. When he was thundering away in his moral sermons, he sometimes said things with which any Christian—and most non-Christians—could agree. However, when he tried to take a plunge into the deep waters of Christian metaphysics, which, just as music, requires intuition and aptitude, he failed miserably.

His hagiographers tend to say that already in his early life Tolstoy showed signs of a strong faith. It was indeed faith, but not as we know it. Taking his cue from Spinoza's and Rousseau's pantheism, Tolstoy believed in the perfection of nature which is identical with God, in the happiness man can find by dissolving himself in it. This belief found its way into his writing from the very beginning. Uncle Yeroshka in Tolstoy's early novella *The Cossacks* already sees himself as a part of nature. He lives like a fowl in the sky, unworried about death: "I die, grass will grow." In another early story, *Three Deaths*, Tolstoy takes pantheism to its extreme by equating the deaths of the carriage driver Fyodor, a rich woman, and a young tree chopped down. And Andrei Bolkonsky, one of the principal characters in *War and Peace*, feels something similar when, looking at an old oak, he contemplates death. Combined with Tolstoy's denial of a reason higher than his own, which is to say God, such natural mysticism can easily cross the line between pantheism and atheism.

Natural mysticism is not a religion, though it can be the first step along the way.[2] Mysticism is like water seeking a vessel to flow into, uncertain which vessel will suit it best. Only religion can steer a man to God, by crystallizing a vague longing into faith and offering a molded shape which the longing can fill. The shape is well defined: whereas mysticism has to remain abstract, religion is always concrete. There exists no religion in general. There only exist specific religions, each with its own revelation, dogma, and rituals—its own way of looking at God and his world.

Mysticism, on the other hand, can only exist in general, and in that sense it is not only different from religion but opposite to it. That is why many who flirt with mysticism only ever use it as a stick with which to beat religion on the head. As religion is both higher and grander than mysticism, it tends to subsume it, channeling it into religion's own mold. But mysticism sometimes refuses to be diverted into that shape. One can say that mysticism relates to faith the way anarchy relates to liberty. When it is particularly recalcitrant, it may rise against religion so as to protect what may appear to be its freedom, but is in fact its lack of self-discipline.

Thus, while "an atheist Christian" sounds implausible, "an atheist mystic" does not. However, by driving a wedge between mysticism and faith, Tolstoy set out to prove that one could become both. With the obtuseness of an inveterate solipsist, Tolstoy recognized truth only when it came out of his own mystical experience and was validated by his own reason. Being an egocentric, he both felt no need for the revelation himself and denied that others may have experienced it. In general, he had no time for the spiritual experience of others, either individual or—especially—collective. So, to remain logical, Tolstoy had to deny both history and culture, which are either the context or the expression of such collective experience. And of course he loathed the church, the guardian of it.

Tolstoy's solipsism, unlike his so-called faith, came from his viscera. That is why it led him to a narrow-minded, often vulgar and crude, intolerance of the religion of others. This did not prevent him from making lofty claims for his own brand of Christianity. Yet a true Christian life is fed not only by mystical longings but also by the love of other people's religious experience. That is why true religious feeling always reaches tropistically for the church, which alone can pool together everyone's limited personal experience. But Tolstoy, who went to misguided extremes in demanding subjugation of the personal to the collective in ethics, went to the opposite extreme in religion. There he forever remained a slave to his own egotism.

That is why he was never for one second a Christian, never mind "one of the greatest Christians ever." His own commonsensical reason, incapable of high metaphysics, could only crawl, nimbly bending around difficult corners, along the low ground of utilitarian do-good rationalism, albeit tinged with mystical touches. He could never, for all his fulsome protestations to the contrary, accept a religion founded by someone who declared that his kingdom was not of this world. There were other religions, or rather philosophies, such as Buddhism, that appealed to him more, as they often do to godless Westerners.

But Tolstoy was no solitary truth seeker. He was a compulsive and hugely gifted communicator. So he sensed that his audience, weaned on Christianity, would never accept a sermon attacking Christ while proclaiming the truth of Buddhism, Hinduism, Taoism, or any other Oriental creed inscribed on Tolstoy's metaphysical banners. To make people march to his tune, he had only one option available: to come up with his own religion, while claiming that it actually was Christianity. And if his audience ever wondered why his Christianity was so different from what they knew, the only logically possible answer was to declare that his Christianity was true, while everyone else's was a lie.

The ruse did not fool Vladimir Soloviov, Russia's greatest philosopher at the time. In a private conversation, he said,

If Count Tolstoy, in laying down his theology, didn't support it with the authority of Christ, I would consider him perfectly within his right. Anyone is entitled to create a moral system and hold it up for debate. But the trouble is that the count passes the fruits of his own creation for a true, purified Christianity—and many can believe him, as serious knowledge of religion is nowadays a great rarity.

It is even a greater rarity these days, and we see hordes of unwitting Tolstoyans everywhere. They are the people who claim they have their own faith; need no intermediaries between themselves and God; look for God only within themselves; believe in an abstract deity, someone who "wound up the clock," and not in any specific religion. Most of such people end up, often without realizing it, as their own gods. Looking for God only within themselves, they find only themselves there. Trying to concoct their own faith, they are left with none.

What Eric Voegelin called "the privatization of the spirit" first turns the man into his own priest and then, if he is consistent, into his own God. And one's own God demands one's own creed. Tolstoy was an exceptionally bright man, so he set out to found a new religion at the barely postpubescent age of not quite 27, when he seemed preoccupied with writing brilliant stories and cavorting with gypsy and serf maidens of easy virtue. His diary entry of March 5, 1855, is especially revealing:

Talking about divinity and faith has led me to a great, immense idea, one I feel I can devote my whole life to fulfilling—founding a new religion in agreement with the history of mankind and Christ's religion, but cleansed of all faith and sacraments; a practical religion that, rather than promising future bliss, gives bliss on earth.

If he thought that such a religion could ever have anything to do with Christianity, he was sorely misguided. Actually, his creed does not sound like a religion at all, any more than his other pet idea of "the gospel of Christ the materialist" sounds like the Gospel of Christ. In fact, it sounds suspiciously like Marxism and other social utopias, draped in quasi-religious camouflage.

Lest you might think this was just youthful bravado, a silly idea the youngster fancied but soon abandoned, Tolstoy repeated it word for word in his last, posthumously published book *The Way of Life*. (That time he attributed it as "after Kant," which is only partly true. Though Kant did talk about a rational religion, he never went as far as Tolstoy in attacking God. He may not have believed in God, at least not in any traditional sense, but he felt no need to fight him.)

This puts a different slant on Tolstoy's watershed work *A Confession*, in which he described the spiritual evolution leading to his "conversion," his seeking of God. That "conversion" supposedly occurred about 25 years after Tolstoy first stated his intention to found a new religion "without faith," and about 30 years before he last did so. In the intervening 55 years, none of Tolstoy's writings suggested any fundamental change in his views. So the "conversion" had to do with tactics, not strategy.

Unfortunately for Tolstoy, successful new religions are founded not by seekers but by finders, people who think they have received the truth by the grace of God. Whether or not they really possess the truth, they do not feel they need to look any longer. The last thing they resemble is headless chickens running into endless religious dead ends, which is roughly how Tolstoy describes his search for God.

Apparently Talleyrand was once visited by a man who claimed to have founded a new religion. Alas, he complained, he had few followers. What should he do? "All I can suggest," smiled the old cynic, "is that you get yourself crucified, die and then rise again the third day." He was right, as old cynics so often are. In a world brought up on the miracle of Christ, a new religion cannot get off the ground without sacraments, miracles, faith—all those things Tolstoy and Kant, his fellow anticlerical thinker, despised so much.

Knowing all this, we shall be less likely than Malcolm Muggeridge to be impressed by *A Confession*, or indeed to trust its veracity. But judge for yourself, for it is time we looked at this work in greater detail.

CHAPTER 5

A CONFESSION THAT WAS NOT QUITE

Every day was for Tolstoy a journey of 20,000 leagues around himself.

Gleb Uspensky

In *A Confession* Tolstoy depicts his relationship with Christianity as that of a shuttle train that follows the same track back and forth. But all he succeeds in showing was that he never was a Christian, even remotely.

At one point he realized that the menial labor of peasants, accompanied by their Christian faith, was the meaning of life. Ergo, decided the count with his usual logic, he should share the peasant's labor so as in due course to end up sharing his faith. This ignores the obvious fact that both in Russia and elsewhere there never was a dearth of peasant atheists. And many Russian peasants in particular successfully combined protestations of Christianity with the most savage pagan rituals, such as self-mutilation, self-castration, mass orgies supposed to exorcise the devils, and so forth.

It was only as an extension of his religious populism that, for a short time, Tolstoy tried to follow the faith and rites of Orthodox Christianity. At the risk of being accused of over-reliance on hindsight, one may suggest that such a road could only have one destination, the one Tolstoy reached: a rebellion, first hidden and then open. Tolstoy turned to Christianity not for its own sake but as part of his populist deification of the peasant. Wrong reason, awful result.

As most of Tolstoy's beliefs, his rebellion against Christianity was weak on positive content but strong on nihilism. The nihilism was reductionist: by ridding Christianity of "faith and sacraments" Tolstoy reduced it to nothing but a moral teaching. Reducing even further, he boiled the entire moral teaching down to the Sermon on the Mount—and even that he either misunderstood or willfully perverted by depriving the Christian ethic of its eschatology (it was not for nothing that he perused *The Critique of Pure Reason*). Yet Judeo-Christian morality is about people's relation to God, not just to one another. This is what the first four commandments deal with, and they are not the first ones just in sequence.

Actually, Tolstoy's focus on morals lacked originality: he was not the first to sense the timeless, immortal nature of moral life. Many Eastern religions, along with Aristotle and his medieval followers (especially Averroes), the stoics, modern pantheists, and others all came up with a moral philosophy similar to Tolstoy's. But none of them passed sanctimonious moralizing for the true teaching of God. However, even though Tolstoy did not believe in the divinity of Christ, he touchingly could not—mostly, one suspects, for tactical reasons—tear himself away from what Jesus was supposed to have taught.

He starts out by admitting that as a youngster he was not innately attracted to God.

I was baptized and raised in the Christian Russian Orthodox faith. I was taught it during my childhood, boyhood and youth. But when I left university...at the age of eighteen I no longer believed anything of what I had been taught. Judging by some recollections, I never did believe seriously, but only had trust in what I was taught...but this trust was very shaky.

It has to be said that this lamentable situation was not going to change. Toward the end of his life, Tolstoy wrote in *The Way of Life*, "Is there God? I don't know. What I know is that there exists the law of my spiritual being. It is the source...of this law that I regard as God." Any pantheist could have said the same thing. Or a Buddhist. Or an agnostic. Or a deist. Or even, at a weak moment, an atheist.

But getting back to *A Confession*, "I remember reading Voltaire as a young man, and his mockery amused rather than appalled me." It is true that in later years Tolstoy fell out of love with Voltaire—but not with the contemporaneous philosophers of the Enlightenment, and particularly not with Rousseau. However, one thing we could say for Voltaire is that at least he mocked with a light touch. His chosen weapon was the rapier, not the bludgeon favored by Tolstoy. Alas, when the count swung his bludgeon at religion, he only succeeded at smashing his otherwise unrivalled power of observation.

Here is a glaring example.

One can't tell on the basis of a man's actions whether or not he is a believer. If there are any obvious differences between those who practice Christianity and those who reject it, they are in favor of the latter. Then and now, the open acceptance and practice of Christianity is mostly seen among stupid, immoral, cruel and self-important people. While intelligence, honesty, openness, good nature and morality are mostly found among the people who regard themselves as non-believers.

One can only gasp and sit back. For the "stupid, immoral, cruel and self-important people" who practiced Christianity in Tolstoy's lifetime included most great Russian writers, such as Gogol, Tyutchev, and Dostoyevsky, and every Russian philosopher of note, with many of whom Tolstoy was on a first-name basis. I have already mentioned Soloviov, Leontiev, Fyodorov, S. Bulgakov, Berdiayev, Florensky, Frank, Lossky, and Merezhkovsky in a different context, but they were all both Tolstoy's intellectual superiors and practicing Christians. In fact, Bulgakov and Florensky were later ordained as priests, while Leontiev took monastic vows in the last year of his life.

Those religious thinkers who had not died earlier were in the couple of decades after Tolstoy's death either murdered or banished by the very people who "regarded themselves as non-believers." While they were at it, those same people unleashed the kind of carnage never before seen in history, eventually murdering 60 million victims. Granted, Tolstoy had no premonition of the macabre events to come, but even in his lifetime the monsters Dostoyevsky described as "the possessed" were already going strong. The same atheists who, according to Tolstoy, had exclusive rights to "intelligence, honesty, openness, good nature and morality" were at the time he wrote busily setting up the hell Tolstoy missed so narrowly by dying in 1910.

By the time *A Confession* was published, *The Possessed* had been out for seven years. Dostoyevsky based his prophetic novel on the widely publicized instances of revolutionary violence tearing Russia to shreds. In the intervening period the well of blood uncapped by Tolstoy's beloved atheists—and partly in the name of atheism—had been gushing higher and higher. Several attempts on the life of the "Liberator Tsar" Alexander II had been made, and, when *A Confession* was about to come out, one of them succeeded—to the chorus of hosannas in the left-wing press led by the good-natured atheists Tolstoy extolled.

Interestingly, the left-wing intelligentsia did not care much for Tolstoy's great novels. This is understandable: by being unabashedly hierarchical, genius goes against the grain of liberal egalitarianism. While the Left turned up their noses at both *War and Peace* and *Anna Karenina*, such conservative critics as Katkov, Strakhov, and Dostoyevsky welcomed Tolstoy as a grandiose phenomenon of world literature. All those critics were among the "stupid, immoral, cruel and self-important" Christians, but Tolstoy was prepared to overlook that failing at the time.

The Left, however, later hailed Tolstoy's turgid philosophy, correctly detecting in it the predominantly destructive impulse they themselves shared. As a result, they lauded *The Resurrection*, Tolstoy's weakest novel, which abounds in virulent attacks on the church. That's more like it, decided Russia's "public opinion." Love the strident message, adore the insipid writing. In Tolstoy's lifetime *The Resurrection* went on to outsell *War and Peace* and *Anna Karenina* combined.[1]

But let us not emulate Tolstoy's tendency for sweeping generalizations and tar all atheists with the same brush. There are many who do possess the fine qualities Tolstoy ascribed to most of them. A kind person can do good works without being inspired by religion. A decent person does not have to be a practicing Judaist or Christian to love his neighbor. A tolerant person may respect other people's views and even their religion, in spite of having none himself. And though my empirical evidence is different from Tolstoy's, I would find it hard to prove that there are more of such good people among believers than among atheists. I think there are, but I cannot back up my belief with reliable data, and neither for that matter could he. But on general principle, perhaps someone who knows he will be held accountable for his actions no matter what, in this life or the next, would be less likely to commit a crime than someone who answers only to his own reason—and believes, as Tolstoy did, that there exists nothing higher.[2]

The count then goes on to confirm our growing suspicion that he was a crypto-atheist. "I can't say what I believed in. Among other things, I believed in a God or, rather, I didn't deny God, but which God I couldn't say. Nor did I deny Christ and his teaching, but here again, I couldn't say what the teaching was about."

Where does one begin? Believing in a God without being sure which one implies that there are many—or more probably none. That is paganism at best, atheism at worst. And if someone who was taught Christianity throughout his childhood still does not know what it is, then the standards of religious education in Russia must have been even lower than in today's West. Or else, more likely, those Kazan University professors were right when concluding that Tolstoy was "neither willing nor able to learn."

God being unavailable, literature was the only salvation. "At that time, driven by vanity, greed and pride, I began to write." For once, Tolstoy is being too harsh on himself. Artists with a gift of his magnitude may have all those abominable qualities, but that is not why they write. They do so because they have to—such a gift imposes its own responsibility. The Gospel that Tolstoy professes to love states this unequivocally: "For unto whomsoever much is given, of him shall be much required" (Luke 12:48).

In literature Tolstoy found a vehicle for his innate didacticism: "Our [writers'] calling is to teach people." That may be, but a story is not a seminar, and a novel is not a tutorial. They are works of art, and an artist must never sell his soul for a pot of message. As Tolstoy was in an ideal position to know, a novelist teaches people not by preaching to them but by uncovering the secrets of their condition, by looking at life with a sharper eye than they themselves possess. When a writer tries to teach overtly, his lesson becomes weak and so, usually, does his writing. Tolstoy's artistic talent was so great that his art survives his didacticism, just, even though the reader has to suppress the odd wince. That is more than one can say for his philosophical works, where the wince becomes insuppressible.

Actually, the belief that the purpose of literature is to teach people how to live was not unique to Tolstoy. For by then literature in Russia had assumed a role it never had played anywhere else. The intelligentsia had largely broken up with the church, abhorred religious philosophy (in Russia, there really was no other worthy of the name), and was nihilistic toward the state with its every institution. Since the intelligentsia had nowhere else to go, they began to look to iconoclastic writers as prophets. Much like today's "opinion formers," progressivist scribes became media celebrities, pronouncing with an air of authority on every subject. They were seen not just as writers but as prophets, God surrogates—and rewarded accordingly.

Professing hatred for the rich and powerful quickly became a lucrative occupation, which is yet another example of Russia presaging the shape of things to come elsewhere. The religious thinker Leontiev led what the writer Rozanov described as a "miserable quasi-life of grief and sorrow." The conservative critic Strakhov often could not even afford to offer a cup of tea to his visiting friend Dostoyevsky (who himself lived in a bedsit favored by cabbies and prostitutes).[3] But their inferiors Dobrolyubov, Mikhailovsky, and Chernyshevsky were parlaying progressivism into a life of renown and power. Contrary to modern falsifiers of history, it was those clamoring for the destruction of the traditional civilization who became "the Establishment", while the loyal, church-going conservatives were the true rebels. Thus Tolstoy's avowed mission was in accordance with the Zeitgeist.

But then he experienced the kind of crisis most people have at some time in their life. This comes from the inevitable realization that at some point, at three score and ten, give or take a few years, one's physical existence will end. Fear of death has led many to ponder the meaning of life. The answer they come up with usually depends on the exact make-up of the fear. Which component is the strongest? Just the biological reluctance of an organism to turn to dust? Feeling that the mission of one's life will remain unfulfilled? The altruistic dread of leaving one's family bereft and in dire need, material or emotional? Fear of the unknown? Anticipating and fearing the Judgment?

Our fear of death always includes one of these constituents, sometimes most, sometimes all. And if the fear is hypertrophied and unaccompanied by the kind of hope that can only come from faith, we can find ourselves in a manic crisis similar to Tolstoy's. Indeed many of us do, which is reflected in modern existentialism, deconstructionism, and other doctrines of hopelessness. All those Derridas and Foucaults owe a self-acknowledged debt to Tolstoy.

I was telling myself, "All right, you'll be greater than Gogol, Pushkin, Shakespeare, Moliere, every writer of the world—so what?"[4] . . . The question was: "What will come out of whatever I do today or will do tomorrow? What will come out of my life?" 'Does my life have a meaning that is not inevitably wiped out by death?

Despair took over. There was no ready answer. Nothing would come out of anything. Life had no meaning.

My life stopped. I could breathe, eat, drink, sleep because I couldn't help breathing, eating, drinking, sleeping; but there was no life for there were no desires I found reasonable enough to satisfy. If I desired something, I knew in advance that, whether or not I satisfied that desire, nothing would come out of it.

What, not even deflowering serf girls in the woods? But let us not be facetious; the man is obviously in trouble.

"The thought of suicide came to me as naturally as thoughts of a better life had come before." That makes sense. Panic-stricken at the very thought of death, Tolstoy considers hastening it. Here one is reminded of what Ezra Pound said about A.E. Housman: "He says we will all be dead pretty soon, so we ought to act as if we're dead already."

This is yet another proof, and *A Confession* provides many, that Tolstoy is like a beached fish when throwing himself out of his natural, artistic habitat. Just compare this helpless thrashing about with his sublime description of the death of Ivan Ilyich in the eponymous novella, which Nabokov described as "the best ever written" in his *Lectures on Russian Literature*. When ostensibly seeking realism, Tolstoy was able to rise to metaphysics. When ostensibly seeking metaphysics, he only succeeded in losing any tangible link with reality.

Where could he look for salvation? Books? Science? No, none of those.

I was looking for [salvation] in all kinds of learning and not only failed to find it but became convinced that all those who, just like me, had looked for it in learning had, just like me, failed to find it. And not only did they fail to find it, but they recognized clearly the same thing that drives me to despair— the meaninglessness of life is the only undoubted knowledge accessible to man.

It is not. This kind of knowledge is exclusively accessible and undoubted only to someone who seeks no other—and consequently reads only those tracts that scream hopelessness and obsession with death. The sages, into which category Tolstoy placed Socrates, Spinoza, Schopenhauer, Solomon, Buddha, Confucius, Lao-Tzu, and obviously himself, were all pessimists. (Illogically, he made an exception for the Enlightenment prophets of progress.) In particular, Buddha and his apologists, such as Schopenhauer, were among Tolstoy's favorite sources, and he quoted them much more than he did any Christian thinker.

In fact, one detects in Tolstoy considerable disdain for the great Fathers of the Church, especially the post-Nicaean exegetes. One could hazard the guess that this disdain was accompanied by scant familiarity: the only Western Father of the Church he sometimes cites is Tertullian. Tolstoy no doubt felt great affinity for Tertullian's moral maximalism and tendency toward heresy, which eventually drove him away from Catholicism and toward Montanism.

But the phrase that Tolstoy loves to quote from him happens to be one of the few demonstrably unwise thoughts ever uttered by a Father of the Church: "The human soul is by nature Christian." Tolstoy found this idea to be consonant with his own Rousseau-inspired belief in the inherent goodness of man. But had he read Tertullian in greater depth he would have found another maxim contradicting the one he quotes: "Christians are made, not born." This appears only a few pages later in the same book, *Apologeticus*, but then Tolstoy was a past master of selective reading. The thought surely is correct. The human soul is not Christian by nature. It can become Christian either by the grace of God or by painful exertion or by a combination of the two.

So the world was meaningless, life was ugly, and Tolstoy could not for love or money understand the elation Christians feel when rejoicing at the beauty of God's world. "These people have such stupid imaginations that they can forget all that bothered Buddha so much: the inevitability of illness, old age and death."

At last we have some clarity: Anyone who does not share Buddha's pessimism is stupid. Admittedly, it would indeed be stupid to forget the inevitability of illness, old age, and death. However, it would take more intelligence than Tolstoy possessed, or else a different kind, to understand them in the light of Christian metaphysics. Illuminated that way, those calamities appear not as the end of the road but steps along the way—or else punishing blows delivered to the same part of life man himself has corrupted.

Finding himself at an impasse, Tolstoy could think of only four possible ways out. The first way was that of ignorance: neither knowing nor being able to realize that life is evil and meaningless. "People of this type—mostly women, and also those very young or very stupid—have not yet understood the question of life that confronted Schopenhauer, Solomon, Buddha."

So women's ability to understand life is equal to that of either very young or very stupid men. No feminist then, Tolstoy. However, one does not have to be either very young or very stupid—or even, God forbid, a woman, the breed that, according to Tolstoy, was only good for one thing—to ponder those same questions and come up with different answers. Unless, of course, one regards Christ and all his followers as stupid, which Tolstoy probably did.

The second possible way was hedonism (enjoying oneself without worrying one's pretty little head about serious things); the third way was that of "strength and energy" (suicide); the fourth way was that of weakness (just getting on with life, knowing in advance it is meaningless). None was acceptable: damned if you do, damned if you don't. And faith was no better either:

My situation was horrific. I knew that I'd find nothing along the way of rational knowledge but denial of life; while there, in faith, I'd find nothing but denial of reason, which is even more impossible than denial of life. . . . According to faith, I, so as to understand the meaning of life, had to renounce reason, the very thing that demanded a meaning.

Augustine had faith, yet he did not renounce reason. Neither did Aquinas. Neither did Pascal. Neither did de Maistre, from whom Tolstoy borrowed his philosophy of history. Neither did Soloviov and Dostoyevsky. They all regarded reason as a gift they had received by the grace of God—and used it for the glory of God. None of that nonsense for Tolstoy though.

"But the moment I talked to scholarly believers or read their books, self-doubt, discontent, argumentative rage appeared within me, and I sensed that the more I listen to them, the further away from the truth I move, and the closer to the precipice." He still refused to recognize, or at least to admit, that his "argumentative rage" was directed at God and not just those who believed in him. In fact, Tolstoy claims he came to realize that one could not live without some faith—as long as it was not Christianity. Or perhaps, at a pinch, even Christianity could do; all those faiths are essentially the same anyway: "Where there is life, from the time mankind was born, it's faith that makes it possible to live, and the main features of faith are always and everywhere the same."

The "main feature" of the Christian faith is Jesus Christ, fully a man and fully God, who died on the cross to redeem our sins, then rose from the dead to go to heaven and sit at the right hand of his Father until such time that he comes again to judge the quick and the dead. I am not aware of any other faith that has these same "main features," and neither was Tolstoy, for there is none. What he meant was that he could find in any creed elements justifying his own religion "without faith or sacraments," one that was already fully formed in his mind. All he had to do was to move some "features" from the periphery of other faiths to the center of his own.

His religion may have been partly formed under the influence of freemasonry. Historians still argue whether or not Tolstoy actually belonged to a Masonic lodge, and hagiographers like Havelock Ellis deny it out of hand. But there is no disputing Tolstoy's inside knowledge of Masonic ritual and dogma, or the presence of Masonic overtones in much of his work. In this instance, the Masons are supposed to respect every religion, but above all they are expected to display tolerance and love toward one another. The Masons absorb what they regard as eternal in every religion, usually meaning nothing but ethics. They declare as their goal moral self-perfection, non-resistance to evil by violence, mutual assistance, and the spiritual brotherhood of the whole of mankind. All these "main features," and practically nothing else, are abundantly present in Tolstoy's teaching.

Embracing all religions can only mean embracing none. Also, reason—the way Tolstoy understood it as the ultimate virtue proclaimed by the Enlightenment—cannot lead an intuitive atheist to God, no matter how assiduously he applies it. That is precisely what Tolstoy proves by his next pearl of wisdom: "I was now ready to accept any faith, as long as it didn't demand that I renounce reason outright, which would have been a lie. And I studied Buddhism and Islam from books, and most of all Christianity from books and living people around me."

Unlike Buddhism, Christianity is not a school of thought, though it has spun off a great philosophy as a by-product. One cannot accept Christianity just by learning about it. One can only do so by embracing Jesus Christ, and Tolstoy was incapable of that. There was no point anyway, for people who did embrace Christ were no better than those who did not. In fact, and this was Tolstoy's recurrent theme, they were often worse:

> The believers of our social circle, just like me, lived in luxury, trying to increase and maintain it, were scared of deprivation, suffering, death and, just like me and all of us non-believers, lived satisfying their lusts, lived as badly as the non-believers, if not worse. . . . Only actions showing that their lives had a meaning that prevented them from fearing what I feared—penury, illness, death—could have convinced me. But I saw no such actions among various people of our circle. Quite the opposite, I saw such actions within our circle only among the greatest non-believers—but never among the so-called believers.

Ignoring for the moment that non-believers rate the superlative "greatest" while believers have to make do with "so-called," at this point we are confused. According to what we have read so far, fearing "penury, illness, death" should have been the highest praise in Tolstoy's book. These were after all the things that sent Prince Siddhartha round the bend when he walked out of his palace, saw a beggar, an old man and a funeral, and became Buddha. We have already learned that people who disagree with Buddha are stupid; so those who agree must have a shot at being clever. Thus it is "the greatest non-believers" who were stupid, as they did not fear those dreadful things. Tolstoy does not seem to have thought these things through even within the rickety framework he is trying to erect.

So does life have any meaning at all? It does. It is its own meaning—provided, of course, it is the life of Russian peasants:

The conviction that only life can help one understand the truth made me doubt my way of life; I saved myself only by abandoning my exclusivity and seeing the real life of common working folk—and by realizing that only this is real life. . . . The common working folk around me were the Russian people and so I turned to them and to the meaning they give life. . . . The people draw this meaning from the faith conveyed to them by pastors and by the tradition residing within the people, which is expressed through legends, proverbs, tales. This meaning was clear to me and close to my heart. But among our non-schismatic people[5] . . . this meaning was linked with much of what repelled me and seemed incomprehensible: sacraments, church services, fasts, veneration of relics and icons. The people couldn't separate one from the other, and neither could I.

That completed a simple syllogism: only the peasants had virtue; the peasants had faith, albeit sullied by "sacraments, church services, fasts, veneration of relics and icons"; ergo, Tolstoy was ready to give their faith a go. He even began to follow church rituals, and "for a while my mind didn't rebel." However, it was a very short while:

I desired with all my heart to be able to merge with the people, following the ritual part of their faith; but I couldn't do that. I felt that I would be lying to myself, mocking everything that's sacred to me, if I did it. . . . Almost two thirds of the rituals either couldn't be explained at all or I felt that, by trying to explain them, I lie, thus completely destroying my relation with God, losing any possibility of faith.

We have already had ample opportunity to see that "everything that was sacred" to Tolstoy was Tolstoy. No reason higher than his own existed, so it was out of the question that he could countenance the filial obedience implicitly demanded by church rituals. Of course rituals cannot be explained. It is not a case of explanation but, as Wittgenstein put it, of entering a world. Accepting Christian rituals is the payment for embarking on a long journey to eternity. You pay the fare, check the baggage of your ego at the gate, and you are off. But hold on a moment, perhaps Tolstoy only meant he loathed the minor rites? Alas, he did not.

Throughout his life, Tolstoy was scathing about three of the main tenets of Christianity: the Incarnation, the Eucharist, and the Resurrection. The first is the Word becoming flesh; the second, flesh becoming the Word; the third, flesh coming back to life. The common element is flesh: the same substance that dominated Tolstoy's existence, the same substance he deplored, fought against, but could not conquer. Thus, his rebellion against Christian sacraments and dogma was as egotistical as the rest of his outlook: it was largely a rebellion against his own flesh, a form of intellectual asceticism. But he would not own up to it:

"The main holiday had to do with the Resurrection, the reality of which I could neither imagine nor understand...the ritual of the Eucharist...was completely incomprehensible to me." In fact, the greatest problem was caused by "my taking part in the most common rituals, those regarded as the most sacred: baptism and communion." And why was that? Here for the first time "one of the greatest Christians of all time" finally says what he really means:

"When...the priest made me repeat that I believe that what I'll swallow is the real body and blood, I was struck in my very heart: not only was it a false note, it was a cruel demand from someone who obviously never knew what faith was." Tolstoy must have known who was the originator of that "cruel demand." But in case it slipped his mind for a moment, here is a reminder:

Then Jesus said unto them, Verily, verily, I say unto you, Except ye eat the flesh of the Son of man, and drink his blood, ye have no life in you. Whoso eateth my flesh, and drinketh my blood, hath eternal life; and I will raise him up on the last day.[6] For my flesh is meat indeed, and my blood is drink indeed. He that eateth my flesh, and drinketh my blood, dwelleth in me, and I in him.

(John 6:53–56)

Actually, Tolstoy did not need such reminders. He knew exactly what he was saying: it was Jesus Christ himself who was that "someone who obviously never knew what faith was." This was not a slip of the tongue, and he was to say many things along the same lines elsewhere. True enough, Jesus never knew what Tolstoy's faith was, but he must have had some idea about his own. Thus Tolstoy's faith—by then clearly formed, not subject to change, and not resulting from the search Tolstoy here describes so disingenuously—had nothing to do with Christianity. Merezhkovsky is correct when writing that

"Tolstoy's mockery of Christian sacraments and rituals . . . [fills] . . . the most shameful pages of Russian literature."

When people veer away from the religion they are born to, and especially when they try to replace it with another, the Gods of the old faith often turn into demons of the new. The rituals of the old creed now appear as magic and sorcery, usually of a perverse sort. That happened, for example, in the original Aryan religion described in the Vedas: the ancient deities turned into evil spirits. And that happened to Tolstoy who saw nothing in the Eucharist but an awful, incomprehensible combination of cannibalism and vampirism.

The peasants were fortunate to be so ignorant and stupid that they could accept the church dogma. "Only for poor me it was clear that the truth is interwoven with the finest thread of lies, and that I couldn't accept it in that form." But, having sorted Christ out, "in spite of all those doubts and tortures, I stuck with the religion." Then down fell the last straw, breaking the back of Tolstoy's brittle faith with a deafening crack. How could one believe in the Christian truth if Christians themselves could not agree on what the truth was?

At the time, my interest in faith drew me to people of different confessions: Catholics, Protestants, Old Believers. . . . I wanted to be these people's brother. And? The religion that promised to unite everyone in love and faith, that very religion told me that these were all people living a lie, that what gives them the strength to live comes from the devil, and that we alone possessed the only possible faith. And I saw that all those who practiced a faith different from ours, are considered to be heretics by the Orthodox, exactly as the Catholics and others regard Orthodoxy as a heresy. . . . The statement that you live a lie and I live the truth is the cruelest thing one man can say to another.

One could think of a few crueler things to say, such as that, because Christianity has different confessions, it has no meaning. Or that Christian sacraments are all savage and stupid, as are the people who follow them. Conversely, it would be not cruel but true and actually quite helpful to say, for instance, to a believer in human sacrifice that there just may be something wrong with that practice. One has to agree with Tolstoy though: there is indeed something incongruous about various Christian confessions being at odds with one another. Something incongruous—and something very human.

The underlying faith is the same for all Christians; it is only the religion built on the faith that has split up into many sub-divisions. The reasons for this are inherent to Christianity, and they reflect both its strengths and its weaknesses. They also reflect the strengths and weaknesses of human nature. The strengths are mostly metaphysical and theological; the weaknesses are mostly practical and psychological. By essentially holding its human element against religion, Tolstoy commits an egregious metaphysical error, one he will repeat in various contexts throughout his life. In fact, one could say that every idea he ever espoused was based, directly or indirectly, on the same metaphysical blunder: belief that, by his own efforts, man can achieve the kingdom of God on earth, and only on earth. And if it has not been achieved yet, then it is the church that is to blame. This mistake is worth correcting before we go much further.

Since the time of St Paul one function of the church has been trying to find a compromise between the truth revealed from heaven and the life lived on earth. The static perfection only achievable in the kingdom of God has had to be balanced against the dynamic human nature made imperfect by the Fall. This is not the Eastern balance of things similar in nature. It is a balance coaxed out of a clash between opposites: perfection and imperfection, one of them divine, the other human, but both extreme. That is why the balance is so precarious and why it has to be vigilantly observed: one step too far in either direction, toward either the sacred or the profane, and a precipice beckons. One or the other end of the seesaw will shoot up violently, tossing either God or man into the gaping abyss.

The kingdom of God is the ultimate goal of human development. Therefore by definition it is the end of human development: man will no longer travel, he will have arrived. The coming of this kingdom will signify the end of time, for God lives outside that category, as we cannot. And the end of time means the end of this world. The church maintains, and Christians believe, that such an end is to come when God wills it. But until then life has to be lived, if only as a way of edging toward the destination. One has to travel in order to arrive.

This duality of the temporal and the eschatological is the exact mimicry of the antinomian nature of Christ. The Scripture states that mankind will reach the kingdom of God when Christ returns, but not before. That is why the church has to reflect the duality of Christ to make it possible for the Christian community not only to expand but indeed to survive until that time—while following an unwavering course toward its sacred destination.

In other words, the church has to find a compromise between absolute perfection, as reachable only in the kingdom of God, and the relative imperfection of human nature, as precipitated by original sin. This the church achieved during the period demarcated by Paul at one end and Aquinas at the other. But in doing so it laid itself open to subsequent attacks from critics, from Wycliffe to Hus to Luther to Jansen to Tolstoy, who could always find its everyday practices wanting when held up against the absolute ideal postulated in, say, the Sermon on the Mount. That has been either the essence or at least the tactic of all reformations and most schisms, including those as ill-conceived as Tolstoyism.

However, had the church not found a compromise between man and God, Christianity would now be remembered at best as a timid attempt to reform Judaism in the early days of the Roman Empire. It would not have become a world religion—and neither would it have had the chance to civilize the world. Therein lies the strength of the church. But therein also lies its weakness. For, trying to adapt to the relative imperfection of human nature, the church itself had to become relatively imperfect.

Also, trying to fashion a religion that could thrive among peoples of different history, culture, and national character, Christianity had to adapt more and more to the local conditions, especially as the monolithic Roman world was dissolving into separate nations. Adapting to the character of each nation meant varying its own character to some extent from one place to the next. As indirect proof of this, the Venerable Bede (672–735) testifies that already by his time the barely post-natal English church had acquired traits peculiar to it— long before the great schism occurred or Henry VIII was born. The underlying faith of, say, an Englishman, a Gaul, and a Corinthian was the same. But, when their cultural idiosyncrasies were taken into account, it was a safe bet that their religions would not stay exactly the same for ever. Thus an institution created to spread the absolute truth had to, by its very nature, overlay its mission with potentially deadly relativities.

That was not just a rhetorical conundrum; it was a disaster waiting to happen. For, trying to be all things to all men, the church had to delve deeper into worldly matters than was good for it. However, during and immediately after the disintegration of the Roman Empire, worldly matters could use the help of a universally civilizing spiritual authority. Responding to the dire need, while still mostly preoccupied with things that are God's, the church had to claim some authority over things that were Caesar's. Somebody had to, for civic order was at the time in danger of imploding, thereby burying the Christian community under its rubble.

For a while this arrangement worked well. Christendom was seen as the single mystical body of Christ within which the sacred and secular realms worked hand in hand. It was not for nothing that Charlemagne's empire was called Holy Roman. It was indeed both and not neither, as Voltaire quipped with his usual lightweight wit.

In a way, during that period the church functioned not only within the state but also as the state. *Pax Romana* became *Pax Christiana*. Yet an institution that fills the vacuum left by the Caesar inevitably assumes some of his characteristics, including his vulnerability. Caesars can be deposed; they can be cut to pieces. To a large extent this is what happened to the church. As the remnants of the Roman world went their own way, the church found itself on the receiving end of divisive nationalist pressures that often adopted sectarian slogans, sometimes mostly for tactical reasons (arguably Catharism and definitely the Hussite movement are examples of this). It thus had to fight from a defensive and increasingly vulnerable position. As a result, the church had to forfeit much of its flexibility, its talent for finding various versions of the Pauline or Thomistic compromise. It had to erect a less and less permeable fence so as to separate itself from the secular realm it could no longer control. But inside that fence the church still had to balance the human with the divine.

This balance was delicate—an inch here, half an inch there, and it could be upset. This is what happened to the church, more than once. Consequently there always was much to criticize it for, as there still is. Moreover, it is the duty of all good Christians to do so, in the hope that constructive criticism proceeding from love can get the church back on track, help it find a new, workable dispensation.

For many of Tolstoy's Russian contemporaries, such as Soloviov, Leontiev, Danilevsky, and Dostoyevsky, such criticism often included a call for ecumenism, albeit with Russia leading the way as *primus inter pares*. One may disagree with that, but at least one can detect real minds seeking a real remedy for real pain. However, to use the problems experienced by the church throughout its history as a reason for attacking either the Christian faith or the Christian religion *in se*, as Tolstoy did, is morally indefensible and intellectually weak.

A real religious thinker, the Metropolitan Philaret (1782–1867), said that the partitions between various Christian confessions do not reach all the way up to heaven, but even if Tolstoy had heard this brilliant aphorism, it would not have made the slightest difference. He desperately needed yet another justification for his assault on Christianity, and anything would do. Such as that old chestnut: If the church follows Christ's teaching, then how come we have wars, not to mention executions?

And I noticed what was being done in the name of faith and gasped in horror, and I almost abandoned Christianity. The other attitude of the church to life was its attitude to wars and executions. At that time Russia was at war. And in the name of Christian love the Russians began to kill their brothers. One couldn't help thinking about that. It was impossible not to see that murder is evil, contrary to the first principles of any faith. And yet the Church prayed for victory, and teachers of faith accepted the murder as something following from the faith.

It was Aristotle, with his unsentimental reading of human nature, who wrote in *Politics* that "there must be war for the sake of peace." Tolstoy implicitly disagrees with this maxim, as he does with the way the church views war. We shall come back to this when discussing Tolstoy's take on Christian ethics. Let us just say for now that Christianity, while accepting that war is evil, still believes that there exist evils that can be even worse. If such evils can only be stopped by violence, then in that instance violence is to be condoned. This is why the church, including such seminal figures as St Augustine (whose *The City of God* first expressed the concept of just war in Christian terms) and St Thomas Aquinas, has always blessed righteous war for as long as it remained righteous—and damned unjust war for as long as it was unjust. At the unsophisticated time of Tolstoy, protecting a defenseless Christian nation, in that instance Bulgaria, against a cruel Muslim predator fell into the category of righteous war. And this happened to be the kind of war Russia was fighting against Turkey while Tolstoy was confessing away.[7]

No such arguments for him though. Say what you will, but any way he looked at it, Christianity was a lie—even though the saintly peasants believed in it. Again he had a conflict between two pieties: agnosticism and populism. Again agnosticism won over. "Even though I saw that the people had less of that lie that repelled me than did representatives of the church, I still saw that even in the faith of the people there was a lie mixed in with the truth."

That got Tolstoy back to his pet idea: his own rational religion "without faith and sacraments." Christianity had been submitted to the litmus test of Tolstoy's reason and turned neither red nor purple. It remained colorless.

I want to understand everything that seems inexplicable to me not because my mind's demands are wrong (*they are right, and I can understand nothing outside them*[8]) but because I see the limits of my mind. I want to understand everything so that every inexplicable idea appears to me as a necessity of my reason and not as a duty to believe.

Tolstoy is being coy here; he did not really "see the limits" of his mind. Otherwise, he would not have insisted on understanding every inexplicable idea to his reason's satisfaction. In any case, it was St Augustine who first argued that Christianity could only be understood from within, not from outside. You do not understand so that you may believe, you believe so that you may understand, wrote Augustine, echoing a similar thought in Isaiah. When Tolstoy did try to achieve understanding without faith, he found himself in the ungainly mess he thought was a new religion. The mess is so tangled up that it is hard to sort out. Yet I shall try to do so in the next chapter.

But before we look at Tolstoy's religion in closer detail, let us linger on his "conversion" for a while longer. That I invariably put this word inside quotation marks, suggests distrust. True enough, it does not appear that at the time he described, when he was about 50, or in fact at any other time, Tolstoy underwent any crisis of faith: his faith had been the same for decades before the "crisis," and remained the same for decades after.

As if to prove that, shortly after he had published *A Confession*, Tolstoy acted on his youthful promise and produced his own version of the Gospel, from which he expunged everything that suggested or even hinted at Christ's divinity: his genealogy, miracles, and resurrection. To counterbalance the omissions, he made some additions as well. Those the great writer integrated into the text so seamlessly that it takes a keen eye to see where, say, Luke leaves off and Leo picks up. He was confident that he was closer to Jesus than was anybody else, including the apostles and the evangelists. In that spirit Tolstoy felt justified in doing what he could to help us understand what Christ really had meant but presumably forgotten to mention. For instance, he ascribes to Christ five commandments that do not all appear as such in the real Gospels:

1. Do not be angry, whatever the provocation.
2. Do not have sex.
3. Do not swear any oaths.
4. Do not resist evil, do not judge, and do not appeal to human justice.
5. Do not discriminate on the basis of nationality; love foreigners as much as your own people.

The book was complete with Tolstoy's own imaginative translation and his own commentary, mostly of the kind that one would not expect even a sane atheist to commit to paper. Some of his comments presaged by about 40 years the frenzied invective of Yaroslavsky, head of Lenin's "League of the Militant Godless." But Tolstoy was an early bloomer, and he had stated his attention to bowdlerize the Gospel roughly 30 years before he actually did so. In his diary entry of October 13, 1850, he puts this with touching bluntness: "During the funeral[9] an idea came to me of writing a materialistic gospel, the life of Christ the materialist."

It would be easy to cite many such passages that would show conclusively that Tolstoy underwent no religious crisis at the age of 50. But this does not mean there was no crisis at all. There was, but not a crisis of faith. Trying to analyze it, I am bound to indulge in some conjecture, but without—one hopes—crossing the boundaries of plausibility. After all, some logical induction is often the only road leading to psychological understanding.

Long before his "conversion," having become perhaps the most venerated writer in the world, Tolstoy suddenly had realized to his horror that he was being pigeonholed. The greater the artistic fame he would acquire, and the more he would foster it with further masterpieces, the more the world would see him as a mere artist. But artists do art. They do not found their own religions, and we have seen already that doing so was the self-admitted mission of Tolstoy's life. Religions are founded by prophets, seers, demigods—and, critically, by those the world accepts as such.

That must have been the psychological cause of the crisis: Tolstoy realized with horrifying clarity that his public persona was getting in the way of his private war. Unless he did something drastic soon—for at some point he would die!—his mission would remain unfulfilled and his life would have been, on his own terms, rendered meaningless. Not knowing what to do about it left him in despair, and being, to put it kindly, an unbalanced man, he might indeed have contemplated suicide. Such an act would have been a death verdict on himself for having failed. "We do not tolerate failure," hiss movie villains. Neither did Tolstoy.

So, in order to have a sporting chance of fulfilling his mission, Tolstoy had to change his public persona—to engage in a lifelong exercise of, to use the modern marketing cant, repositioning and repackaging. (Let us not forget that Tolstoy was primarily a communicator, not a contemplator.) He had to make the world accept him not just as a writer but as a God-like figure, a Christ surrogate.

But, perceptive artist as he was, he knew that he would always remain only a parody of the real thing, that people would always see him as second best no matter how loud his voice or apocalyptic his message. This explains the seething resentment of Christ that resurfaces throughout Tolstoy's work. It also explains his incessant attempts to drag Christ down to earth, where the chasm between him and Tolstoy would be less noticeable.

The stratagem he favored was to ignore, or even to reject, the divine person of Jesus, while reducing him to the moral sermon that was not so different from Tolstoy's own. And, while lowering Jesus's person down to his own level, Tolstoy had to raise himself up to what the public would perceive as some approximation of Christ.

In the beginning was the Word, and Tolstoy knew his texts well. But that Word was uttered not in ink on paper but in the flesh, in the incarnated person of Jesus Christ. Naturally, Tolstoy did not believe this for a second, but he knew that most of his potential flock did. To sway them, he had to do a bit of mimicry, to embody his own Word not just in his writing but also in his person.

Hence his strident declaration of the futility of all art, accompanied by his undertaking to devote himself to the truth, not to frivolous writing. Hence his public striving for what he saw as Christ-like self-simplification. Hence his cultivated appearance that made him look like a dead ringer for Michelangelo's God in the Sistine Chapel. Hence his propaganda of celibacy, which he did not practice, and of vegetarianism, which he did. Hence his half-hearted attempts to give away his property. And hence his vicious attacks on the church and what he called "church Christianity," which is to say Christianity. Christian clergy was for Tolstoy what the Pharisees and Sadducees had been for Jesus.

All these were not the genuine urges of a troubled soul but the calculated moves of a chess player. Christ was the opponent to beat. Elements of various other creeds, including atheism, were Tolstoy's pieces, and he had to deploy them all in order to checkmate his adversary. It is only in this light that one can make any sense of *A Confession*—or indeed of the patchwork quilt of Tolstoy's religion.

CHAPTER 6

TOLSTOY'S FAITH, SUCH AS IT WAS

L. Tolstoy believes in neither God, nor in the Son of God, nor in Christ the Savior, nor even in "the wisest and most righteous of all people, the man Jesus"—he believes in nothing.

Dmitry Merezhkovsky

1

Tolstoy was unique, but he was not unique in every respect. In many ways he was the product of his time and of his nation, reflecting and sharing their characteristics. His nihilism, for example, owed a great deal both to the Zeitgeist and to the peculiarities of the Russian character—it was not for nothing that the word "nihilism" was invented in Russia when Tolstoy was in his thirties. New words appear when they are needed to describe notions that may have existed for a while but are now so all-pervasive as to demand a terse definition.

The Russians are not known as builders of the new on the foundations of the old. They generally believe in razing the old off the face of the earth, dredging the site, and only then, if they get around to it, beginning to build. Being by nature impetuous (Tolstoy is a prime example of this), they often run out of steam halfway through that process and stop at destruction.

Thus Peter I felt he had to smash old Russia to bits before making it over as a European state. The first part worked to perfection, the second not quite. Paul I started out by repealing many of his mother's laws, most of them good, and replacing them with his own, most of them bad. Lenin and his friends grabbed power without first having given the slightest thought to what they were going to do with it—apart from looting the country and destroying everything and everyone they disliked. When they took over, the painter Malevich, not yet the non-person he would soon become, spoke out in favor of pulling down the Kremlin, St Basil's Cathedral, and the Bolshoi theatre. Those buildings, he announced, were obsolete. They ought to be replaced, Malevich ranted, with the kind of forward-looking abominations his like-minded architectural colleagues were slapping together in the 1920s, and still are.

Tolstoy's attitude to Christianity was not far off. He raved and ranted, stabbing an accusing finger at God, the church, its founders, dogma, and ritual with so much venom that only a blind man would have failed to see the destructive animus. Yet the moment Tolstoy felt satisfied with the hatchet job and had to turn his inflamed mind to the sort of religion he wanted to replace Christianity with, the focus disappeared. His vision narrowed and the outlines became blurred, as if he was myopically squinting at his faith through a dirty window, having forgotten to put his glasses on.

His life gives the lie to the widespread notion that it takes physical hardship for a man to begin to contemplate the higher meaning of life. Tolstoy's "crisis" occurred when he had every outward attribute of happiness: worldwide fame, unfettered creativity, wealth, loving family. And suddenly, out of the blue, came the thrusts of an assassin's dagger: Why? What next? For I—the most talented, powerful, moral Me—am going to die! My mission will remain unfulfilled! I shall be remembered merely as a writer!

His animalistic terror of death partly explains Tolstoy's religious and cultural nihilism, although the same fear can drive others in the opposite direction. He even extended this dread of death to erotic love, to the power of women whom he consistently despised throughout his life. Sex, food, wine, and other earthly delights all triggered the same panic. He could no longer have a life because he knew it would end in death.

Tolstoy's obsession with death (expressed so trenchantly in *The Death of Ivan Ilyich* and elsewhere in his fiction) is at the foundation of his heresy, or rather heresies, for there were many. Death dominated Tolstoy's mind, leaving little room for life. Gorky leaves a record of this in his *Reminiscences of Lev Nikolayevich Tolstoy*, quoting Tolstoy as saying,

If a man has learned to think, all he thinks about is death. All philosophers are like that. How can there be truth if there is death?... Then he began saying that there is one truth for all, love of God, but on this subject he was talking in a cold and tired way.

True, Plato and Aristotle regarded philosophy as merely preparation for death. But all philosophers? How about Pascal? Aquinas? Newman? Or, closer to Tolstoy's home, Soloviov? That is the beauty of saying unsupportable things either on paper or when talking to worshipping sycophants. There is no one there to contradict you.

Tolstoy's main heresy was denying the cornerstone of Christianity: the divinity and resurrection of Christ. Accompanied as it was by Tolstoy's rationalistic rejection of the very possibility of a miracle triumphing over matter and down-to-earth reason, this led him to a view of Christianity that was close to Arianism. But Tolstoy was too big a man to squeeze his religious bulk into one tiny heresy. Like Samson, he wanted to push at the constricting walls. Like Samson, he did not realize that the ceiling might come crashing down on his head.

A scan of what he claims to be his Christianity reveals a stew of many heretical ingredients, most sampled by Tolstoy at the same time. A very incomplete overview shows:

Arianism—Belief that Jesus was a created being, denial of his divinity

Gnosticism—Manichean dualism of darkness and light, accompanied by rejection of the body as evil and a claim to special knowledge that will lead to salvation. Belief that the two testaments deal with different Gods

Chiliasm—Belief that the kingdom of God will eventually arrive without God's help

Pelagianism—Belief that man is unaffected by the Fall and can keep all the divine laws

Socinianism—Denial of the Trinity. Jesus is a deified but not divine man

Catharism—Belief that the physical world is definitely meaningless and possibly evil

Eckhartism (Free Spirit heresy)—Belief that it is possible to reach perfection on earth through a life of austerity and spirituality

Add to these the ever-present overlay of non-Christian components, such as pantheism, Buddhism, Taoism, Hinduism, and agnosticism, and one realizes that Tolstoy collected isms the way some people collect ancient coins. We have already seen that such eclecticism is not necessarily to be accepted at face value—it was not a genuine spiritual evolution but a trial-and-error search for the right offensive weapon. Yet many people did take Tolstoy's religion seriously, and some still do.

The important thing to keep in mind when trying to understand Tolstoy's faith is that his main motive was to wipe the slate clean of any Western belief, especially Christianity. Only when the slate was pristine could he scribble his own fiery message, hoping that people, shielding their eyes from the blinding light, would exclaim "Ecce homo!" or words to that effect. But his fire could only scorch, not illuminate. There was no light. There was nothing but incessant attempts to reduce God's message to Tolstoy's own rationalist, moralizing musings. There was no God but reason, and Tolstoy was its prophet.

The way he puts this in *The Way of Life* is revealing. "Both before and after Christ, people were saying the same thing: that inside man lives a divine light sent from heaven, and that this light is reason—which alone must be served, in which alone one can find the good." The implication is that one is supposed to feel sorry that Christ interfered, albeit temporarily, with this consistently rationalist vision.

That Tolstoy saw reason as an offensive weapon against God is confirmed by endless sources, such as his own letter to a friend, the poet Fet, with whom he conducted extensive correspondence in 1859–60:

Pray to whom? What is God when perceived so clearly that one can communicate with him? Whenever I imagine a God like that, he loses all his grandeur....A God who could be asked or served is an expression of feeble-mindedness. He is God precisely because I can't imagine his essence...all God is, is power and law....May this page remain as a monument to my conviction of the power of reason.

Yet again, this is a direct dig at Christ who not only told his followers to pray to God but, in the Lord's prayer, told them how to do so. So it is he who is the target for the accusation of "feeble-mindedness." At the same time, reducing God to "power and law" seems to take us into the first part of the Bible, and away from the second. Yet Tolstoy, just like one of his idols Kant, made a point of rejecting the Old Testament out of hand. On numerous occasions, not least in his commentary on the Gospel, he denied that the Old Testament had any value whatsoever: "Christ rejects all, absolutely all Jewish teaching. Really, this is clear and irrefutable to such an extent that one feels somehow embarrassed trying to prove it."

Again, the rivalry explanation comes in handy. The Old Testament God may have been largely about "power and law," but the wrong kind, which is to say not Tolstoy's kind. Therefore that God had to go. Actually, a deity that exists only as a one-time law-giver is not even the God of the Old Testament. It is the ill-defined deistic God of Locke and Rousseau, the dead God of Nietzsche, the moralizing, rationalistic God of Tolstoy.

His impaired vision of God has little to do with the Gospels and even less with the New Testament in its entirety. Once again, reason to Tolstoy is not Logos but "common sense," which in this case is indeed very common but not very sensible. And it is certainly not Christian. Searching for a religion based on belief in an "eternal service to reason, in which alone one can serve the good," we have to veer east of Jerusalem and keep going until we get to the Far East of Confucius and Lao-Tzu, then turn right and go to the land of Buddha.

If Tolstoy based his metaphysics on anyone Western at all, it was not so much Christ as the moralizing, rationalizing deists and pantheists of the seventeenth and eighteenth centuries. But in reality he did not follow anybody. He would take his multitude of sources, Eastern or Western, and do a Procrastes on them, chopping off a bit here, stretching out there, until in the end they could all fit into the squeaking bed of his creed.

That is why most critics of Tolstoy tend to shy away from taking issue with his metaphysics. In a way, his eclecticism is like a wide net of decoys designed to divert potential attacks. Are these real fortifications or cardboard cutouts? Real battlements or sand castles? Charging knights or windmills? Critics shrug, fire a few tentative salvos, and then usually decide not to waste their ammunition any further, preferring instead to fight Tolstoy's practical prescriptions, such as non-resistance, rejection of culture, civilization and the state, and his moral dicta. Only in those areas there seems to remain some room for dialogue. His metaphysics only leave room for scorn.

Take his affection for Buddhism, for example, and other subcontinental creeds. They all attracted Tolstoy mostly because they fit his purpose of grabbing God's ankles and dragging him down to earth. This begins with cosmology, the origin of the world. The Judeo-Christian God made the world as a free act of absolute creation, that is out of nothing. As a result God stays above the cosmos, thus remaining absolutely free. Conversely, the Vedic gods—just like their Greek colleagues—did not create the cosmos; they merely made it orderly. They both begin and end within the world, sharing its cosmic non-freedom and never being able to break out of it. The road to freedom is paved with contemplation, meditation, and asceticism, and it may be open to some people, but never to their gods. That is why the Vedic gods are inferior to any great ascetic and certainly to Buddha who, unlike the gods, have all won their freedom by following certain inward-looking practices.

By now we know enough about Tolstoy to understand why such religions appealed to him. He would find irresistible any concept of a God who, rather than viewing man from an unreachable height and demanding prostrate obedience, seemed to be there for the over-taking. Buddhism, though falling short of Tolstoy's requirement of promising "bliss on earth," had many elements of the "religion without faith" that Tolstoy saw in his mind's eye. He was also attracted by the self-centered mysticism of the Buddhist, and his ability to rise higher than any god. At the same time, this kind of religion offered the weapon of predestination that in Tolstoy's eyes made the God of the Bible ever so vulnerable.

He had a point there. For logical theodicy—defense of God—is no straightforward matter within the doctrine of predestination, especially when it is maintained as rigidly as in Buddhism. Even Luther[1] struggled trying to reconcile theodicy with predestination, stating paradoxically that, if it were in any way possible to understand how God who is so wrathful and unjust can be merciful and just, there would be no need for faith. Such abject intellectual surrender is odd, considering Luther's Augustinian background. For it was Augustine who first resolved the seeming conflict between predestination and free will, though his explanation is not the only one possible.

To a Christian thinker the idea of predestination is fused with justi-fication by faith and the relevance of good works to salvation. The link is unbreakable but subtle, not lending itself easily to simplistic reduc-tions so beloved of Tolstoy. For predestination only has a transcendent but not always an immanent meaning. It is rooted in the timelessness of God's life, as opposed to the temporal existence of man. God has neither the past nor the future; they are both the present to him. From his timeless height, God looks down upon earthly time the way a space traveler would look down upon the earth from a faraway star. Viewed from that perspective, time—and therefore human life before and even after death—is reduced to an infinitesimal dot that only looks like a continuity from immanent proximity. From the vantage point of transcendent timelessness, our customary difference between a good and sinful life looks the way the difference in height between a seven-foot giant and a four-foot midget would appear from the sun. Hence both the predestination of man and the prescience of God.

But as we descend to the immanent world and get closer to the dot, it begins to grow and continues to do so until it unfolds into a seemingly endless line. The difference between the giant and midget becomes visible—and the difference between good deeds and bad vital. Time becomes a meaningful concept, and within it man's ability to choose between good and evil is paramount. Justification by faith as the route to salvation, when lowered to the immanent level from its original niche in the timelessness of God, suddenly needs help from man's good deeds. God, while remaining omniscient, at this point chooses not to exercise his omnipotence—just as he left Adam and Eve to make their own choice between good and evil, even though he knew in advance which way they would go.

The Christian doctrine of free will within time and predestination outside it can thus obviate, or at least reduce, the need for Lutheran paradoxes. And it can also help even rigorous Protestants to activate their own moral resources in good cause. No such help for the Buddhists or for Tolstoy.

The God of the Old Testament can punish our sins, Jesus can forgive them, but Buddha says we can never escape the consequences of our karma. This means that, if God predetermines every human action, then God is solely to blame for all evil done in the world. He therefore has forfeited the moral right to punish anybody, even the worst criminals. The guilt is God's own, not the sinner's. And if God himself has no right to act as a judge, then mortal men certainly cannot. This gives Tolstoy another opening to attack the church and every Western institution, including the state with its justice. And such openings were all he really sought.

Buddhism's cyclical view of existence was another feature that had to attract Tolstoy. Reducing life to a series of predetermined cycles means that history is meaningless, and this makes Buddhists fatalistic and indifferent. It also gives Tolstoy a justification for his nihilistic rejection of Western history and culture. Both after all represent linear development toward the eschatological goal. So, having decided in advance that history has no meaning and culture no value, Tolstoy found in Buddhism—and its various Eastern spin-offs—a creed that made such nihilism plausible.

All that the Buddhists retain of faith, in our understanding of the word, is the joy of a good conscience, with all the power this gives to live a graceful and forgiving life of love. However, human life is somehow pointless since each rebirth is but a *samsara*, "wandering on" in the baseless hope that one day we will reach nirvana. Yet according to some Buddhist traditions, nirvana will never be reached, for we must pass through infinite worlds in our development cycle, always returning to square one. Ask a Buddhist to define nirvana, and he will be unlikely to have a clear idea. The best one can get is vague allusions to the further shore...island amidst the flood...cave of shelter...beyond the realm of reason. It is impossible to put meaning into these words, and the result is that Buddhism offers neither definable, understandable hope nor any sense of the direction in which we should be heading.

The biblical doctrine of the kingdom of God is dramatically different, though of course not to Tolstoy. Christ offers believers spiritual renewal in God and a one-time rebirth through baptism in water (John 3:3–5). As a result they will enter the kingdom of God when Christ returns, thus erasing the boundary between heaven and earth. The rebirth Christ offers is therefore a rebirth to eternal life, whereas all Buddhist rebirths end finally in death. And their idea of reincarnation, though superficially reminiscent of the Christian resurrection, is in fact its opposite. The Buddhist's soul does not reach the ultimate perfection of resurrection—it merely hops from one body to the next. Christianity saves man from death; Buddhism saves him from life. "Death is the transition from one consciousness to another, from one image of the world to another," says Tolstoy. Buddha himself could not have put it better.

For a Christian the absolute is unknowable completely. For a Buddhist the absolute is completely unknowable. It lies beyond human understanding, and paradoxically that appealed to Tolstoy's rationalism. To him there was nothing higher than his commonsensical reason. Therefore whatever lay outside common sense, such as God, either did not exist or may as well not have existed. To Tolstoy, rationally unknowable meant non-existent. So mixed with Western rationalism, Buddhism naturally segues into Western godlessness.

Hence Tolstoy's never-ending flirtation with Buddhism and other Asian creeds: when transplanted from the Ganges valley to the spiritual area currently irrigated by the Jordan, they justify atheism. More important, they allow Tolstoy to take God down a peg. Thus in his hands Buddhism, a peaceful and harmless philosophy in its native habitat, becomes a weapon of religious destruction—and this is mostly how it has been used in the West ever since. Such misuse is predictable. For it is harder for a Westerner to become a genuine Buddhist than for, say, an Indian to become a genuine Christian.

Every religion begets a complex behavioral system. When it has been in existence for millennia, it has entered the genes and begun to interact with people's personalities in all sorts of intricate ways. The religion absorbs behavior, and behavior absorbs the religion. This is a meandering, millennia-long road, and the only shortcut can come from a revelatory experience or its approximation. That avenue is open to would-be Christians, but not to would-be Buddhists (their "enlightenment" relates to the Christian revelation roughly the same way as their reincarnation relates to the Christian resurrection). That is why most Westerners who describe themselves as Buddhists really are not. They simply dislike Christianity but, as we do not live by bread alone, feel they ought to like something in its stead. This is negation rather than assertion, and Western Buddhists, the J.D. Salingers and Richard Geres of this world, ought to thank Tolstoy for having shown the way.[2]

There are many historical sources confirming Tolstoy's flirtation with Buddhism. For example, Gorky, who, before he was anointed by Lenin, had been Tolstoy's friend and disciple, recalls in his *Reminiscences of Lev Nikolayevich Tolstoy*: "He said I ought to read the Buddhist catechism.... Of Christ, he talks particularly badly. His words lack enthusiasm and pathos, not a single spark of the heart's fire. I think he regards Christ as naïve and pitiful and though he—sometimes—admires him, he hardly loves him."

Immediately following *A Confession*, Tolstoy wrote *Critique of Dogmatic Theology*, his own abridged—very abridged—translation of the Gospels, and the pamphlet *What I Believe*. He made no bones about the purpose of those works: the count set out to debunk "the false Christianity of the church" so as to "assert its true meaning." As ever, his criticism proceeded from "common sense." He insisted in no uncertain terms that the church conform to the demands of elementary reason. And since it could not do that, Tolstoy triumphantly rode roughshod over it. Having first attacked the church for being too human, he now attacked it for being too divine.

Empirical mysticism, rationalism, and solipsism are the principal constituents of Tolstoy's religiosity. He desperately tried to be a religious rationalist, along the lines of Aquinas. But true religious rationalism, such as St Thomas's, never turns away from the revelation. This is proved by much theology and philosophy based on church dogma. Actually, Tolstoy's positive ideas are as far removed from sound common sense as they are from faith. He only showed rationalism in the negative part of his religion, in his attacks on established Christianity.

But even there his appeal to common sense was highly selective, an ace pulled out of Tolstoy's sleeve whenever it suited him. By and large he used only his own mystical experience, often without thinking it through properly. That is why his criticism of the church, for all its energy and passion, was never deep. He rejected the church without first taking the trouble to understand it.

Feeling constricted, suffocated within the ecclesiastical confines, Tolstoy acted the way claustrophobic people often do when finding themselves on a crowded bus—he began to push others aside. He himself believed that the dogma, miracles, and sacraments of Christianity were all one big, awful lie. But rather than treating with kindness those who derived from these the deepest solace, he treated them with cruelty, venom, and malice, shoving them aside as if they were inanimate obstacles blocking his way. When doing so, he often shunned the very common sense in whose name he supposedly acted. Witness, for example, how Tolstoy describes in *The Way of Life* the martyrdom of the early Christian reformer John Hus (1370–1415):

In 1415 John Hus, because he was exposing the false faith of the Catholics and the evil deeds of the Pope, was found to be a heretic, tried and sentenced to death without bloodshed, that is by burning. He was executed beyond the city gates, amid the gardens.[3] When Hus was brought to the place of the execution, he knelt and began to pray. When the executioner told him to enter the pyre, Hus got to his feet and said loudly, "Jesus Christ! I am going to my death for preaching your word and I shall suffer with resignation." The executioners stripped Hus and tied him to the post; Hus's feet stood on a bench. They put kindling and straw all around him. The kindling and straw reached up to Hus's chin. Then the officer in charge approached Hus and said he would be reprieved if he recanted and withdrew everything he had said. "No," said Hus, "I'm not guilty of anything." When the executioners lit the fire, Hus chanted the prayer, "Christ, Son of living God, have mercy upon me!" The fire rose up high, and Hus fell silent. Thus people who called themselves Christians confirmed their faith.

It could end here, but in fact there is one last sentence after this, with which Tolstoy sums up the story. Can you guess what it is? Here is a multiple choice: (*i*) there must be something about that faith for people to be ready to die for it; or (*ii*) there are some people for whom the love of God is stronger than the fear of death; or the atheist option, (*iii*) people are different from animals in that they are prepared to die for an idea, even one as false as religion.

The answer is, none of the above. This is how Tolstoy ends the story: "Is it not clear that this was not a faith but the crudest possible superstition?" What is clear is that the ending is a *non sequitur*, but then it did not come from Tolstoy's mind; it came from his viscera. In one stroke Tolstoy dismisses Christian martyrdom as savagery. One detects a strong resentment there, as if God had led Tolstoy up the garden path, landing him smack in the middle of a religious maze. Messrs Marx, Engels, Lenin would have been proud of such a punchy payoff line. As they would be of Tolstoy's other snappy phrases, both their meaning and style: "The concept of Christ as the Son of God is lunacy," "The doctrine of revelation is nonsense." Such lines of Tolstoy are strewn about his corpus of work. If pulled out of their actual pages, they could easily fill a longish volume, his 91st.

2

Tolstoy, individualist though he was, stepped onto a path to God that was well trodden by many others. He realized, rightly, that life can only have the kind of meaning that is not cancelled by death. In other words, he sensed that outside God the question of the meaning of life can neither be answered nor indeed asked. Therefore his self-deification led him into a cul-de-sac: only God could provide the meaning of life, Tolstoy could not do so, ergo: He! Was not! God! The thought was too much to bear, and that was part of what made him go off the rails, causing his much-vaunted crisis.

Tolstoy never perceived the reality of God, but he perceived the need for him. That was his link, however tenuous, with God and thus with the meaning of his own life. But somehow that did little to assuage Tolstoy's fear of death—the critical element of immortality was missing. For, having found himself at a spiritual crossroads, the path he took to immortality diverged from Christianity and led him nowhere.

Following Christ's words and the known facts of the Gospel, the Christian church believes in the resurrection of the whole person, body and soul. But Tolstoy not only emphatically rejected this promise of Christ but also denied that such a promise ever had been made. In *What I Believe*, he says "Christ . . . never uttered a single word suggesting personal resurrection and a person's immortality beyond the coffin."

True enough, Christ never uttered a single word suggesting personal resurrection in the Gospel as "translated" by Tolstoy. In his real Gospel, however, Christ said many words about it. Here is a brief sample:

And thou shalt be blessed; for they cannot recompense thee; for thou shalt be recompensed at the resurrection of the just.

(Luke 14:14)

But they which shall be accounted worthy to obtain that world, and the resurrection from the dead.... Neither can they die any more: for they are equal unto the angels; and are the children of God, being the children of the resurrection.

(Luke 20:35, 36)

And shall come forth; they that have done good, unto the resurrection of life; and they that have done evil, unto the resurrection of evil.

(John 5:29)

Rejecting the resurrection of the flesh, Tolstoy comes up with his own explanation of Christ's passion: what Christ sees as the opposite to earthly life is not afterlife but collective life. Christ, as interpreted by Tolstoy, teaches the immortality not of individuals but of mankind, which is the true Son of God. He goes on to say, "Belief in afterlife is a base and crude notion common to savages, from whom church dogma borrowed it."

I can no longer doubt that, while my personal life perishes, the life of the world—by the will of our Father—does not, and only this makes salvation possible. But how small it is compared with the elevated religious belief in personal immortality! Well, it may be small, but it's true. (*The Kingdom of God Within You*)

He is half right there: it is indeed small. His concept of immortality reduces the person to an insignificant cog in the wheel of the collective juggernaut—it is socialism by other means. By implication, it reduces the person of Christ to an irritating irrelevance. Moreover, this collectivism run riot paves the way not just for any old socialism but for its nastier forms, those that deny the intrinsic significance of the individual altogether, totally subjugating the personal to the collective. Incidentally, the idea of replacing individual immortality with the immortality of the species comes straight from Aristotle, or rather Averroes's interpretation of Aristotle. Closer to Tolstoy's time it was postulated by one of his heroes, Kant, who may have borrowed it from Aristotle, along with his ethics based on "the starry sky above me and the moral law within me." Here and everywhere, in selecting his sources, Tolstoy follows his ground rule of ABC: Anything But Christianity.

This kind of collectivism is immortality according to Leo but not according to Jesus. Tolstoy introduces the concept of the Son of God here as part of his general tendency to reshape Christ's words to suit his own purposes. He uses this concept, as he does many others, seemingly for assertion but in fact for negation, in this case of personal immortality and resurrection.

To Tolstoy mortality and immortality merely reflected the conflict between the personal and the collective. As a man is mortal, he exists within a certain time frame. However, mankind, which according to Tolstoy is the true Son of God, is immortal and therefore timeless. Thus, in order to become immortal, a man has to reject his personal happiness, his own personal self, dissolving it in the collective happiness of mankind. In this way Tolstoy justifies his characteristic amalgam of affection for humanity in general and indifference to human beings in particular.

Once again, everything Tolstoy says on any subject is a transparent cover for his own experience. In this context, he writes non-stop about devoting one's life to the good of mankind, what with individual happiness being unattainable. Peeking under the cover, though, one discerns in Tolstoy a craving for just such individual happiness, and bitterness over not having been able to attain it. His religious system was also built exclusively on the skimpy foundations of his own experience, and he borrowed from the Gospels only what agreed with it. That this is the case is proved by Tolstoy's lifelong attempts to create a religious system without the revelation of which he himself was deprived. In doing so he persisted in referring to biblical tests in the hope of finding support for his own faith. That was a vain hope from the start.

For the unique essence of Christ, as revealed in the Gospels, lies in the ontological mystery of his very person, not only—dare one say, not so much—in his teaching. Christianity is not just the teaching of Christ; it is the teaching about Christ. Jesus is not a seeker of truth and not just a teacher of it; he carries it within himself. He not so much preaches the truth as shows it. But Tolstoy remains blind to this. The Gospels are valuable to him only because they contain a fragment of his own universalist creed, with many other fragments scattered over the books of assorted sages. Hence his tiresomely endless litanies of religious teachers: Solomon, Buddha, Mohammed, Confucius, Socrates, Lao-Tzu, Spinoza, Rousseau, Kant, Schopenhauer, Feuerbach—all grist to Tolstoy's mill, all fulfilled within Tolstoy's own creed. Christ is another one of those teachers, nothing more.

Because of his emotional ignorance of the person of Christ, Tolstoy's religious equations had to take the human person out as well. His starting points were pantheism and universalism.

Everything personal, particular, and individual was dissolved in Tolstoy's amorphous universal mix. Consciousness, what constitutes the essence of individuality in the physical world of space and time, stops being individual outside that realm.

Yet again he finds himself in a mess. On the one hand he proclaims the primacy of reason, understood not as Logos but as plain common sense. On the other hand, true reason for Tolstoy is extra-personal and therefore eternal. Personality is thus a stifling restriction; it stands in the way of true reason.

But he is wrong about that: reason is not extra-personal. For all its urge to generalize, to seek universal values, human reason remains part of the psychological makeup that we call personality. A person's reason is inseparable from the person. The metaphysical and psychological mystery of an individual personality is such that, while seeking universal values, it does not cease to be an individual personality. This parallels the mystery of Christ's duality, in which resides the unity of God and man. But Tolstoy strips the mystery to its bare bones. Having detected the universal aspect of reason, he sees no other, divorcing it from the person and making it pale and insipid.

If everyone's reason is collective rather than individual, then it is the same for all. Moreover, it is the same as God's reason. This is where pantheism begins, something Tolstoy could never quite escape. For if individual reason is identical with God's, God is thus equally "divided" (Tolstoy's expression), fractured among all souls. Reason, being greater than the person who possesses it, eventually becomes constricted within the narrow confines of a personality and breaks out. When that happens, the person dies, but the higher reason continues to live in other people.

Immortality is thus separated from the individual: the only immortal aspect of man is impersonal, the same for all. It is not a man who is immortal but mankind. And if Tolstoy rejects the immortality of the person, he automatically has to reject resurrection in any physical or even spiritual sense. In other words, immortality exists, but it is natural and universal, not personal. By maintaining this Tolstoy becomes a pantheist, a mystic of universality.

That is why, whenever he goes through the roll call of his pantheon, Spinoza's name invariably pops up. For Spinoza, God was virtually identical with nature, and we can see why Tolstoy found that idea attractive. But, in the Western, which is to say Judeo-Christian, tradition, equating God and nature is worse than pantheistic, and even worse than atheistic. It is illogical—unless of course we deny the Creation altogether.

After all, if God created the world, he also created nature, which is one aspect of the world. Logically, a creator cannot be identical with his creature. Thus, if we maintain that God and nature are the same, then we have to believe that God did not create the world. The world stops being an objective, indivisible entity, instead becoming something that does not exist outside the perception of man's senses. In effect, this means that man himself is nudged towards the center of the universe. In all but name, he ousts God. God now finds himself on the same plane as man, which in this case spells not the elevation of man but the downgrading of God.

This takes us back to the God of Plato and Aristotle, or else to the Vedic gods, none of whom was the Creator. One must not deny, however, that their contemporaneous believers had faith, as they knew it. But since we know better, for us to hold similar beliefs means ignoring two millennia of Christian culture with its sublime metaphysical philosophy. That is akin to continuing to believe that the earth is a flat plate resting on the backs of three whales, an idea once espoused by respected scientists but now held only by cranks. Atheism begins to loom large, but Tolstoy still bandies the word "God" about so as to camouflage his godlessness for old times' sake. Empty word, impotent faith.

According to any Western religion, God's creation of the world was an absolute act in that he used no materials previously available. Nor did he detach a part of himself to put into the world, for God is always whole and indivisible. That is why the world as created by God is a wholly new entity, not just an extension of divine self-expression. There is no equivalence, either total or partial, between God and nature. Therefore every form of pantheism is logically false, be it Spinoza's monism that preaches a complete overlap between God and the world, or the more nuanced teaching of, say, Plotinus who believed, as Tolstoy did when he felt like it, in a partial overlap.

God's being is not exhausted by his self-expression in the world: he is a universe that is infinitely higher than the world. Judeo-Christians reject the logic of pantheism because, if God is super-systemic and the world is a system he created by an absolute act, then there exists an ontological separation between the Creator and his creature, between God and the world.

Christianity, with its teaching of the dual nature of the Logos made flesh, bridges the ontological gap between God and the world he created. But, unlike pantheism, Christianity does not equate God and his creature. God's omnipresence in the world is not a total overlap with the world, nor even a partial one, for this would diminish both God and, by depriving it of its freedom, also the world. God, according to Christianity, lovingly follows his creatures wherever they choose to go, extending his helping hand to anyone ready to take it. That is why, even though a Christian is aware that the hand of providence is discernible in the world, he would never agree with Tolstoy that God is an unlimited all, of which man sees himself as a limited part.

In his 1898 diary, Tolstoy found a slightly different expression for his pantheism: "I felt God clearly for the first time; that He existed and that I existed in Him; that the only thing that existed was I in Him: in Him like a limited thing in an unlimited thing, in Him also like a limited being in which He existed."[4] Translated from the Tolstoyan, this means that God and Tolstoy overlap—either completely or, as he here seems prepared to concede magnanimously, at least partially. And he did not feel this "clearly for the first time" when he was 70 years old. This feeling was ever present throughout his life.

The cul-de-sac turns into a cage, a steel gate slams shut behind him, there is no exit, and Tolstoy feels trapped within the closing walls of his own ratiocination. In *The Critique of Dogmatic Theology*, he inadvertently hints at the inadequacy of his own reason. "What is outrageous about Christianity is that it poses questions for which there neither is nor can be an answer." One detects here Tolstoy's dissatisfaction with his own "small but true" teaching. The nature of the dissatisfaction is again self-centered. Collective immortality of mankind is all good and well, but the burning issue is still his own personal death, and for this his mind provides no satisfactory answer.

He goes on to say that "what convinces one that an afterlife is necessary is not arguments but when, having gone through life hand in hand with another person, this person disappears into nothing, and you yourself stop at the end of that abyss, peeking into it." This terror of death is as far as individual quasi-religious experience can go. But although that clearly was not far enough for Tolstoy, he—predictably—could not find an answer in his own life. For a Christian, the news of personal immortality is a divine revelation, grounds for hope and the reason to rejoice. For this is where the solution to that metaphysical problem lies. Yet by rejecting the resurrection of the flesh, Tolstoy kept this solution off limits.

He was aware that his reasons for denying personal immortality were weak, but his pride prevented him from accepting it. Add to this his one-sided mystical rationalism, leaving little room for intuitive faith, and it becomes clear that agnosticism was the only position Tolstoy could take when he had to retreat from pantheism. And if agnosticism is anything, it is an admission of failure, both religious and intellectual.

However, pantheistic mysticism that colored most of Tolstoy's philosophy does not have to be all wrong. In fact, it can fit snugly as a small element into a large religious picture. Indeed, as the world was created by God, God is eternally reflected in everything. But equally eternal is the person, the particular as well as the universal. In this way the world fulfils the Trinitarian God, the mystery of the universal and the personal intertwined. If the Trinity is roughly the outside possible limit of human understanding, then pantheism can eventually direct one's mind toward it.

Nor was Tolstoy's emphasis on the ethic of Christianity useless in itself. Our minds are too weak to accommodate the totality of the vital questions both posed and answered by religion. That is why there are people, and they may well be in the majority, who single out the one aspect of Christianity which they feel can help them come to faith. This aspect can be either metaphysical or ethical, or both, or but a fragment of either. It can even be aesthetic, as it was for the sublime Russian pianist Maria Yudina who wrote in her diary, "Music is the only way to God open to me, though I know that there exist others."

There is no harm in that; we all find our own way to God. But that is why the church Tolstoy detested is so essential: it preserves the revelation in its fullness. An individual understanding of Christianity, however limited, is perfectly legitimate but only as long as it does not try to pass a part for the whole. And that is precisely what Tolstoy did. By trying to take "faith and sacraments" out of Christianity, he effectively took out Christ. By reducing the endless spiritual range of Christianity to an ethical system based on ascetic denial of the flesh, he reduced it to a do-it-yourself guide to salvation achievable in this world.

The apostles who, it ought to be remembered, learned their Christianity at source, saw things differently. Though by no means ignoring the teaching of Christ, they drew potential converts to the miracle of his person, the truth of his divinity. Never once did they as much as mention the Sermon on the Mount. To Tolstoy that could only mean one thing: the apostles did not have a clue. That is the brief summation of the following passage in *The Way of Life*:

From the earliest time the apostles and first Christians misunderstand Christ's teaching to such an extent that they teach converts to Christianity to believe first of all in the resurrection of Christ, in the magic ritual of baptism, in the coming of the Holy Spirit etc., but they say next to nothing about the moral teaching of Christ, as is evident in the apostles' words written down in the Acts. Faith in miracles, confirming, in their opinion, the truth of the Revelation, is the main thing, while faith in the very teaching of Christ is a secondary thing, often either completely forgotten or misunderstood.

The count's effrontery knew no limits: Tolstoy, with his mishmash, hodgepodge quasi-religion of refreshingly impudent heresies tossed with some Oriental creeds, understood the meaning of Christianity better than did the apostles. They were the people who spent at least a year breathing in Christ's own words, who followed him to Calvary, took his body down from the cross, wept over his death, saw him come back to life and ascend to heaven—and then carried his message to the world. They were reviled, scourged, tortured, and finally killed for Christ, imitating the destiny of their Lord. It is thanks to them that Christianity became the world religion it still remains, for all of Tolstoy's efforts.

Then again, he too made sacrifices for his faith: the count stopped eating beef stroganoff and made life hell for his family. These sacrifices relate to those made by the apostles the same way as Tolstoy's understanding of Christ relates to theirs. His replacing the person of Christ with a perverted version of the Sermon on the Mount can suggest only two things: either a lamentable misunderstanding of Christianity or a willful attempt to sabotage it.

Plato believed in reason soaring above physical reality, which often led him to despise the immanent world. He lived within the cave of his own mind, with reality merely casting shadows on the wall. But already Aristotle showed that logic can only have value when rooted in empirical life. Empirically, Christianity, for all its spirituality, is different from gnosticism, Buddhism, and Tolstoyism. It does not teach salvation *from* the flesh but salvation *of* the flesh, which is the meaning of the Resurrection.

Tolstoy got hopelessly bogged down in his own contradictions here. He was both a Platonist and an anti-Platonist: his own reason was the sole spiritual reality, and yet he remained riveted to the day-to-day physical happiness of real people in the material world. He was both an Aristotelian and an anti-Aristotelian: he prayed at the altar of logic but could not make it tally with empirical evidence.

When he tried to explain his take on Christianity, the subtle artist in Tolstoy often turned into a vulgarian. Witness, for example, this statement in *What I Believe*, which Merezhkovsky described as "crude and vulgar": "the teaching of Christ has a most simple, practical *meaning* for the life of every person. This *meaning* can be expressed thus: Christ teaches people not to do stupid things. That is the simplest *meaning* of Christ's teaching accessible to all."[5]

One has to disagree. In purely practical terms, Christ teaches people to do things that most materialists would regard as stupid. His entire ethical system—when pushed down to the ground and never allowed to soar above it—is stupid. His Sermon on the Mount is stupid, and was seen as such by many of those present. Can you, for example, imagine loving your enemies and not resisting the evil they do to you? Loving, say, Bin Laden and instructing the security services to do nothing to thwart acts of terrorism? Or, looking back, not shooting down Hitler's bombers over London? What can be more stupid than that?

It is only when we follow Christ's road to heaven that we realize that his ethics are not stupid but sublime. It is only when we remind ourselves that Christ was not just fully a man but also fully God, and the ethical perfection he describes can only be achieved in the kingdom of God, that his moral teachings stop being stupid and become divine.

Tolstoy could not—or would not—do that. That is why his ethical system is as weak as the metaphysics whence it came.

CHAPTER 7

THE GOSPEL ACCORDING TO LEO

And he said unto them, Ye are from beneath; I am from above:
ye are of this world; I am not of this world.

(John 8:23)

As Tolstoy felt he had to make his faith credible by veiling it in
Christ's shroud, he was obliged to make continuous appeals to the
Gospel. The trouble was that the Scripture stubbornly refused to
show a Tolstoyan Christ—a mortal, agnostic, vaguely Buddhist guru
preaching touchy-feely morality and nothing else. Any critic of Tolstoy
could easily turn the Gospel against him, and many did. To someone
as hubristic as Tolstoy this could only mean one thing: inasmuch as the
Gospels disagreed with him, they were wrong. But he could not have
come out and said so openly, while still claiming to be a Christian.

That left only one course of action open. Tolstoy had to show that
the Gospels, along with the rest of the New Testament, were later
deliberately mistranslated or misinterpreted by the dastardly church.
Where that could not be claimed with even a modicum of credibility,
it was the early apostolic church, including the evangelists, that had
to be blamed for having either misunderstood or willfully distorted
Christ's meaning.

We have already seen that, according to Tolstoy, "the apostles and first Christians misunderstand Christ's teaching." (Unless
otherwise specified, all quotes in this chapter are from Tolstoy's
gospel—*Chetveroevangileye*.) Fair enough, the apostolic church was
thus at odds with Christ. But where does this leave the Scripture,

the only source of our—and even Tolstoy's—knowledge of Christ's words? After all, two of the four evangelists, Matthew and John, probably were apostles themselves, while the two others were decisively influenced by two other apostles, Mark by Peter and Luke by Paul.[1] And the rest of the New Testament was either written by the apostles or described their lives. Moreover, in the 30–50 years that had passed between Christ's death and the Gospels being written within (not against, as Tolstoy seems to have believed) the church, Christians had worshipped Christ as the ultimate revelation of God.

Tolstoy's only way out of this conundrum was to produce his own version of the Gospel, the gospel of "Christ the materialist," as he once described it with appealing frankness.[2] Thus he had to become the fifth, and to him the only trustworthy, evangelist. To do so, the count had to go to the source. But as the earliest extant source was in Greek, Tolstoy had to learn that language first. Mercifully, he was linguistically gifted: his French and German were of the highest native quality, and his English was fluent. Still, it was no mean achievement for a middle-aged man to sit down and learn Greek to a point where he could argue the meaning of obscure words with professional scholars. That he did so is a tribute not only to Tolstoy's towering talent but also to his maniacal persistence.

What resulted from this herculean labor was a 750-page book merging the four Gospels, as translated by Tolstoy, into one. This text was accompanied by his extensive commentary on the contentious verses and his explanations of why his translations were superior to anyone else's. It must be said that even an uncompromising critic of Tolstoy's theology has to applaud the audacity of undertaking such a project. Equally impressive was the mental agility involved in filing away the uncomfortable angles of the square-peg Scripture so that it could fit into the round hole of Tolstoy's faith.

This book, known in its abridged form as *The Gospel in Brief*,[3] had a massive influence on Wittgenstein. As a foot soldier during the First World War, he carried Tolstoy's gospel in his rucksack, claimed it kept him alive, and drove his comrades to distraction by reading excerpts from it on any pretext. This is not the place to analyze Wittgenstein's complex relationship with religion, but at the time he was no doubt attracted to Tolstoy's emphasis on the ethics of Christianity, as opposed to its metaphysics. Kant, who exerted a strong influence on both Tolstoy and Wittgenstein, also believed in the primacy of ethics over religion. Just as the Russian did, the Prussian and the Austrian sometimes tended to confuse the two, but it is the Russian who interests us here.

And Tolstoy, let us remind ourselves yet again, saw Christ as nothing but a rational moralist like Socrates, reducing his whole passion to the Sermon on the Mount. But the Gospels do not show that kind of Christ. He was neither a philosopher nor a moralist, at least not in the accepted meaning of these words. Also, divorced from his eschatology, Christ's moral dicta, or something similar, could be found in the teaching of the Old Testament prophets and many pagan philosophers, both in Greece and in the East.

Thus Tolstoy faced the task of making Christ sound Tolstoyan (which is to say a moralizing rationalist who taught the world "not to do stupid things"), while expurgating every suggestion of the divine miracle-worker Christ really was. St Augustine must have had a premonition of Tolstoy when he wrote that if you believe what you like in the Gospel and reject what you do not like, it is not the Gospel you believe but yourself.

A similar project had been undertaken a century before Tolstoy by Thomas Jefferson. He too had practiced a selective approach to Christianity: some of it was acceptable to him, some was not. So he clipped the acceptable passages out of the Bible and pasted them into a notebook, thus creating his own Scripture. One can argue that possibly all Protestants and certainly all deists go through the same exercise in their minds, if not literally. Tolstoy, however, did nothing merely in his mind. Once a thought occurred to him, it had to be turned into a written gift for posterity.

Making Christ over into a fully paid-up Tolstoyan is an impossible task, one would think, and so it would be for anyone less nimble than an intellectual Houdini. But Tolstoy's agility made the great escape artist look like a clumsy bungler—and his gospel is there as testimony to his attainment. Now, obviously one cannot go through a book of this length in any great detail without writing even a longer book on that one subject. I shall have to give you only a few selected snippets that, in my view, are characteristic of the book as a whole. This leaves you only two options: either to take my word for it or to read the book yourself so as to form your own opinion. You are, obviously, welcome to do the latter but I advise against it: if you are a believer, you will be enraged; if you are an atheist, you will be indifferent; in either case, you will be bored.

So to begin, let us start from the beginning—of the world, that is. Tolstoy disagrees with the way St John describes the event. Or rather his problem is not with the original Greek but with its translation into Russian (which is the same as its translation into English). "In the beginning was the Word, and the Word was with God, and the Word was God. The same was in the beginning with God" (John 1:1, 2).

According to Tolstoy, "This is not a translation of a thought but a translation of words. The thought does not come across, and every word is given a mystical and arbitrary interpretation." Prepare yourself: for Tolstoy—here and everywhere—anything that is mystical in the Scripture has to be arbitrary. This is how he thinks these verses ought to be rendered in a non-mystical way, with nothing arbitrary anywhere in sight: "The beginning of all was the understanding of life. And the understanding of life acted as God. It was this understanding of life that became God. It became the beginning of all instead of God."

Sure enough, there always have been many arguments about the meaning of the Greek word *Logos*. What gave rise to the arguments was partly the slight variations in its meaning, depending on who was using it, and when. For example, to Greek pre-Socratic philosophers, specifically to Heraclitus, Logos stood for divine reason that gives order and shape to the cosmos. This is similar to the way the word functioned in Vedic religions. Plato and the Jewish Platonists of Egypt used it to describe a self-differentiating divine unity, giving Gibbon an opening for one of his many anti-Christian jibes (to the effect that St John's revelation had been taught in Alexandria 400 years before it was written down). But in Christian theology, and definitely in the Gospel of St John, Logos describes Jesus as an eternal, cosmological hypostasis of God—the Word, ultimately uttered in Christ's flesh at the Incarnation. Thus, though Logos was indeed not unique to Christianity, the Word uttered in flesh was. Moreover, it is what Christianity is all about.

On the basis of what we already know about Tolstoy, this meaning of Logos was not something he would ever countenance. When used that way, the word points at the divinity of Christ—which was beyond Tolstoy's commonsensical reason and therefore a lie. But even if one can see his point, his own version of these verses makes no sense at all this side of the lunatic asylum.

Understanding of life? Whose understanding? God's? Surely not: according to Tolstoy, this understanding "became the beginning of all *instead of* God." If Entity A acts instead of Entity B, then A is not B. Whose understanding was it then? Of the people alive at the moment of the Creation? But by any sensible definition, there were none—the world was created first and only then populated. Tolstoy's? Now we are getting warmer. For, in his unauthorized version, it was his role to replace God at present. Therefore it made good sense to hint that he had been acting in that capacity from the Logos go.

Christ is not the only victim here. Tolstoy's version of this passage is not just anti-Christian but also more broadly anti-God. For, to a Judeo-Christian, nothing ever became God. God has neither beginning nor end, which is why St John specifically says "was," not "became." To imply that God came out of something else betokens either ignorance or stupidity or atheism. And Tolstoy was far from being either ignorant or stupid.

Getting back to miracles being off limits, Tolstoy leaves St John for a while to take issue with St Matthew—specifically, with the way that gentleman was hung up on all that nonsense about Immaculate Conception. Tolstoy considered himself, with some justification, to be an expert on conception (references available upon request). In his experience, it never was immaculate—a little hanky-panky always was involved. And in matters of religion, as in everything else, his own experience was all that mattered. So Matthew was a liar. Or, more likely, the perfidious church had played fast and loose with his sacred text, leaving it for Tolstoy to sort out its sharp practices.

Clearly, the evangelist could not have meant what he is alleged to have written: "Now the birth of Jesus Christ was on this wise: When as his mother Mary was espoused to Joseph, before they came together, she was found with child of the Holy Ghost" (Matt. 1:18). What he really meant, and trust Tolstoy to have got to the bottom of it, was, "This is how the birth of Jesus Christ was: when his mother was married to Joseph, before they mated, she turned out to be pregnant." In case we did not get it the first time, Tolstoy kindly expands on the delicate situation in his subsequent explanation, using the plain language even we can understand:

There was this girl Mary. This girl got pregnant by nobody knew whom. Her husband took pity on her and, hiding her shame, took her in. It was to her and an unknown father that a boy was born. The boy was named Jesus. (And that Jesus was the understanding in the flesh. Allegedly, it was he who revealed to the world a God whom no one knew and we still do not.) And that Jesus was the Jesus who gave the world the teaching that John talks about and that is described in the Gospels. . . . The meaning of this verse is that it justifies the shameful birth of Jesus Christ. It was said that Jesus Christ was the understanding,[4] that he alone revealed God. And that very Jesus Christ was born in what was regarded as the most shameful conditions, to a maiden. All these verses are in essence justifications of this shameful birth from a human point of view. Jesus's shameful birth and his not knowing his physical father are the only features of these verses that have any bearing on the subsequent teaching of Jesus Christ.

Why not just call Jesus a bastard and Mary a loose woman and be done with it? And exactly what kind of "bearing" does Christ's "shameful birth" (mentioned several times in the same passage) have on his "subsequent teaching"? I get it. Perhaps being a bastard, like all those children Tolstoy spawned in the woods around Yasnaya Poliana, Jesus had to prove himself. Psychoanalysts, a breed that was coming into its own at the time of Tolstoy, would find this perfectly plausible. Add to that a domineering mother, which Mary probably was (she was a Jewish woman after all, and Tolstoy cherished his stereotypes), and there we have it in a nutshell. Jesus was deeply traumatized as a child. By way of compensation he worked harder than the children of more fortunate nativity and eventually became a useful teacher of morals, almost as good as Tolstoy. Señor Torquemada, please come back. All is forgiven.

In general, Matthew was obsessed with miracles, do you not think? As, for example, when he ascribed some mysterious healing powers to Jesus, a normal man like you and me, if ever so slightly inferior to Tolstoy. "And Jesus went about all the cities and villages, teaching in their synagogues, and preaching the gospel of the kingdom, and healing every sickness and every disease among the people" (Matt. 9:35). To Tolstoy the teaching part was fine, but what was all that nonsense about healing? Out comes the blue pencil: "I omit the words 'healing every sickness and every disease' as unnecessary and related to the miraculous proofs of the teaching."

When Nikolai Nekrasov, Tolstoy's editor, changed a few words in his first story, Tolstoy threw a tantrum and fired off not one but several indignant letters. Who did Nekrasov think he was, messing around with his prose? One can sympathize with that outburst: any writer will know how Tolstoy felt. But at least Nekrasov had explained the reasons for the changes, and most of his suggestions were good, such as using more full stops. He had dismissed nothing out of hand as "unnecessary." Here it is Tolstoy who is acting as editor, with Matthew as greenhorn writer. You want to talk miracles, Matt? Do it in someone else's book. And who are you calling arbitrary?

Tolstoy's next point of disagreement with St Matthew concerns the count's pet subject: morals, specifically the issue of anger. The Russian translation of Verse 5:22 is the same as in the Authorized Version: "But I say unto you, That whosoever is angry with his brother without a cause shall be in danger of the judgment." Tolstoy eliminates the words "without a cause." These words, he says, are apocryphal:

One does not need to explain that this is an obvious insertion. Anyone can see how crudely these words contradict the meaning of the whole teaching, how they are simply stupid. If it is only no good being angry without a cause, then it's fine to be angry with a cause. And who, pray tell, will judge what constitutes a cause?

Is it St Matthew who was stupid or his translators? Or perhaps the church at large? Maybe even Christ himself? But leaving out the knockabout bits, one must mention here that some scholars agree with Tolstoy on this score (and some do not). In fact, some of the other versions of the Bible make the same omission. Who is right? This is an involved theological issue, but we are not here to sort those out. It is Tolstoy we are interested in, and his approach to this verse is characteristic.

Every time, whenever there was the remotest possibility of a choice between a softer or more absolutist version of the same moral dictum, Tolstoy in his translation went for the absolutist. We shall discuss his reasons in the chapter on ethics. Suffice it to say now that Tolstoy had a vested interest in moral absolutism. This was an essential part of his "religion," to be used, like the rest of it, as an offensive weapon in his war on what he called "church Christianity." It was necessary for him to show that the church had perverted the real teaching of Christ for its own nefarious purposes. Thus the stricter his own moral rules seemed to be, the easier it was for him to scream that the church had transgressed against them. This is observable everywhere in Tolstoy's work, but especially in his pronouncements on ethics, and in the way he insisted this was what Christianity was all about.

In this case the Russian (and the King James) version sounds truer than Tolstoy's and other similar versions. It is clear from many passages in the New Testament that Jesus distinguished between righteous and unrighteous anger, proscribing only the latter and freely indulging in the former. For instance, his own behavior in the Temple was not that of someone who thought anger was *ipso facto* wrong, righteous or otherwise.

It is equally clear that Christ's concept of brotherhood was not so all-inclusive as Tolstoy tried to picture it: "my brethren are these which hear the word of God, and do it." As we can see on numerous occasions, "brother" was to Jesus a fellow believer and usually not a Pharisee, to name one group. Often when he talks to or about them, Jesus does not sound very brotherly. Nor does he pull his punches: "The fool hath said in his heart, There is no God." Or "Ye fools and blind." Or "Ye fools, did not he that made that which is without make that which is within also?"

The received text may still be wrong; this is something for academic theologians to argue about. But it demonstrably does not "contradict the meaning of the whole teaching," and neither is it "simply stupid." It just fails to portray Christ as the ever-smiling, all-forgiving, happy-go-lucky moralizer of Tolstoy's or Renan's imagination. Jesus did come to redeem our sins, and he did preach brotherly love. But it was not going to be all beer and skittles in the process: "If any man come to me, and hate not his father, and mother, and wife, and children, and brethren . . . he cannot be my disciple" (Luke 14:26). And, "Think not that I am come to send peace on earth: I came not to send peace, but a sword" (Matt. 10:34).

Tolstoy did not realize, or perhaps care, that it was difficult to derive one single ethic from the Gospels. Jesus was by his very nature antinomian, and his message was full of seeming contradictions.[5] That is why any interpreter of the Scripture needs to come to the task armed with the ability to understand the delicate balance of Christ's teaching, the chiaroscuro of the canvas he paints. But when it came to such matters, subtlety was hardly Tolstoy's middle name. The words "bull" and "china shop" spring to mind when one considers his approach to intellectual tasks. And in any case his intention was not to understand Jesus Christ; it was to make him redundant and his church universally reviled.

Nowhere is this more obvious than in Tolstoy's crude interpretation of the beatitudes. For example, he noticed with his eagle eye that Matthew and Luke have a divergence in their versions of the first one. According to Matthew, Jesus said, "Blessed are the poor in spirit." According to Luke, he simply said, "Blessed are the poor." According to Tolstoy, for whom asceticism was more important than faith, this can only mean that the beastly church inserted the words "in spirit" into Matthew 5:3 for some ulterior motive. Perhaps the count felt that the church was in the service of the rich and was instructed to say they were the only ones to be blessed. Or else it simply misunderstood the message in Luke. Or perhaps Matthew was an impostor.

One way or the other, according to Tolstoy "poverty of the spirit is meaningless." These words "express nothing not already expressed more strongly and appropriately elsewhere in the gospel. . . . And that is why I omit the incomprehensible words 'in spirit.'. . . This omission changes nothing in the meaning of the sermon." Were these words added in Matthew or omitted in Luke? To Tolstoy it is clearly the former, and no disagreement is possible. But some of us would rather not be quite so decisive until we have examined the nature of this divergence between the two evangelists.

First, Jesus delivered more than one sermon. It is possible that, though they seem to have come at roughly the same time, the Sermon on the Mount in Matthew was not the same as the Sermon on the Plain in Luke. In that case Christ could have been talking about two different kinds of poverty. And Tolstoy is wrong when saying that "poverty of the spirit is meaningless." It certainly is not meaningless in the everyday sense (just look at tattooed, facial-metaled fans of pop music) and neither was it meaningless in the context of the Sermon on the Mount.

Pope John Paul II made a telling point when observing in his encyclical that the church's "preferential option for the poor is not limited to material poverty, since it is well known that there are many other forms of poverty, especially in modern society—not only economic but cultural and spiritual poverty as well." And St Paul indirectly explained the concept when talking about justification by faith—as opposed to the laws of the intellectual Pharisees and Sadducees. But then of course Paul was not much of a Christian, according to Tolstoy: "Paul was not familiar with the ethical teaching in the gospel of St Matthew and preached therefore a strange Christ."

Then, even if we assume that both evangelists were among the listeners (which is not undisputed in the case of Luke, who, according to some scholars, was even unfamiliar with the geography of Judea), they could have read some of themselves into what they heard—especially considering that they wrote several decades after the event. Different evangelists pursued slightly different theological ends, and Luke was much more preoccupied with asceticism and poverty than Matthew was. Matthew's interests were more spiritual. He did not believe that asceticism was by itself sufficient for salvation, and this comes across throughout his Gospel. Incidentally, the Dead Sea Scrolls, produced by the ascetic Qumran community, include the same thought as the first beatitude in a version closer to Matthew's than to Luke's.

Then again, and here we begin to understand why the poor in spirit are blessed, both evangelists were Jews (although some scholars claim Luke was not), and in their native Aramaic the word for "poor" (*anav*) describes someone so destitute that he has to rely only on God, and not on his own resources, whether material or spiritual. That is why the Greek translators of the original Aramaic text of the Scripture would frequently render the word *anav* (needy, dispossessed) not only as "poor" but also as "meek" or "humble." For example: "My soul shall make her boast in the Lord: the humble shall hear *thereof*, and be glad" (Ps. 34:2). Or, "But the meek shall inherit the earth" (Ps. 37: 11).[6] Thus it is not the materially poor but the meek or humble in spirit who are blessed. That makes the difference between the two versions a moot point. But to Tolstoy this interpretation would have been unthinkable. His own spiritual resources were so replete with wisdom that he had no need for God. Asceticism, on the other hand, was an important ingredient in his religious stew: once his busybody flesh was mortified, he felt his spirit would live forever.

To sum up, the words "in spirit" are neither "meaningless" nor "incomprehensible." But to be comprehended, their meaning, like that of any other words in the Bible, ought to be pondered with reverence, humility, and love. These were demonstrably missing in Tolstoy. And surely the great stylist should have realized that sputtering venom at the evangelists would destroy whatever little credibility his pronouncements had in the first place. Alas, the red mist in front of his eyes rendered Tolstoy the thinker blind to the sort of subtleties that came so naturally to Tolstoy the artist.

What he does display in his hatchet job on the Gospels is a great deal of mental enterprise, and nowhere is it more evident than in the way he treats Christ's main commandment. Here the count would have had to choose between two versions, Matthew's and Mark's:

Jesus said unto him, Thou shalt love the Lord thy God with all thy heart, and with all thy soul, and with all thy mind. This is the first and great commandment. And the second is like unto it, Thou shalt love thy neighbor as thyself.

(Matt. 12:37–39)

And Jesus answered him, The first of all the commandments *is*, Hear, O Israel; the Lord our God is one Lord: And thou shalt love the Lord thy God with all thy heart, and with all thy soul, and with all thy mind, and with all thy strength: this *is* the first commandment. And the second *is* like, *namely* this, Thou shalt love thy neighbor as thyself.

(Mark 12:29–31)

Tolstoy faced a hard choice. On the one hand, Matthew's Jesus prioritizes the commandments even more unequivocally than Mark's. Such a pecking order ran across the grain of Tolstoy's makeshift religion, which was wholly based on loving one's neighbor to bits. To Jesus and to any Christian, love for others is derived from love for, and of, God:

Beloved, let us love one another: for love is of God; and everyone that loveth is born of God, and knoweth God. He that loveth not knoweth not God; for God is love. In this was manifested the love of God toward us, because that God sent his only begotten Son into the world, that we might live through him. Herein is love, not that we loved God, but that he loved us.

(1 John 4:7–10)

Such love is inseparable from its eschatological aspect: we love others because God loves us, not because, as Rousseau and Tolstoy preached, they are all equally lovable. Only because the faithful believe in Christ can they love those who otherwise might not deserve affection. However, Tolstoy's faith did not go higher than the ends of his disheveled hair—it stayed close to the ground. Heaven was an abstract construct that had no value for him whatsoever. So both Matthew's and John's verses were suspect in his eyes.

On the other hand, Mark's Jesus repeats word for word the prayer every pious Jew says several times a day, the last prayer he says before dying: "Sh'ma Israel, adonai eloheinu, adonai ehad." This shows Christ praying, which was heretical to Tolstoy. And it directly contradicts Tolstoy's assertion that "Christ rejects all, absolutely all Jewish teaching...which is so obvious that one feels almost embarrassed trying to prove it."

Mark's text makes this not so much embarrassing as impossible to prove. Especially since elsewhere Christ is unequivocal on the subject: "So verily I say unto you, Till heaven and earth pass, one jot or one tittle shall in no wise pass from the law" (Matt. 5:18). So the count must have thought long and hard before making his choice. But then he probably realized that his groundless assertion on the Old Testament had come 450 pages earlier in the book, and no reader would be likely to remember that far back. It was this pragmatic consideration that must have swung him toward Mark in the end. In any case, Tolstoy knew that his prodigious, if somewhat impressionistic, translating skills could take him around any potential pitfalls.

And so they did. With his uncanny ability to make a single word count, Tolstoy stood Mark's version of Christ's second commandment on its head by replacing "thyself" with "himself," meaning God. That effectively puts God and man on the same footing: both must be loved equally. Such leveling not so much raises man to God as lowers God to man, or rather to one particular man, Tolstoy's Number One. But his "translation" is a fallacy: Christ teaches unequivocally that we must love others as much as ourselves, and God more than ourselves. This is as clear a statement of a hierarchy as one is likely to see anywhere.

But that hierarchy did not feature Tolstoy at the top, so it would not do.

The last excerpt that we shall look at concerns the cornerstone of Tolstoyan metaphysics: the kingdom of God within us. He used this concept to justify his threadbare religion wholly based on ethics. There is some logic to it. If the sole location where the divine kingdom can be found is within us, then moral self-improvement is all it takes for us to become a part of it. And even that may not be crucial. After all, the kingdom is already inside us, it is not going anywhere, so we can choose to enter it at a time that suits us best. But is it really *within* us?

Well, at least this is how the preposition is translated in both the Authorized and Russian versions of the Gospel, meaning that the kingdom of God is in our hearts and minds. For once Tolstoy does not argue with the received translation. And for once I shall, siding on this one occasion with other versions of the Scripture, such as the Revised Standard Version, Jerusalem Bible, and New English Bible. They translate the Greek preposition not as "within" but as "among" or "in the midst of." According to *Vine's Complete Expository Dictionary of Old and New Testament Words*, *entos* can indeed mean either "within," "among," or "in the midst of." Actually, in Elizabethan English the word "within" could also mean "among," not just "inside." But the way *entos* is translated in the Russian Bible, it definitely means "inside."

The difference between "inside" and "in the midst of" is important: the former internalizes God completely and unconditionally, the latter does not. Which did Christ mean? This is a difficult question because under different circumstances, and depending on his audience, he could have meant either. In other words, he could have taught that the kingdom of God is already *within* some people, but still only *among* some others—and therefore, depending on the context, both meanings of *entos* would be correct.

So let us look at the circumstances in which these words were uttered. "And when he was demanded of the Pharisees, when the kingdom of God should come, he answered them and said, The kingdom of God cometh not with observation: Neither shall they say, Lo here! or, lo there! For, behold, the kingdom of God is within [or among] you" (Luke 17:21). This is the only place in the Gospels where Christ uses *entos* in relation to the kingdom of God.

And Jesus said those words when talking to the Pharisees. So if we accept that *entos* means "within," "inside," we must also accept that Christ taught that the kingdom of God was, among other places, within the Pharisees' hearts. To see whether this is likely, let us look at a couple of other passages: "Then the Pharisees went out, and held a council against him, how they might destroy him" (Matt. 12:14). Or, "And the Pharisees went forth, and straightway took counsel with the Herodians against him, how they might destroy him" (Mark 3:6). The Pharisees were thus out to destroy Jesus. It is then no wonder that, as we have already seen, St Matthew shows Christ describing the Pharisees as "blind" or "fools" or both.

And blind they were, spiritually, for they did not recognize that Jesus Christ, the embodiment of the kingdom of God, was already *in their midst*. Thus Jesus was not patting his audience on the back by saying the kingdom already was in their hearts—he was castigating them for rejecting it. Within them? This is what Christ really thought was *within* the Pharisees: "And the Lord said unto him, Now do ye Pharisees make clean the outside of the cup and the platter; but your inward part is full of ravening and wickedness" (Luke 11:39). Full. Of ravening. And wickedness. Not much room left for the kingdom of God there.

Elsewhere, Christ is even more specific in showing that the Pharisees will not be admitted to the heavenly kingdom: "For I say unto you, That except your righteousness shall exceed *the righteousness* of the scribes and Pharisees, ye shall in no case enter the kingdom of heaven" (Matt. 5:20). The kingdom of God is thus something we can only enter having first paid the admission charge of righteousness, and, according to St John, baptism—a price that Christ's Pharisee audience never paid. That is why we must be more righteous than they are to be considered for admission into the kingdom. It follows that it is not the kingdom of God that is inside us but we who are—or rather conditionally can be—inside it. It also follows that Tolstoy built the edifice of his whole "religion" on termite-eaten foundations.

The edifice came down, burying many underneath. Whereas in his gospel Tolstoy only touches upon the internal nature of heaven, he later wrote a whole book about it, *The Kingdom of God Within You*. It was this best-selling essay that turned Gandhi into a Tolstoyan, along with many others. And it was this idea, spun out of its true meaning, that has had such a destructive influence on modernity.

These days we are all encouraged to delve deep inside ourselves, paying meticulous attention to every little fancy we find there, confusing it with the kingdom of God. We can forgive ourselves every wickedness, every evil thought, for they come from inside, which is to say from the kingdom of God or any of its modern surrogates. Freudians and other mountebanks encourage us to look even deeper, or shall we say lower, and we go along with them because anything inside us is good or at least significant. Because that is where the kingdom of God is.

For a great part of this decadent egocentrism, we have misinterpreters of the Gospels to thank—while not forgetting the popularizers of their folly, chief among whom is Leo Tolstoy.

His attempt to interpret the Scripture was not undertaken in good faith, and so distortion was not only a possible result of his effort but indeed the desired one. But this points at a general pitfall, teaching a lesson to us all: Interpret the Bible at your peril. This endeavor can only be undertaken successfully by someone endowed with a first-rate philosophical mind and profound knowledge of both theology and philosophy. After all, every word in the Scripture has already been interpreted by some of the greatest minds the world has ever known.

This is not to say that no one can ever add anything to the interpretation of, say, Origen, Gregory the Great, Ambrose, Augustine, Jerome, and Aquinas—or even take issue with the odd point. Only that, if one's credibility is not to suffer terminal damage, doing so requires a mind of similar subtlety, a soul of similar depth, and a faith of similar purity. Tolstoy was not the only one who fell short when judged by those criteria. He just tumbled from such a great height that we can still hear the reverberations of the thump.

CHAPTER 8

DESPERATELY SEEKING
GOLGOTHA

What does it take to see clearly? Not to look through oneself.

Pyotr Chaadayev

Tolstoy always tried, though not always managed, to be logical. Once he decided on the course of personal mimicry of Christ, he had to stay it consistently to the inevitable end: martyrdom. In search of it, he kept attacking the state in general, and especially the Russian state in particular. The thunder of this offensive was neatly harmonized with his broadsides against the church—not only against some of its objectionable practices, of which there were many, but against the institution as such.

The tsar's government usually took a dim view of that sort of thing, so even the intrepid publisher of one of Tolstoy's harangues served six months in prison for the offence. And the count's faithful hangers-on Chertkov and Biryukov were exiled from Russia, eventually ending up in London where they launched a worldwide PR campaign for their guru. But Tolstoy himself was not even charged, never mind convicted.

The count upped the tempo, and the salvos of his clamor became a barrage. He was begging to be punished, for he knew that personal martyrdom, preferably minus the cross and nails, would add firepower to his batteries. Like Christ, he wanted his person to be both the medium and the message, both the prophecy and its fulfillment. Alas, the tsar's government of Russia proved to be less obliging than the Roman administration of Judea. They simply would not come out and play: no crosses were erected; the nails stayed in the toolbox.

No matter how strident Tolstoy was becoming, no matter how subversively nihilistic was the message he screamed all over the world, the government clearly felt that punishing him would be more trouble than it was worth. Censorship was the only measure they took, and Tolstoy's most incendiary works were banned. But then the Russian Empire was no USSR, and it was easy enough to get around the ban.

Here Tolstoy followed the same stratagem as did the émigré bolsheviks with their blood-thirsty pamphlets. He used the good offices of his disciples Chertkov and Biryukov to publish his works abroad, mostly in London, and then smuggle them into the country. As they came out in Russian, Tolstoy's excuse that they had not been meant for the Russian public sounded lame, but the government was prepared to accept it up to a point. The works of course did reach the Russian public, for smuggling forbidden literature into the country was easy, and Chertkov was good at exploiting the burgeoning network of Tolstoyans to that end.

Yet the martyrdom Tolstoy craved still would not come, as the government stubbornly refused to go along with the ploy. Never mind Radishchev's penal colony. Never mind the death penalty, commuted to penal servitude, to which Dostoyevsky had been sentenced for much lesser offences. Never mind Aksakov's incarceration or Chernyshevsky's "civic execution" followed by imprisonment. Tolstoy could not rate even a puny exile. Granted, the police looking for banned literature did search his house once and jimmied a couple of drawer locks. But that act, objectionable as it was, could not quite be stretched to martyrdom however hard Tolstoy tried, however loudly he ranted.

Moreover, Pobedonostsev, Procurator of the Holy Synod and one of the ablest minds in Russia at the time, was openly dismissive about Tolstoy's vituperative arguments, refuting them with contemptuous ease whenever he could be bothered to do so. But then at last, in 1901, came the godsend. Pobedonostsev's patience had run out, and Tolstoy was excommunicated—to a chorus of indignation, mostly coming from the kind of people who had nothing to do with the church and hated it as much as Tolstoy did.

Even Lenin (you know, the chap who later went on to rob and destroy most churches, while having 40,000 clergymen murdered in just one year of 1922) was indignant: "The Holy Synod has excommunicated Tolstoy. So much the better. This act will count against it in the hour when people take vengeance on the cassock-wearing bureaucrats, gendarmes in Christ, on the macabre inquisitors who supported Jewish pogroms and other heroic deeds of the tsar's black-hundred gang."[1]

Lenin was as good as his word. His hour of vengeance did come, in the shape of water poured over priests in freezing temperatures, turning them into pillars of ice; monks castrated, dismembered, nailed to the wall; nuns gang-raped and eviscerated, not always in that order; church valuables plundered; believers shot out of hand; cathedrals blown up. Tolstoy was fortunate to have supporters who kept their promises.

It is worth mentioning that excommunication was not something the church practiced widely. For example, it never applied this measure to such self-proclaimed atheists as Pisarev, Dobrolyubov, or Chernyshevsky. Nor did it excommunicate Chaadayev and Soloviov for openly expressing pro-Catholic sentiments.[2] It excommunicated neither Vladimir Pecherin, who eventually became a Catholic monk in Ireland, nor Russian converts to Buddhism, such as the painter Roerich.[3] It did not even excommunicate Lenin. Tolstoy was singled out because he not only maliciously, insultingly, tactlessly attacked the church with all its rituals and dogma, but because he also maintained that he remained a Christian, and only his Christianity was true. By doing so he excommunicated himself, and the Synod simply endorsed the *fait accompli*.

In the Russian Orthodox Church, excommunication is neither anathema nor damnation, though either would have been justified in Tolstoy's case. It is not even expulsion from the Church. It is simply the exclusion of a baptized communicant from the Eucharist. The action is reversible: once the punished Christian has repented he could be welcomed back. Considering the venom of Tolstoy's attacks on the sacrament of the Eucharist, and the fact that he had not gone to communion for several decades anyway, one might think he could have let the punishment pass without batting an eyelid. In fact, he even could have welcomed it. But the count saw his chance of creating a big splash, and plunged in headlong.

Illogically, Tolstoy would not take his excommunication lying down. Ever so sensitive to slights, and alert to publicity opportunities, he protested against it by writing to the Synod an open letter in which he portrayed himself as an innocent victim. Moral damage apart, Tolstoy claimed that as a direct result of the outrage he had suffered he had received hundreds of obscene and threatening letters from Christians.

As usual, he treated his data selectively here. He did not mention the thousands of letters of support he also had received, many with multiple signatories. For instance, one such letter, from Kiev students, had 1,080 signatures. And workers of the Maltsev glass works sent him a hunk of green glass with a gold engraving, saying, "You have shared the fate of many great people who are ahead of their time, dear Lev Nikolayevich. Let those Pharisee First Priests excommunicate you all they want...."

So even such a child's play of martyrdom was working! The people themselves, unprompted this time, were drawing parallels between Tolstoy's excommunication and Christ's martyrdom! Clearly, he was on the right track! Just imagine the effect that an exile or imprisonment would have had! Nonetheless, Tolstoy's sense of style demanded that the Holy Synod be rebuffed. After all, when queried by Pilate, did Christ not object that his kingdom was not of this world? And anything Christ could do, Tolstoy could do better. However, reading his rebuff, one wonders how different it would have been had Tolstoy written to agree with every word in the Synod's ruling, rather than to take exception to it.

He draws the battle lines early: "The Synod ruling...is illegal, unfounded, untrue and, moreover, contains libel." Now, Tolstoy's publicly expressed view was that the state has no right to pass and enforce any laws. And his version of one of Christ's commandments said that we must never appeal to legal authorities. Against that background, invoking legality was a bit like, say, Richard Dawkins begging God to save him from his critics.

Also, Tolstoy was excommunicated for having placed himself outside the church. As he regarded the ruling as groundless and libelous, then it followed logically that he still considered himself to be very much within the church, and therefore entitled to take communion. How dare that devious institution not recognize this? And even if he did not share any of the church's faith, specifically its belief in the Eucharist, so what? Who says one has to be a believing Christian to stay within the church? Certainly not anyone Tolstoy knew.

As he points out, "not only many, but almost all educated people in Russia share my unbelief." This constitutes *argumentum ad populum*, a rhetorical fallacy. The "great thinker" here uses the logic of a crank who avers that, because many people believe in UFOs, they exist. Or, because millions of people think Elvis is still alive, he is.

Tolstoy's appeal to majority opinion sounds particularly odd considering that he had nothing but contempt for pluralism in state institutions. And if majority opinion is so wrong in politics, how can it be right in religion? In any case, he does not cite any statistics to support his assertion. Nor does he tell us if his fellow non-believers are all as confident as he is that theirs is the only true Christianity. In the absence of such information, the statement is meaningless. And we must never forget that those same "educated people" Tolstoy refers to were only 16 years away from unleashing hell. Surely, the great thinker ought to have sensed the causal link between "unbelief" and what Pushkin described as "the Russian rebellion, senseless and merciless"?

Then comes the kernel of the ringing protest. Tolstoy goes on to say:

That I have rejected the church that calls itself Russian Orthodox, is perfectly true.... I've come to the conclusion that in theory the teaching of the church is a perfidious and harmful lie, while in practice it is a collection of the crudest superstitions and sorcery, hiding completely the entire meaning of Christian teaching.... It is perfectly true that I reject the incomprehensible trinity and the myth, these days meaningless, of the fall of the first man, the blasphemous story of a god born of a virgin to redeem the human race.... You say that I reject all the rituals. That is perfectly true.... This [the Eucharist] is horrible!

If this is protest, methinks the count doth protest too little. Every word in this "protest" screams visceral hatred for the church and everything it stands for. Just look at the adjectives: "perfidious," "harmful," "crudest," "meaningless," "incomprehensible," "blasphemous," "horrible." The rhetoric of bolshevik dynamiters of cathedrals had nothing on Tolstoy's harangues.

Now just imagine, in a flight of fancy, what would have happened to a holder of similar beliefs, and a launcher of similarly hysterical public attacks, not only in the carnivorous Spain of Torquemada but even in a relatively herbivorous Elizabethan England. But then of course in those days our civilization still had enough confidence in its rectitude to defend itself. Westerners were prepared to strike out for their faith because they were prepared to die for it. But the people who inherited Christendom were not just culturally but also viscerally different from those who had built it. As proof of this, the action of the Russian government (of which the Synod was a department) represented weak-kneed liberalism at its most suicidal. That is why taking umbrage the way Tolstoy did at the featherlike slap on his wrists was tasteless, not to say borderline insane.

But it was not all negative—he then goes on to explain what makes him such a uniquely good Christian: "This is what I believe: I believe in God whom I see as a spirit, as love, as the beginning of all. I believe that he is in me, and I am in him. I believe that God's will is expressed most clearly and understandably in the teaching of the man Christ, whom I believe it to be the greatest blasphemy to worship and to pray to."

Most of this is not even true, never mind devout. Tolstoy did not believe God was the beginning of all, in the sense in which Judeo-Christians believe it, or in any other sense. In his commentary on the Gospel he totally rejects the Old Testament, which is the source of Christian cosmology. "I don't read the Old Testament," he writes, "...We cannot accept the continuity of faith from Adam to our time.... The alien faith of the Jews only has curiosity value for us, like the faith of, say, the Brahmins....[4] It was the church's mistake to have accepted the Old Testament." By inference, the church was wrong to accept the Old Testament truth that "God was the beginning of all." And Tolstoy's interpretation of John (1:1, 2) shows that he believes not that God created man but roughly the other way around.

Neither did Tolstoy, as we have seen on numerous occasions, believe that God dwelled in him. He thought God *was* him, which is why in his pronouncements he always tried to internalize the deity totally. Of course God is in every believer's heart. But to identify, as Tolstoy invariably does, that organ as the only place where God can be found is to proclaim that God and the believer are coextensive. That, in effect, makes God redundant, which was Tolstoy's aim in the first place.

And he did not really believe that "the man Christ" expressed God's will "most clearly and understandably." He knew for sure that such clarity of expression had never been achieved before the great theologian of the Russian land got around to it. However, given the nature of the document he was producing, Tolstoy must have felt he had to say something nice about Christ—so as to offset partly the many nasty things he had said before and planned to say in the future.

Yet what he did say, that Jesus was merely a teacher, is false, as were Tolstoy's repeated assertions that Christ had never "uttered a single word" on his own divine nature. He uttered such words throughout the Gospels, especially that of St John ("I and the Father are one" in John 10:30). If Jesus was telling the truth, he was divine. If he was lying, he was either a lunatic or an impostor, and even Christ's enemies never claimed he was either. One thing he absolutely could not have been was a mere teacher.

Depending on how you feel about Christianity, you will have to decide which is more blasphemous: to worship—and pray to—a divine Christ, or to regard him as merely a man. But even the most fervent of atheists will have to agree that the Holy Synod of the Russian Orthodox Church could only see this dichotomy one way.

Of course, courtesy of Ernest Renan's book *La Vie de Jésus*, published some 40 years before Tolstoy's excommunication and still a bestseller in Russia at the time, describing Christ as merely a man was the currency of the day. Only the really dense atheists felt they had to deny the very existence of a historical Jesus any longer.[5] The more subtle among them, taking their cue from Renan's flowery prose, realized that Christ could be debunked more credibly not by sweeping rejection but by fulsome elegies to his sagacity and goodness–but only as a man.

That ploy was custom-made for Tolstoy, and he used it *ad infinitum*. This fits in with the syllogistic justification for the mission of his life: Jesus was a sage and good man; Tolstoy is a sage and good man. Ergo, we do not need Jesus, who has been dead for 2,000 years anyway, when Tolstoy is very much alive and so much more understandable.

In effect, that one word "man" dismissed one rival. To conclude, Tolstoy invokes Coleridge to dismiss another. "I," he writes, "love the truth more than anything else. And so far the truth has coincided with Christianity, as I understand it." We have already seen that the way he understood Christianity coincided neither with the church's understanding nor with Christ's nor with that of any Christian living or dead. If the count had not been blinded by his own hubris, he would have realized he was simply being ridiculous here. Chaadayev's advice of not looking at life through oneself could have stood Tolstoy in good stead.

But the real aim of this passage was to take a hidden swipe at Dostoyevsky, who had stated that he loved Christ above everything else, including the truth. "If someone proved to me that Christ is outside the truth, and if indeed the truth were outside Christ, I would rather stay with Christ than with the truth," was how Dostoyevsky had put it. This was simply a rhetorical flourish on his part: for Dostoyevsky the thought that the truth could have been outside Christ was unthinkable at any moment of his life. But the stylistic device he used in that passage left an opening, and you could trust Tolstoy to take it with alacrity.

Dostoyevsky was a lesser rival than God, but a rival nonetheless. For that reason Tolstoy had never bothered to meet Dostoyevsky when he was alive. And he now took the opportunity to kick the author of *Crime and Punishment* when he was dead.

CHAPTER 9

SEX, LIES, AND ETHICS

What is good is also divine. Queer as it sounds, that sums up
my ethics.

Ludwig Wittgenstein

1

We have already discussed the problems springing from the
dichotomy of the church being a human institution that upholds
divine truth. The same dichotomy applies to ethics, which is the subject of this chapter. At the risk of repeating myself, the root of all those
problems lies precisely in the juxtaposition of "human" and "divine."

The church had to make sure that some harmony between the two
existed so that the Christian community could survive as both Christian and a community. To that end, given the fallibility of human
nature and the consequently imperfect character of all institutions
reflecting it, the church had to compromise not only its humanity but
also its godliness. The only alternative to such a compromise would
have been to go back to being a semi-clandestine sect that could only
survive for as long as the lions were sated.

The Christian soul would thus have lost its institutional body, and
with it any chance of having a profound influence on the world. As
Christ's words to Peter suggest, that was not an outcome he desired:
"And I say also unto thee, That thou art Peter, and upon this rock I
will build my church; and the gates of hell shall not prevail against it"

(Matt. 16:18). Apart from showing that sometimes even the Savior could not resist the odd pun, these words state unequivocally that his church must be built lest the gates of hell might prevail. Hence the balancing act of all subsequent Christianity, and its refusal to stake survival on a roll of monistic dice. Christendom would not emulate the moral rigorism of the Qumran community because it did not wish to emulate its physical demise.

Tolstoy, with his artist's perspicacity, could not fail to notice the gaping cleft between the moral demands of the Gospels and the actual life of the society that called itself Christian. But instead of trying to understand the inevitable nature of this divergence, the "great thinker" went on the attack: "If life here and now cannot confirm Christ's teaching on life," he writes in *What I Believe*, "then this teaching is false." And since anyone could see that the world demonstrably did not follow the Sermon on the Mount to the letter, then to Tolstoy the falsehood of the whole faith had been proven beyond a shadow of doubt. But do not despair: under his spiritual leadership there was a way of getting mankind back on track.

In order to reshape "life here and now" according to Christian principles, Tolstoy offers his usual extremist solution. Either you reject all physical life if you believe in Christ's Gospels, or you reject Christ's Gospels if you believe in physical life. Black or white, no compromise is possible, no shades exist in between.

"The teaching of Christ ... demands complete perfection, i.e. confluence of the divine essence of every person with God's will," continues Tolstoy. This is undoubtedly true, but Christ saw complete perfection as the end of the journey, not the point of departure. That was not good enough, as far as Tolstoy was concerned. There was no reason to have to wait for a long time, especially since he himself did not have much time left. Absolute perfection could be achieved at the drop of his top hat, along with his other Western clothes.

"The coming of that hour depends on no one other than people themselves.... The moment everyone starts doing what we should all do and stops doing what we shouldn't do ... the kingdom of God on earth will come." So God has no say in the exact timing of his kingdom's arrival. But what if he has other ideas on the subject? No matter. Who asked him anyway?

Tolstoy's maxim is another way of saying that people can be saved merely by their own efforts, no outside help necessary, thank you very much. That leaves God unemployed, and a redundancy note will arrive any time now. QED, as far as Tolstoy was concerned. Unfortunately, taking "God" out of "good" only leaves one letter "o." At best, it can function as an implied question, but never as a definitive answer—even though some Englishmen may try to use it that way.

Tolstoy's moral message to the world was as unrelenting as it was uncompromising. He had to repeat it countless times, for his "religion" left much slack to take up. Moral, or rather moralizing, extremism was all there was, and it had to be twisted every which way in an attempt to plug many metaphysical holes, creating the impression of real faith and coherent religion. The way this was expressed centered around the Sermon on the Mount, which Tolstoy insisted ought to be obeyed literally, instantly, and universally. Add to that a few personal touches, such as not eating meat, not having sex, not washing regularly, not drinking alcohol, and not looking after one's teeth, and there we have it—Tolstoy's religion in all its non-existent glory.

Origen warned against biblical literalism 17 centuries before Tolstoy, so his insistence on the literal following of Christ's commandments lacked even novelty appeal. Holding the church down to the letter of the Scripture has been for ages the stock in trade of church haters. Jonas could not have lived in the belly of a whale? So the Books of Prophets mean nothing. Christ could not have walked on water? So all of Christian metaphysics is a lie. Jews could not have wandered around a smallish Sinai desert for 40 years? So there is no God.

To be sure, there have been saintly people throughout history who not only preached but, unlike Tolstoy, also practiced moral absolutism. For example, John Chrysostom called for the same kind of purity 1,500 years before Tolstoy, St Francis of Assisi 600 years before him, and Dietrich Bonhoeffer, the Lutheran pastor who shared the fate of his flock at Flossenberg, 30 years after Tolstoy's death. But their demand for moral perfection was inseparable from the person of Christ, the cornerstone of Christian ethics. Yet Tolstoy claimed that his call for biblical purity attacked not just perversions of the church doctrine but the doctrine itself. Then of course by now we know that Tolstoy's religion was an offensive weapon with which to assail Christianity, and therefore such assaults sprang from its very core.

Though ostensibly a maximalist, in fact he did not seem to think that people should change their lives very much. If we stopped copulating, drinking, smoking, eating meat, and killing one another, the kingdom of God would arrive. We would then all live in bucolic countryside communes, joyously digging up just enough potatoes to keep body and soul together and loving one another to death. This description of Tolstoyan love is not just a figure of speech. For, as love Tolstoy-style excluded sex and therefore procreation, the pastoral bliss of his imagination would only last one generation. The perfect humans of Tolstoy's fancy would grow old in the state of ideal love and eventually keel over, their varicose hands dropping their Zimmer plows onto the shallow, zigzagging furrows.

Nor is this perfect state particularly hard to achieve, according to Tolstoy. He says as much in *What I Believe*: Fulfilling the teaching of Christ is easy. And it should not take long—we can become perfect straight away, without waiting for some nebulous kingdom to come. "The ideal of perfection laid down by Christ is neither a dream nor the subject of rhetorical sermons, it is the most essential moral guide accessible to all." And how are we to achieve this ideal? In practical terms? Surely this may take a while?

Not at all, replies Tolstoy. All we have to do is read *The Kingdom of God Within You* along with other chapters of his moral canon and—presto! The kingdom will arrive with the flourish of Tolstoy's pen. "People are by nature good," says Tolstoy, repeating *ad nauseam* the fallacy of his idol Rousseau. "The moment people are told, and their eyes are opened, they will understand."

Of course, it is natural for a writer to believe in the power of the word, preferably his own. But to believe in it that much bespeaks the last stages of emotional instability. Or, more likely, Tolstoy is simply being logical here for a change. After all, his erroneous metaphysical premise relies on the perfectibility of man in this life. Tolstoy swept the doctrine of original sin, along with the rest of the Old Testament, under the carpet. He did not realize that in the process he had lost the only basis for morality that can be validated not just by Christian metaphysics but indeed by the evidence before our very eyes. Socrates joins Rousseau here: as people are good, they do rotten things only because they do not know they are rotten. Tell them, convince them they are wrong, and their reason will wake up with a jolt. They will instantly realize the error of their ways and turn into perfect little angels.

A beautiful thought, that, but alas it does not quite tally with the evidence gathered over the last five millennia. For people have been told thousands of times for thousands of years—by Confucius and Buddha, by Moses and Plato, by Lao-Tzu and Christ. So why have we always fought wars, killing progressively greater numbers of God's creatures? Why, only a few years after Tolstoy delivered his moral sermon, did the very same Russians who had been hanging on to his every word go on to commit atrocities on a scale never even approached until then?

The Judeo-Christian religion provides a clear answer to all these questions: original sin. The Fall makes us all fallible. Created as an ideal being, man then fell from grace because he chose wickedness over virtue. From then on, man forfeited the right to the presumption of goodness, though each of us retains the free choice of restoring personal virtue through lifelong effort.

But this answer is at odds with Rousseau and just about every other constituent of Tolstoy's "religion." So he sweeps it off the table with such a broad stroke that Jesus himself is dumped on the floor as well. That was no accident—the great Christian felt it was time to sort Christ out once and for all. "A fish starts rotting from its head," says the Russian proverb. A firm believer in homespun wisdom, the count must have felt that, if a religion had gone bad, its founder could not be absolved of the blame.

Thus, according to Tolstoy, it is Christ personally, and not only subsequent "church" Christianity, who has had a deleterious effect on the spread of Christian ethics. "It is a terrible thing to say," he writes in *The Kingdom of God Within You*,

but I sometimes think that if Christ's teaching, with the church teaching that has grown out of it, never had existed, then those who call themselves Christians would be nearer to the truth of Christ—that is to a reasonable understanding of what is good in life—than they now are.

There probably never has been any other moral preacher in history to mouth such a thought with so much bold-faced effrontery. Baudelaire did say "were God not to exist, religion would remain holy and divine," but he did not mean it the way it sounded. Tolstoy did. For the inner logic of his "religion" demanded an utterance along these lines, and he again ought to be admired for his consistency.

Translated from the Tolstoyan, this thought means that Christ gets in the way of his own truth. But even Tolstoy would have realized that this is nonsensical—the argument does not hold water even at the most elementary logical level. Without Christ there would have been neither any "truth of Christ" nor any of "those who call themselves Christians." What he really means is that Christ gets in the way of Tolstoy's own version of Christ's truth. If Christ had never existed, Tolstoy would be there to fill the vacancy. But since Christ did exist, there was no vacancy to fill, and our hero must have been aware of that. That is why, outside his letter to the Holy Synod, Tolstoy's affection for Jesus was so understated.

But he does have a point: the person of Christ invalidates any one-dimensional interpretation of his words. A real God seeker would have realized that a dichotomy existed and therefore would have looked for other dimensions. The starting point of such a search would have been humility: the seeker would have assumed that, if his ideas did not agree with God's, then there was something wrong with him, not God. But such an act of loving submission was of course not something the count would even have considered.

What Tolstoy and his ilk either did not realize, or refused to accept, was that Christ's teaching was no more monistic than his person. The God in Christ laid down the ideal moral standards for his future kingdom. The man in Jesus knew that this kingdom would have to be constructed out of available building blocks: human nature, as revealed through both individual deeds and collective history.

In other words, the kingdom of God is the metaphysical structure to be built, while people are the physical materials. The two came together in the person of Christ who established the link between God and his world, between the physical and the metaphysical. Christ revealed the idea of human perfection and realized it through his own life. Son and hypostasis of God, Jesus set an example of the ultimate good made flesh. But "ultimate" is the key word here. It cannot be universally replaced with "immediate," much as Tolstoy claimed that was possible.

A developing individual, the microcosm of a world in flux, must at the end of the road reach the terminal point at which his own personality is no more; it becomes dissolved in the collective personality along with all others—above all, in the person of God. The history of mankind can be seen as striving to achieve this ultimate end, the kingdom of God. And the ideal purpose of any development is the end of the development: having got there, man would not progress any further. This is another way of saying that man would no longer live, in the sense in which we define living on earth.

This process is not only collective but also individual: we all walk to the same destination. But each of us walks at his own pace. Asceticism, physical escape from a sinful world before physical death, is the last stage of earthly existence, entry point into the kingdom of God. Yet as we move at different speeds, we cannot arrive at that door all at the same time. The road leading there is labyrinthine and fraught with all manner of physical and spiritual dangers. It is also sometimes hard to find. That is why mankind needs path-finders, people able to take the point and raise high the lantern that could light the way for the rest of us. Such people reach the kingdom of God before everyone else.

They are called "saints," and they deserve the right to demand moral absolutism because they live by it.

They, people like Chrysostom, Francis, or Bonhoeffer, earned this right by having gone all the way—but first by having learned from personal experience that Christian eschatology is as indispensable to Christian morality as Christian morality is indispensable to Christian eschatology. Tolstoy, on the other hand, demanded perfection without the eschatology, thus losing all credibility not only as a theologian but also as a thinker in general.

He divorced this world from the next, snipping off the connecting links and letting heaven drift away into a hazy nothingness. That took Christian ethics out of its context and turned it into an indigestible ingredient of a pie in the sky. In this he yet again showed familiarity with the works of Kant who also thought that it was ethics that led to God, not the other way around. Tolstoy hails Kant as the genius who made his ethics independent of metaphysics. Good always leads to the knowledge of God, he quotes the Prussian with approval. But Kant differed from our hero in that he never ignored the significance of the individual. His whole moral philosophy revolved around the person. However, I think he was wrong about ethics being independent of metaphysics. Though also suspect, the narrower statement that ethics could be independent of *religion* would have been just about tenable.

Unlike Tolstoyism, Christianity proceeds from the assumption that people are not an amorphous, collective mass. They are individuals, and each chooses a different path in life. Some paths are as straight as Roman roads; they lead to perfection with a minimum of travel time. Some are winding, with many barriers along the way. And some actually go backward, rather than forward—people who take those paths will never reach the glorious end unless they backtrack and change direction.

In response to this understanding of human nature, Christianity had to develop a doctrine with enough subtlety to account for individual differences—and enough strength ultimately to subsume them when the world ends. Hence the fullness of religious truth, the fine balance of Christianity. On the one hand, it preaches ultimate departure from this world; but on the other hand it sanctifies this world. That is why the person of Christ is so vital: it unites the flesh of the world with God's flesh. This flesh, unified at long last, ends not in death but in resurrection, eternal life.

And that is why, as we have already discussed, Christianity does not throw a uniform light; it is a chiaroscuro with its sharp contrast of light and shadow. The shadow is the ultimate departure from this world; the light is the wondrous joy of the world. Like in a great canvas, the light and shadow form an indivisible whole. Christianity balances the morals of asceticism and monasticism with the secular ethics of day-to-day existence. It knows that some people are far enough gone along the road to God to forgo earthly joys for the sake of sequestered, contemplative asceticism. It also knows that others are not quite there yet. Most people are expected to make a living, enjoy the pleasures of life, and procreate—always provided they do not commit too many sins along the way, or at least repent them if they do.

It takes all sorts, says the church—and so it accepts all sorts. If Tolstoy had read the Gospels less selectively, he would have known this. The marriage in Cana, friendly suppers with some publican or even the odd Pharisee, joy in food and wine, pity for human grief over the death of children or parents, the healing of all comers, taking joy in a child's face or in flowers of the field—there is so much in the Gospels that would be impossible to reconcile with Tolstoy's demand of unsmiling asceticism for all. But the counterweight of asceticism is of course also there (e.g. Matt. 19:12) for Christianity to make sure that neither end of the seesaw shoots up, making the other end hit the ground.

In other words, Christianity is big enough to contain two morals, or rather two aspects of the same ethic. One, lying outside time and space, is determined exclusively by life in God; the other, existing in history, takes into account the imperative needs of everyday life. Eventually the two will converge, but so far they have not done so. That is what Tolstoy, with his dour monism, either misunderstood or willfully misinterpreted.

In a way, one can sympathize with his difficulties. Reconciling the moral height of the Scripture with the lower reaches of life in general, and modern life in particular, is indeed an ungrateful task. Without resorting to a tendentious selection of quotations from the New, and particularly the Old, Testament, a demand that the two be fused into one "here and now" is implausible. And it becomes impossible when one excludes the essential link, the person of Christ, who according to Tolstoy was not only unnecessary but actually harmful. In this Tolstoy comes close to Dostoyevsky's Grand Inquisitor: both would crucify Christ again if he came again, one for getting in the way of the Catholic Church, the other for getting in the way of Tolstoyism.

In *The Kreutzer Sonata*, Tolstoy mocks the dualism of Christian morals, springing from the dualism of Christ: "As the Christian ideal is unachievable, it can only be dreamed about, but it is not applicable to life." This is a vulgar reduction of the church's doctrine to something it never said. Tolstoy puts these words into the mouth of Christianity the better to mock it.

The church does not think the Christian moral ideal is unachievable. In fact it does its best to help people achieve it. But because, unlike Tolstoy, it also accepts the doctrine of original sin, it has to fashion a religion that recognizes the difference between saint and sinner—and excludes neither of them. We have to live on earth before we go to heaven, or before the heaven comes to us on Christ's return. Thus the harsh reality of this life is that we can only talk about varying approximations to moral perfection, not the absolute ideal "here and now." Accepting this does not mean issuing a blank license to immoral behavior. It only means admitting, with sadness, the fallibility of man, which will persist for as long as man does.

Had Tolstoy been able to accept—or understand—this, both his spiritual and physical life would have been less tortured. He would have had the answers to the questions he claimed were tearing him apart, especially the question of personal immortality—something he desperately needed to answer, yet just as desperately could not. For if earthly life in general, and the life of every man in particular, is not the end in itself but merely an intermediate step along the way, then the end lies elsewhere.

The existence of such an end toward which human life moves, and the fact that it can only be reached when all development stops, along with physical life, means that there has to be life after death. Otherwise the whole process would be meaningless. And it cannot be regarded as meaningless within a metaphysical system based on what the metaphysical philosopher R.G. Collingwood referred to as "the absolute presupposition" of God's existence. However, as this ideal life would be static, it would in no way resemble the physical life on earth which is dynamic by definition.

Defense against attacks based on moral absolutism should thus be easy, or at least easier. We admit the obvious truth that Christianity has not yet taken over the souls of most people. We accept as irrefutable the observation that there still exist war, violence, suffering, poverty, disease, and death—all those outrages that so appalled Buddha and Tolstoy. But this lamentable state of affairs exists precisely because of the transitional nature of life. Its opposite, the ideal life unmarred by misery, belongs to the kingdom of God reachable at the end of the road but not at any point along the way.

It follows logically that loving not only one's neighbor but indeed one's enemy—the active ingredient of Tolstoy's instantly fillable prescription for our everyday existence—is not an ideal most people can fully attain in this life. And during dynamic development this ideal will remain unattainable for most people simply because, according to Christ, it is the summit—not a step on the ladder used to get to it.

That is why in Christian theology only faith in Christ can be a non-negotiable precondition for immortality. It is inseparable from the moral ideal that Tolstoy sees in the myopic eye of his mind, without realizing what it is. Thus, accepting Christ as the ultimate ideal has to be the starting point of the journey to moral perfection. Overcoming evil within oneself is impossible without an ontological link with the Logos made flesh.

The teaching of Christ is not *Debrett's Etiquette for Girls* and neither is it Dale Carnegie's *How to Win Friends and Influence People*. It is the promise of the kingdom of God inhabited by saints and angels. All those heavenly creatures will have achieved the final purpose of dynamic development: loving their neighbor as themselves, loving God more than themselves, and even having some love left over for their enemies. The bodies of these heavenly creatures will have to be different from our bodies, both in function and appearance. They would have no need for food, shelter, sex—they would live by, and create, only the absolute good, absolute beauty, absolute virtue. In other words, they would have no physical life. Their life would be supernatural, as indeed they themselves would be.

That does not mean they would be disembodied creatures, bereft of any physical aspect. On the contrary, corporeality is essential to the fullness of heavenly life, even as the church, the body of Christ, is essential to the fullness of religious life. Neither absolute nor earthly beauty is possible without some physical embodiment. The ineffable grandeur of a Bach fugue would not exist without its physical tones; the aesthetic perfection of a Shakespeare sonnet would not exist without its physical words. The heavenly creatures are spirits made flesh, and their bodies are ideal, free of human imperfections. They are transfigured bodies, like the body of Christ after the Resurrection, which is why people who had known him before the Crucifixion did not recognize him at once. The existence of such bodies is confirmed by the visions of saints and other people blessed by the grace of that experience. And it is accepted by Christians as an essential part of their faith.

In heavenly life, marriage, for example, would indeed be unthinkable. It would not be needed, for historical development achieved through continuity of generations would no longer occur. The family, which on earth is perhaps the most essential institution of all, the inevitable stepping stone in the dynamic development of mankind, would become in an ideal life the most useless institution, one that would serve no purpose whatsoever.

Tolstoy's mistake was to confuse the ideal with the practical. In fact, along with Descartes, he used the adjectives "moral" and "practical" interchangeably. Yet his utilitarian morality is not linked to the kingdom of God, much as Tolstoy claimed it was. He never looked skyward, and his morality was all down to earth. According to him we ought to be good not in preparation for the Judgment but because that would make our lives easier in this world: we scratch others' backs, they will scratch ours. We do not kill so that we shall not be killed. We do not steal so that others will not steal from us. We do not resist violence so that we shall receive none.[1]

Simple, is it not? One almost wishes this could be true in earth, as it will be in heaven. Here is one of the instances where Tolstoy diverges from Kant, but in this case only because of his own confusion. He simply did not realize that he had shifted from the Kantian categorical imperative (innate moral law), on which Tolstoy's moral philosophy had been largely based until then, to what Kant called "hypothetical imperative" (practical ethic). Perhaps Tolstoy did not realize there was a difference, or else he decided it was time to be his own man.

Invoking Christ, who he claimed had taught us "not to do stupid things," Tolstoy declared at the top of his voice that he was offering people a better life. But in fact he only offered them a quicker death.

2

Death was one obsession of Tolstoy's life; sex was the other. Freud, who reduced all human impulses to those two, would have had much fun with him. Unlike death, sex was the subject on which Tolstoy's views—or at least his pronouncements—changed over his lifetime. It is easy to see why.

We know already that Tolstoy's take on anything at all, from religion to love, was solely based on his own experience, however limited that might have been. In the absence of such, it was based on ideology. Obviously, he never experienced death until his last moment, so his idea of it was chiseled in stone at a young age and was not subject to change. Sex was a different matter: Tolstoy's experience in that area was greater than most people's. And, like with most people, the nature of that experience changed with age. So, *pari passu*, did his pronouncements.

And there were many, for Tolstoy, unlike Dostoyevsky or Gogol, always devoted a great deal of attention to that subject. This was another aspect of his work that had such a profound effect on modern literature and, more broadly, modern obsession with the inner workings of human psychology. For Tolstoy weaved psycho-erotic strands not only into his plots but also into his depiction of the inner world of his characters. He attached to sex a more all-encompassing psychological importance than any other writer did at the time, which presaged Freud in many ways. And sex for Tolstoy was inseparable from his moral sermon, just as it was inseparable from his interpretation of the biblical commandments.

At first he only talked about it in general terms, at least outside his diaries, as if afraid that going into any detail would reveal parts of his personality he would rather keep under wraps. Then came the six-year period between his wedding and the publication of *War and Peace*, during which his marriage was quite happy. This was reflected in everything Tolstoy wrote at the time, including the novel itself, where in the end all the surviving main protagonists get married and live happily ever after.

The marital happiness Tolstoy depicted did not include any spiritual camaraderie—he himself never had experienced that sort of relationship with a woman, and so he could neither imagine it nor believe that such a thing existed. Tolstoy was certain that "all happy families are alike." What he meant was that all happy couples were like him and his Sonia in the early stages of their marriage: the man takes care of any serious business, the wife takes care of the man. While she is at it, she must also continue to drop offspring at a rate seldom encountered among humans. In *War and Peace* even Maria Bolkonsky was shown in the end as merely a fertile female completely subservient to her husband, who was by a long chalk her intellectual, cultural, and spiritual inferior.

However, soon thereafter Tolstoy's own marriage began to go sour even on its limited terms, and by the time *Anna Karenina* came out he had begun to have second thoughts about the whole institution. As a result, most marriages in the novel are unhappy, and only that of Lyovin and Kitty resembles the somewhat schematic fecund bliss depicted in the epilogue to *War and Peace*. One senses that Tolstoy's panegyrics to nuptial happiness are becoming ever so slightly qualified.

The time between the publication of *Anna Karenina* (1878) and *The Kreutzer Sonata* (1889) was when Tolstoy's marriage hit the rocks. This is directly reflected in the latter work. Its principal character, Tolstoy's mouthpiece, a sadistic misogynist and in all likelihood a latent homosexual, preaches an impassioned sermon of sexual teetotalism. From then on that theme became constant with Tolstoy and progressively grew in stridency, perhaps partially under the influence of his declining testosterone count. Or else because no one was paying much attention. In response, Tolstoy did what people often do when realizing that the other person either is not listening or does not understand: he began to talk louder and louder until he no longer spoke but screamed.

Thus the evolution of Tolstoy's pronouncements on sex faithfully reflected his experience and hardly anything else. What never did change was his theoretical view that sex in general, even when it has to be permissible in marriage, is something dirty and immoral. Knowing how his personal experience guided everything, one has to believe that these adjectives applied to his own sex life as well. Such a belief would not be wholly unfounded.

The count lost his virginity at the age of 16, to a prostitute, as was common at the time. One detects little joy in Tolstoy's description of that event in his diaries: "The first time my brothers dragged me to a brothel and I performed the act, I sat at the foot of the woman's bed and cried." Nonetheless, the impressionable youth went back for more. And more. In fact, until he got married at the age of 34, Tolstoy's romantic urges, when directed at women, had been more or less limited to prostitutes and serf girls, neither of whom were in a strong institutional position to rebuff his advances.

It is interesting to compare Tolstoy's amorous CV with that of another great, and greatly libidinous, writer Alexander Pushkin, who died eight years after Tolstoy was born. Pushkin too would help himself to the odd serf girl, and patronize brothels even after his marriage. In fact he justified such forays when writing to a friend, "Even if one has a kitchen at home, one can still eat at a restaurant every now and then." However, his reputation as a Lothario was not based on such shenanigans. For Pushkin actively, and successfully, pursued society women, both married and single.

Many of his 100-odd documented affairs led to scandals, all contributing to his notoriety. Among many others, he had flings with his wife's two sisters, the wives of his best friend Prince Viazemsky, of his patron Count Vorontsov and of Prince Volkonsky, Tolstoy's relation. The way Pushkin wrote about his women spanned the full range from the ideal to the profane, from the romantic to the scabrous. But at either end one detects in him the sheer carnal exuberance, a love of women as a reflection of his love of life. He cast his net wide but he could also love deeply. He even died for love, killed by a bullet fired in a duel by his French brother-in-law, the putative lover of Pushkin's wife.

How different, how very different from the romantic life of our dear hero: Tolstoy seldom sought the attentions of his social equals, probably because sex for him had more to do with power than with love. To preclude any possibility of rejection, his urges were aimed low, something he knew and abhorred. But as they were also irresistible, Tolstoy had to regard sex as essentially dirty, with a moralizing element ever-present in everything he wrote on the subject. However, it is interesting to trace the development of his views over a lifetime.

At the beginning he was struggling to come to terms with his sexuality, which was as robust as it was ambivalent. Nor was it always directed at the opposite sex, which he mentions both in his diary and in the biographical trilogy *Childhood, Boyhood, Youth*. He also describes homosexual attraction quite knowledgeably in *The Cossacks* and *Anna Karenina*—and hints at it in *War and Peace*.

Pierre Bezuhoff, Tolstoy's *alter ego* in that novel, finds the erotic passion he feels for his wife, Princess Helen, "dirty and shameful." Why? Is it not normal to desire a beautiful woman, even when one is married to her? Not in this case. For Helen's lovers include her brother Anatole, Pierre's erstwhile friend and companion in numerous orgies. One does not need to be a Freudian to detect a simple transference here, especially since Tolstoy himself hints at it expertly. Pierre clearly fancies Anatole, his wife's brother and lover. And as her "marble-like" flesh is thus doubly associated in his mind with Anatole's, then it is doubly sullied. So lusting after it is indeed shameful.

Yet again Tolstoy tries to use his protagonist to exorcise his own demons, in this case of the sexual variety. He was not the only one to use the trick: witness, for example, Nabokov externalizing his own dark urges in *Lolita*.[2] But Tolstoy used that device perhaps more widely and more literally than any other writer, as he did biographic material in general. Practically every line he ever wrote was either biographical or autobiographical, and most characters in his novels are based either upon himself or on the people he knew well from his own experience or from recent history.

In *War and Peace*, for example, his own personality is divided between Pierre and Andrei, Princess Maria is based on his mother, Vasilyy Denisov on the poet-partisan Denis Davydov, Boris Drubetskoy on Prince Trubetskoy,[3] the old Prince Bolkonsky on Tolstoy's maternal grandfather Prince Volkonsky, all the Rostovs on various members of Tolstoy's family, and so forth. He obviously attached a great value to his own experience, and much of it, including his homoerotic cravings, can be either learned or inferred from his works.

But in the case of his homosexual tendencies, no inference is needed, for Tolstoy was quite open about them in his diaries. In 1851, at the age of 23, he writes in his diary, "I have never been in love with a woman . . . but I have quite often fallen in love with a man." "I shall never forget the night we left Pirogovo together, wrapped in my blanket," he writes later about a fellow officer, "when I wanted to devour him with kisses and weep. Sexual desire was not totally absent." Neither, by the looks of it, was the desire to cry, which is according to Yevlakhov so characteristic of epileptics.

Tolstoy goes on to explain that the only reason he did nothing to act on such urges was that his attraction to other men was exclusively and shamefully physical, whereas he loved women for their spirituality. Most men would argue that he got it the wrong way around, but then Tolstoy was unlike most men. In any event, the nature of his feelings for women must have changed soon, as his wife testifies in her own diary: "Now I see how I idealized him, how I refused to realize that he felt nothing [towards me] but sensuality."

If his wife is to be believed, and she ought to have known, the homoerotic cork did not stay in the bottle for a lifetime. Sofia Andreyevna once accused her husband, then an old man, of having a homosexual affair with his disciple and amanuensis Vladimir Chertkov. Granted, at that time the Tolstoys cordially hated each other, trading all sorts of wild accusations. But in view of his own admissions one has to regard that particular accusation as at least plausible. Especially since the count himself described how at an advanced age he liked to French-kiss peasant men, inhaling their "spring-like aroma."

The more carnality did Tolstoy discover in himself, the more he was merciless to everything sexual—both in himself and others. And in the Bible of his mind it was Eve who was cast in the role of serpent. Observation suggests that many homosexuals, latent or otherwise, are hostile to women, probably because they blame them for leading men astray, which is to say away from the homosexuals. Psychoanalysts may have a different explanation of this, or they may even question the observation. If one unwisely chooses to argue with them, one could always invoke Tolstoy. For example, he writes in his diary, "Women's question! There is indeed a women's question. But it's not so that women would run life, but so that they stopped destroying it."

One way in which women persisted in trying to destroy Tolstoy's life was leading him into temptation, not that he was kicking and screaming every step of the way. Even as a young man, Tolstoy tried, somewhat half-heartedly, to fight his sexuality but "was prevented by wenches" from bringing that battle to a victorious end. Here is how he chronicles one such fight in his diaries (1852–54): "Oh, shame! Went to knock on K.'s window. Fortunately she didn't let me in." "Went to knock on K.'s window but fortunately was prevented by a passer-by." "Went to K. Good job she didn't let me in."

There we see one example of a "wench" who refused to contribute to Tolstoy's downfall, and there must have been others, but then whom else would he blame? Surely not himself, at least not for his own licentiousness. "I reproach myself for being lazy....I also reproach myself for unforgivable indecisiveness with the wenches."[4] In other words, in Tolstoy's eyes "indecisiveness with the wenches" is as reproachable—and as immoral—as his passion for them. Readers who try to model their lives on Tolstoy's must be at sixes and sevens by this time.

Another diary entry: "Regard the company of women as a necessary social evil and avoid them as much as possible." However, judging by his own admission to Chekhov, that he was amorously insatiable, the count did not see women as just a "social" evil. They also contributed sexually to his downfall as the paragon of morality. This is confirmed by a string of his conquests over an endless procession of Gashas, Duniashas, and Aksinias, hearty peasant girls with "strong womanly bodies," none of whom was in a position to say no, and many of whom bore his children.

Tolstoy's easy conquests were always accompanied by moralizing in his diary entries: "What does it all mean? Is what has happened to me wonderful or horrible? Bah! It's the way of the world; everyone does it." Quite. But not everyone makes a moral song and dance about it, or tries to base an ethical sermon to mankind on unsuccessful attempts to resist the simple desire to climax. Nor does everyone lust after his own family, as Tolstoy lusted after his "delicious" and "unique" aunt Alexandra Tolstoy (one of the rare examples of his pursuing a social equal).

"Where is one to look for love of others and self-denial, when there is nothing inside oneself but ambition and indulgence?" he wrote to her. "My ambition is to continue to be corrected and converted by you my whole life long without ever becoming completely corrected and converted." Trust a great writer to create literature out of a sentiment that lesser mortals would have expressed as a prosaic "would you like to sleep with me?" And compare Tolstoy's verbosity with the epigrammatic style of another great writer, St Augustine: "Lord, make me chaste!—but not yet."

Tolstoy was 61 when he wrote the novella *The Kreutzer Sonata*, in which he championed the cause of chastity. Being consistent, in all his subsequent writings he renounced marriage altogether, as according to him a Christian should be a sexual teetotaler. Without missing a beat, in what Sophia Andreyevna bitterly described as "the true postscript to *The Kreutzer Sonata*," the count then made his exhausted 45-year-old wife pregnant yet again. Such an accomplishment was less common in those pre-IVF days than it is now.

As the Tolstoys were growing older, his sex drive remained strong, while hers took a dive—at least with her husband. To have his wicked way with her, the count had to chase Sonia all over Yasnaya Poliana, an exertion for which he blamed his menopausal bride–how dare she inflame his passion to such an extent! One may suggest that Mrs Tolstoy's flagging libido was not all due to menopause. By that time, being ideologically if not morally consistent, Tolstoy had adopted the hygienic habits of his beloved peasants. As a result, he smelled rather ripe, and his feet were covered with dirt and sores. That did not do much to endear him to his wife's erotic fantasies, which were for a while directed toward the sweeter-smelling composer Taneyev. But the man was a confirmed bachelor, in the euphemistic terminology of the day, and therefore what Tolstoy called his wife's "senile romance" did not come to its natural conclusion. However, obsessed by jealousy (an all-consuming emotion he described so knowledgeably through the character of Lyovin in *Anna Karenina*), Tolstoy cast a musician in the role of vile seducer in *The Kreutzer Sonata*.

Toward the end of his life, Tolstoy felt affection for his wife only the mornings after sex, while she frequently cried and threatened suicide. In due course, when Tolstoy and his amanuensis Chertkov secretly began to draft a secret will bequeathing all his works to the public, Sonia accused her husband of using the younger man for sexual gratification, not just as an agent of her fiscal demise. We shall never know if she was right.

Confirming Yevlakhov's observations, Tolstoy would not have been Tolstoy if he had not codified carnality in the numbered order of moral value. Indeed, with his usual thoroughness, he compiled the descending pecking order of lust in his diary:

The best thing one can do with sexual desire is (1) to destroy it utterly in oneself; next best (2) is to live with one woman, who has a chaste nature and shares your faith, and to bring up children with her and help her as she helps you; next worse (3) is to go to a brothel whenever you are tormented by desire; (4) to have brief relations with different women, staying with none; (5) to have intercourse with a young girl and abandon her; (6) worse yet, to have intercourse with another man's wife; (7) worst of all, to live with a faithless and immoral woman.

Tolstoy's dam-busting temperament could not be confined to any one item—he routinely practiced at least five of them. Only (1) was clearly beyond him. It is amusing to examine his priorities though. Surely, (7) refers to the woman's morality and not the man's. Logically, it does not belong in the list at all, but once the count got on his hobby horse there was no dismounting. And how is (3) preferable to (4)? At least (4) presupposes if not love then at least mutual attraction, some emotional basis for sex. Whereas (3) is mechanical and cold-blooded. And surely (6), which is after all proscribed in both Testaments, has to be worse than (7)? We may be too harsh on the man who is trying to do his best. But Tolstoy invites this kind of treatment by his doctrinaire obtuseness divorced from the very commonsensical reason in whose temple he worships.

In *The Way of Life*, Tolstoy adds hysterical overtones to his call for chastity, presumably in response to the widespread argument that sex is good for one's health: "To consider whether it's good or bad for a man's health to have sex with women with whom he is not going to live is the same as considering whether it's good or bad for a man's health to drink other people's blood."

Now, there, let us calm ourselves down. Hyperbole may be a time-honored rhetorical device, and even the Bible uses it:

And if thy right eye offend thee, pluck it out, and cast *it* from thee: for it is profitable for thee that one of thy members should perish, and not *that* thy whole body should be cast into hell....And if thy right hand offend thee, cut it off, and cast *it* from thee: for it is profitable for thee that one of thy members should perish, and not *that* thy whole body should be cast into hell

(Matt. 5:29, 30)

Presumably, Jesus did not expect people to indulge in self-mutilation–he was just making a point forcefully so that his listeners would not forget. But, to paraphrase Terence slightly, *quod licet Jovi, non licet Lyovi*. This goes to show how ideological extremism can deprive even a great writer of an elementary sense of stylistic proportion, his supposed stock-in-trade.

As Tolstoy grew older, all other options faded into the background, and abstinence began to loom large. In striving to promote celibacy, the count had to reach deep into his bag of rhetorical tricks, trying every possible one on for size. He attacked sex from the ontological, religious, sociological, economic, physiological, and religious angles, but for all his efforts human nature still held fast. People stubbornly remained people and Tolstoy was getting desperate. Human nature? What human nature?

"It's not true that chastity runs against man's nature. Chastity is possible and it does much more good than even a happy marriage," he writes in *The Way of Life*. But chastity does run against man's nature, for, if we had been made chaste, there would have been no people beyond Adam and Eve. So marriage, happy or at a pinch even otherwise, is a precondition for the survival of man. And after all, did Tolstoy himself not postulate that the human race was immortal? For it to remain so, some sex ought to be condoned. This objection is so obvious that the count anticipated it. He was forewarned, and he came forearmed:

If some think that by getting married they serve God and people in that they perpetuate the human race, then they are deceiving themselves. Instead of getting married so as to increase the number of children's lives, such people would do better just sustaining and saving the lives of those millions of children who are dying of want and neglect.

(*The Way of Life*)

Here the religious, demographic, sociological, and economic arguments all come together to form one incoherent blob. The Bible is ignored in the process, for the God of the Old Testament was unequivocal on procreation: "Be fruitful, and multiply, and replenish the earth" (Gen. 1:28). In the New Testament, even though Jesus must have known what happens on wedding nights, he blessed the marriage in Cana by turning water into wine. And the religions based on the two Testaments treat marriage as a sacrament.

That, of course, could only mean one thing to Tolstoy: millennia of religious experience had all been one big lie because he only lived for 82 years, and the world both began and would end with him. "Church marriage is not a Christian institution at all," he writes, "because, by allowing sexual intercourse under certain conditions, it moves away from the Christian requirement: striving for greater and greater chastity." Let us leave it for the church to decide what is and what is not a Christian institution, shall we? As they say, you don't play the game, you don't make the rules. And I must continue to insist on the difference between a dynamic, incremental "striving" and a static, final "achieving." Remaining faithful to one's wife is an example of the former; becoming celibate of the latter.

As to "those millions of children dying of want and neglect," presumably including those 20 or so Tolstoy had spawned on the side and then forgotten like a bad memory, modern experience suggests that many of such suffering children come into being out of wedlock.

In fact a functional marriage is the best guarantee against such misfortunes. And in response to the crude Malthusian hint at overpopulation as the cause of all the world's ills, a popular theme at the time, one could object that England has the highest population density in the world, and Mongolia the lowest. On that basis it is hard to argue persuasively that the greater the number of people per square mile, the harder it is to "sustain and save" children's lives.

At this point it would be best to drop this subject quietly, but Tolstoy would not let us. Thus he continues in *The Way of Life*:

One scientist has calculated that, if population were to double every 50 years, as it is doubling now, then in 7000 years one couple will produce so many descendants that if they were to stand shoulder to shoulder all over the globe, then the globe would only have room for one twenty-seventh of all people. To avoid this, all it takes is what has been declared by all the sages of the world and what lives in the souls of all people—chastity, striving for greater chastity.

If all Vassar girls were laid end to end, joked Dorothy Parker, she wouldn't be at all surprised. But one would indeed be surprised if Tolstoy's calculations had a grain of truth to them. This sort of demographic sleight of hand has been refuted both by science and experience. It is not overpopulation that threatens the world, but spiritual paucity and lack of moral fiber. And "*all* the sages in the world?" Chastity "lives in the souls of *all* people?" Really. Sometimes one wishes Tolstoy had thought things through before talking, so one could have a reasonable discussion.

It would be tedious to give a list of "sages" who "declared" quite the opposite. A wild guess says they would outnumber champions of celibacy by a thousand to one. Most sages whom Tolstoy acknowledges as such (Messrs Solomon, Socrates, Mohammed, Spinoza, et al.), and certainly those he never mentions, such as Aquinas, did not "declare" anything like that. And if chastity "lives in the souls of all people," then most people do a useful job making sure it never comes out.

Trying to defend his indefensible bastions, Tolstoy is ready to enter into unlikely alliances, including one with the church, which he reviled his whole life, and science, which he despised for most of it:

They say that, if all people were chaste, then the human race would come to an end. But the church believes anyway that the end of the world is nigh; just like science says that both man's life on earth and the earth itself will end; then why are people so indignant that good and moral life will also bring about the end of the human race? The main thing is that it's not up to us whether the human race will or will not end. What is up to each of us is one thing: to live in a good way. And, in relation to sexual lust, living in a good way means trying to live as chastely as possible.

(*The Way of Life*)

Yet again one does not know where to begin. Every sentence in this statement, after the first one, is nonsensical. The church does not believe that the world will end through human agency within one generation, only when God wills it. Our job is to try to prepare for this end, not to hasten it. Nor does science, at least mainstream science, say anything of the sort—and even marginal science talks in terms of millions of years, not one generation. It is indeed not up to us to speed up the end of the human race. And "living in a good way" means celibacy only to saints, monks, and eunuchs. Most of us are none of these—and nor are we expected to be by any serious religion of which one is aware.

As was his habit, Tolstoy insisted on a literal—and in this case altogether erroneous—interpretation of the Scripture. He would quote non-stop Matt. (5:28): "But I say unto you, That whosoever looketh on a woman to lust after her hath committed adultery with her already in his heart." According to our hero, this was an injunction against lust, which vice he knew from experience was hard to avoid. Yet what Jesus was really saying there was that, much as we ought to try to follow "every jot and tittle" of the Law, we would not succeed. Salvation is thus impossible without faith; the Law alone does not quite do it—a theme that was later reiterated by St Paul. That was too subtle for Tolstoy: all he was looking for were divine mandates to support his own.

Sensing that his arguments do not cut much ice, Tolstoy tries to engage semantics. God is love, he says, so by defining love tightly we can understand God, come closer to him. That thought is solid, if not necessarily original. But then in *The Way of Life* Tolstoy twists it into an unrecognizable shape:

The same word is used to describe spiritual love—love of God and one's neighbor—and profane love of a man for a woman or a woman for a man. This is a great mistake. The two feelings have nothing in common. The first—spiritual love of God and one's neighbor—is the voice of God, the second—sexual love between a man and a woman—the voice of the animal.

The same word is also used, although not by many, to describe love of broccoli. This goes to show that the word "love," like many other words, can be used in various meanings. But in this case the meanings are, or at least can be, close. It is just that Tolstoy himself was incapable of loving a woman in any other than the sensual, "animal" way. Women for him were only good for one thing, or two, or three, depending on the woman and his mood. Elevated, spiritual love for a woman was beyond his ken: as his wife testifies, his women were bedmates, never soul mates. Also, he refuses to acknowledge that, as love of others comes from love of God, the two are related. Of course the types of love a man feels for God, his neighbor, and a woman are not identical. But saying they "have nothing in common" makes one pity Tolstoy, not agree with him.

That argument failing, Tolstoy tries another one: "God's law is to love God and one's neighbor, that is all people equally. But in sexual love a man loves one woman more than others, and a woman one man, which is why it is sexual love that most often distracts man from obeying God's law."

Yet again Tolstoy confuses the two planes of Christian morality, one of heaven, the other of this world. We should love all people equally because that is how God loves all of us. And we shall indeed love all people equally when we are all united with God in heaven. That does not mean you cannot for the time being prefer your best friend to Osama bin Laden or your wife to Amy Winehouse. Tolstoy himself suggested that the word "love" can have different shades of meaning, but then of course that was a couple of paragraphs earlier, so he may have forgotten. And inasmuch as sexual love is focused on one's spouse, God's law is in no way contravened. Tolstoy's law may be, but he was only God in his own mind.

Once again, and we cannot remind ourselves of this too often, the kind of egalitarian, universal, non-discriminating love he talks about is not so much a constituent of moral everyday behavior as a reward for it, the last step before entering heaven. Tolstoy effectively removes every step from the ladder but the top one, not caring that this way no one would be able to climb it.

If we can learn righteousness neither from Tolstoy nor from God as defined by Tolstoy (which is again Tolstoy, according to his 1898 diary: "Come, Father, come and dwell within me. You already dwell within me. You are already 'me'."), we must all change our wicked ways by following the example of animals.

Even as people must learn from animals how to abstain from food—to eat only when they are hungry, and not to overeat when they are full, so must people learn from animals in sex: just as animals, to abstain until puberty, to have intercourse only when one is irresistibly drawn to it, and to abstain from sexual intercourse the moment a child is conceived

(*The Way of Life*)

While we are it, why not learn other things from animals as well, such as drinking from puddles, relieving ourselves where we stand, eating feces, and chasing one another around the block? Tolstoy's idea does not add up even empirically, never mind philosophically: most people abstain from sex until puberty willy-nilly anyway, while having intercourse "only when one is irresistibly drawn to it" is meaningless unless one defines "irresistibly." Some people are irresistibly drawn to sex several times a day, some once a month, some once in a lifetime, some never. And his last recommendation is phrased loosely: we do not know the moment of conception, only the moment when pregnancy is confirmed. There is usually a period of a couple of months in between, so what shall we do in the interim? Can we still have a little fun while remaining unsure whether a child has been conceived?

But the really telling point again is Tolstoy's inability to see the difference between the impersonal coupling of two animals, occurring only because the female is in heat, and the physical expression of love between a man and a woman. His attitude to nuptial love is certainly un-Christian and fundamentally irreligious in any Western understanding of religion. For what can be derived from Christianity is not only monastic squeamishness toward marriage but also the glorification of it as a great mystical union before God.

Tolstoy's views on sex are inseparable from his moral sermon, which in its turn is tainted by his metaphysical failings. The philosopher Shestov pointed out that in Tolstoy's theology God was replaced by the good. Indeed, Tolstoy said many things along these lines. Thus in *The Way of Life*:

In order to live a good life, one must understand what life is and what one should and shouldn't do in it. The wisest and most virtuous people have taught this at all times and everywhere. All these people essentially teach the same things...it is precisely this that is true faith.

This belief that God is the same as the good is not a far cry from Wittgenstein's "what is good is divine," and is identical to Nietzsche's "God is dead." In fact, Tolstoy and Nietzsche had much in common. Both rejected their contemporaneous world, the difference being that Tolstoy did so in the name of morality, and Nietzsche in the name of aesthetics.

Tolstoy read the moral failure of Christianity into his own moral failure. He himself did not become any better even though he considered himself to be a Christian, and therefore neither did mankind. Quite the contrary: under the impact of a civilization described as Christian, mankind, according to Tolstoy and Rousseau, found itself to be even worse off. Hence the conclusion: denial of Christianity, most culture, and the totality of civilization, which, according to Tolstoy, are all based on false values. Step by moralizing step, Tolstoy arrived at a theology without God–just as he earlier had arrived at a Christianity without Christ.

Tolstoy's sermon on sexual or any other morality goes to prove, if any proofs are necessary, that even an intelligent person can amble into a cul-de-sac if he starts off on the wrong foot. The metaphysical foundations of Tolstoy's morality were not put together properly, and they were erected on loose soil. No wonder the whole structure comes tumbling down the moment it receives the slightest push. The same goes for all his prescriptions for other aspects of life, which we shall consider in the next chapter.

CHAPTER 10

AN IMPRACTICAL IDEA
OF A PRACTICAL LIFE

The desire for universal welfare . . . is what we call God.

Leo Tolstoy

1

Some people can sound utterly convincing in their logical constructs, until one realizes that their starting premise is dubious. For example, an astrologist can explain to a doubting layman that everything in life is cyclical, and the cycles recur with regularity. Therefore they can be timed, with the stars acting as the clock. So we astrologists do not say that the stars predetermine events, as you, Mr Layman, claim we do. The stars merely tell us which phase of the cycle we are in, thus enabling us to predict things.

This makes sense until the ambushed layman realizes that not everything in life is cyclical. Some things are, and some are not. Those other things may, for instance, be linear (human life is a good example, unless one is a Buddhist). Or they can even be haphazard, chaotic—and one cannot predict entropy. Usually, this realization sinks in as the rhetorical victim drives home, too late for a retort.

The same happens with Tolstoy's arguments. All we have to do in order to accept many of them is acknowledge that bliss is achievable in this world—and only in this world, for there exists no other. Once this wrong premise has been accepted, everything that comes out of it will make sense. Well, perhaps not quite everything, but something.

However, the moment we realize this premise is a metaphysical blunder, Tolstoy's whole system of thought comes tumbling down like the walls of Jericho. And the epigraph to this chapter shows how terribly confused Tolstoy was about the two antinomian planes of Christianity, and God in general. In fact, his definition of God changed about a dozen times in the course of his life. Out of this confusion spun a deity who by that time had become "the desire for universal welfare in our lifetime." Replace God with communism, and the sentence will make as much sense.

Leontiev, a bitter critic of Tolstoy, was, in *The East, Russia and Slavdom*, merciless in his demolition of this thought: "The idea of collective good, the religion of universal welfare, is the most lifeless, prosaic and, to boot, the most improbable and unfounded of all religions." Tolstoy would not listen. When it came to equating God with earthly happiness, his ardor was not just eudemonic but downright demonic.

Yet material happiness cannot function as a religious desideratum, at least not in any Western religion, and certainly not in Christianity. The religion that brought the West to life had itself been brought to life by the purifying power of redemptive sacrifice. And if we, along with Thomas à Kempis, accept Christ's life as the ideal to imitate, then it is suffering and not happiness that takes on religious significance.

Christianity is unique in history because suffering was a formative experience of both the religion itself and the culture it produced. If we believe that the pain Christ endured on the cross was also the birth pain of Christianity, then suffering has a special place in our hearts. To reflect this, Western religion, whence came Western culture, attaches a deep meaning to suffering, something no other religion or culture ever has emphasized to the same extent. Suffering plays the same central role in Western religion as do peace and harmony in Eastern faiths.

It is important not to interpret suffering simplistically as merely physical deprivation. Christian suffering is more spiritual than physical. It is the anguish in the soul, not the pain in the body, at least not just that. Suffering is a corollary to freedom, the ability to make a free moral choice that is inseparable from Western ethos. Making a free choice is painful in itself and it can also lead to painful consequences. However, the only way to reduce the suffering implicit in freedom is to reduce freedom. Thus an approximation of slavery, sometimes institutional but more often spiritual, is the price we usually have to pay for "happiness." For any Christian this price would be unacceptably high. For Tolstoy it was just right, which is why he equated God with "universal welfare."

Moreover, we know empirically that it is suffering and not happiness that enables people to reach great spiritual depths. It is hard to imagine a great philosopher, artist, or musician as a happy-go-lucky self-content individual. In fact, one cannot think of such a creative man—and Tolstoy himself is certainly not an exception.[1] In any case, universal happiness is achievable not in this world but only in the next. Belief to the contrary takes us away from Christ and puts us into the eagerly awaiting embrace of all sorts of social utopians, from Saint-Simon and Fourier to Owen and Marx.

This was something Dostoyevsky understood much better than Tolstoy. When the liberal writer Korolenko declared that "Man is born for happiness as a bird is born for flight," Dostoyevsky delivered a cutting retort: "Man isn't born for happiness. A man earns his happiness, and always by suffering." However, such spiritual vision was not only beyond Korolenko but also beyond Tolstoy.

As to elevating global welfare to a God-like status, turning it into a religion, Tolstoy probably sensed this was a fantasy, not a realistic aim. But even as far as fantasies go, not only is this eudemonia run riot impractical, but it also has no positive content whatsoever. Real religions all have that: one single God in Judaism, Christ the Savior in Christianity, Mohammed as God's prophet in Islam. By contrast, universal welfare is just a cold-blooded, lifeless, soulless abstraction. And every attempt to find it on earth has so far led to more, not less misery. The only real meaning "universal welfare" could possibly have would be destructive, similar to the moral component of Tolstoy's "religion."

Every human institution could be held responsible for not having achieved this allegedly achievable earthly bliss—and thus slated for destruction. More specifically, the blame could be assigned to the people manning such institutions. That is precisely what non-violent demagogues like Tolstoy and his disciple Gandhi tend to do: they thunder away and then somehow, unwittingly as they will later claim, pass the relay baton on to their violent followers. Then they sit back and feign horror as heads roll. Unable to believe in God, they do not even believe in consequences.

Failing to get either to the Athens of thought or the Jerusalem of faith, Tolstoy stopped halfway, splashing down into the Mediterranean of chiliasm. Such an aborted journey would have spelled a spiritual catastrophe for anyone genuinely determined to get to either place, to build a philosophy or found a religion. But Tolstoy did not particularly care. Building was far from his mind; it was demolition that he really craved. Chiliastic ideology is a tool custom-made for that purpose. It is a destructive heresy: if man can achieve perfection on earth, then there is no need for a redeeming, saving God. Therefore, out comes the same 45-volume redundancy note that Tolstoy was writing to God all his life.

As there is no evidence that another world exists, the divine kingdom must be built "here and now," words that Tolstoy uses almost as often as "stupid" and "asinine." In that sense, chiliastic eschatology is like communism: both deny God and proclaim man's self-sufficient ability to build a perfect world. The kingdom of God thus becomes the kingdom of man. From there it is but half a step to the kingdom of one particular man: Tolstoy himself in all his demiurgic glory, surrounded by lightning-struck apostles and supine Aksinias and Duniashas ready to act out his synthetic idea of the Virgin and Mary Magdalene.

Preaching his millenarian earthly happiness, he therefore had to top his moralistic pie in the sky with the cherry of social utopia. The inner logic of his philosophy demanded this, for social utopias are the secular answer to chiliasm. All such fantasies, whether they come from Moore, Campanella, or Marx, are based on the perfectibility of man, an idea Tolstoy got from his beloved *philosophes* and Rousseau. If man is perfect to begin with and, furthermore, tautologically perfectible, then evil has to be regarded as incongruous. Just tell the people what is what, and they will instantly become as good as gold.

On the other hand, Judeo-Christian ideas are based on the Fall, which made most people imperfect, and some evil inevitable in this world. If the kingdom of God exists beyond death, and only beyond death, and if we believe in the Judgment, then we must accept the existence of evil. Christ certainly did, in the very Sermon on the Mount to which Tolstoy so clumsily tried to reduce all of Christianity.

When Jesus says, "Blessed *are* the merciful," the implication is that mercy will stay in demand as there always will be sinners to forgive. "Blessed *are* the peacemakers" presupposes wars. "Blessed *are* they which are persecuted for righteousness" assumes the perennial existence of unrighteous persecutors. Here in the same breath Christ both tells us how to be good and prophesies the inevitability of evil.

Neither in the Sermon on the Mount nor anywhere else does Christ suggest that it is possible to smooth out all the sharp angles of this world. The rasp to be used for that purpose has not so far been invented. Hence the nature of Christian harmony—under this sun.

It is not the indifferent, serene harmony of the Oriental ideal but precarious balance emerging out of a clash between opposites. It is not gentle, rolling valleys but precipitous troughs and dizzying peaks. It is

Glenn Gould playing *The Art of Fugue* and not, with all due respect, Ravi Shankar strumming his sitar. Our hearts respond to Bach because they are weaned on the same drama, the same desperation.[2] As we listen to his music, we realize how true to life it is, how precisely it reflects the eternal clash between good and evil.

We know that good will emerge victorious—but not in our lifetime. That is why Christendom can only ever aspire to edge toward approximations of the universal, impersonal love of Tolstoy's dreams, not to achieve that ideal in this world. And if millennia of history have taught us anything, it is that such dreams turn into nightmares when we make an attempt to make them come true. We wake up racked by our own pain, hoarse from our own scream.

The same Christian ideas, when transferred from religion to politics, enable us to see evil as a natural adjunct to freedom. At every moment of their lives people are free to choose vice or virtue, evil or good. Evidence shows that some tend to go one way and some the other, even though a certain amount of crossover is inevitable. Logic then suggests that societies have to be organized in such a way that those who have chosen wrong cannot do much damage to those who have chosen right. But first societies have to make up their mind on what exactly constitutes right and wrong.

The American Declaration of Independence says, "We hold these truths to be self-evident . . . ," and these are telling words. A useful definition of a cohesive society would be precisely that: a group of people who share in a collective consciousness by holding certain truths to be self-evident. That those words were committed to paper meant that by then the American colonies had turned, more or less, into a country ready for its own statehood. They were ready to become the United States of America because they already were united in their understanding of right and wrong.

2

The state, which Tolstoy rejected altogether, relates to collective consciousness the same way as religion relates to faith. It is the physical embodiment of a metaphysical fact, an institutional body that pools individual interests, organizing them in such a way so as to produce the least number of conflicts. And just like a workable religion, a workable state cannot proceed from all-or-nothing extremism. Attempts to do so are guaranteed to destroy all and arrive at nothing. For the state is not there to create paradise on earth. It is there to prevent hell on earth.

Yet if one's unspoken aim is neither to create paradise nor to prevent hell but to destroy the existing state, then a demand for all or nothing will do nicely. That is why people who are likely to pursue the destructive aim love to hold human institutions down to the absolute ethical standard. They know that no such institution can pass muster. So it should come as no surprise that Tolstoy rejected the state as being evil and criminal by definition.

"Any sincere and serious person of today cannot fail to see the incompatibility of true Christianity—a doctrine of humility, forgiveness, love—and the state, with its grandeur, coercion, executions and wars," he states categorically in *What I Believe*. "Christianity in its true meaning destroys the state. . . . The state is at odds with love, specifically the commandment of non-resistance to evil by violence," he repeats in *The Kingdom of God Within You*, the essential chapter of the global anarchist canon.

Tolstoy therefore believes that we ought to reject any state, whichever form it takes: "autocracy, monarchy, *Convent*, consulship, empire, constitutional monarchy, commune or a republic." He left oligarchy out, so presumably he would be happy with the Russian post-communist state. But jokes aside, such ideas, coming from a public figure as influential as Tolstoy was at the time, fell on the fertile soil of a pre-revolutionary Russia. Tolstoy himself could segue effortlessly from general criticism of the state to specific attacks on the tottering Russian Empire. But the more practical people could easily discard the general altogether and concentrate on the specific: bringing about revolutionary hell.

It naturally followed that Tolstoy's nihilism toward the state as such was taken up with alacrity by the revolutionary nihilists. In addition to their theoretical objections to the state, in practice they hated the Russian state specifically, right or wrong. Thus Tolstoy, with his empty sermon of non-resistance, regularly joined murderous ghouls on the same side of the barricades. For example in the Russo-Polish war of 1863, both Tolstoy and the revolutionaries were on the side of the ultra-reactionary Polish nobility and against the peasants whom Alexander II tried to liberate from their enslavement in serfdom. And in the Russo-Turkish War of 1877–78, the revolutionary liberals, along with Tolstoy, in effect supported the genocidal expansion of Turkey in the Balkans against the comparatively liberal regime of Alexander II. The subsequent genocide of Bulgarians and Armenians perpetrated by Turkey when Russia was otherwise engaged proves how criminally wrong Tolstoy was.

Yet, for all the wrong reasons, Tolstoy did pose the right question: how do Christians justify the state? It is after all based on coercion. Judicial violence personified by the military, police, prisons, and so forth is part and parcel of any state, be that a democracy, a tyranny, or a democratic tyranny.

Sensing the relativism inherent in the very idea of the state, Tolstoy put it next to his own absolutist demand for the kingdom of God on earth here and now—and saw with relish that the two gears could not quite mesh. There we are then, smirked the count with his usual smugness. And his argument almost carried the day because the counter-arguments of his opponents, such as those of Soloviov, did not quite work either. Soloviov proposed replacing the secular state with a "free theocracy," uniting fallible people under the aegis of an infallible religion. But that too is a fallacy.

No state, including theocracy, can be included in the kingdom of God. That kingdom has to remain stateless, for the state is by definition coercive. However, faith, the ticket to the heavenly kingdom, is a free union between two entities. A man born to a faith usually has the option of not espousing it; the same man born within the realm of a state has no option but to follow its laws on pain of punishment. A theocracy by its very nature cannot accept the freedom of conscience to the same extent as Christianity and most other faiths must.[3] Thus a "free theocracy" that Soloviov[4] dreamed of is an oxymoron. The political ideal of the kingdom of God is not theocracy but Christian anarchy, the elimination of all secular power. In that sense Tolstoy was almost right.

The kingdom of God is the summation of all ethical requirements of the Gospel, including non-resistance to evil. In that kingdom man has no life apart from God, and no one is unique any longer. As there are no individual interests, no state is needed to pool and protect them. But on earth, with time ticking away, the same commandment that tells us to turn the other cheek out of brotherly unity based on universal love also implies that we must prevent evil done to others. Thus it was exactly the same spirit that drove some Christians to monasteries while driving some others on to the Crusades. And it was exactly the same faith that inspired St Bernard both to found Cistercian monasteries all over France—and to preach the Second Crusade from the hill slope at Vezelay.

Tolstoy is wrong in that he sees non-resistance as an absolute that expresses the entire meaning of the Gospels. Any use of force is immoral to him, whether for offensive or defensive purposes.

However, from the Christian standpoint it is not any violence that is evil, but only violence that contradicts the principle of love. Thus Soloviov was right when writing that the existence of nomadic bandits who fry Christian babies alive justifies the existence of a secular organization that harnesses the beast in man by force of arms.

The two men broke lances over this issue many times, with Soloviov demanding to know what Tolstoy would do if he saw a villain torturing a child to death. Would he not, if he could, kill the villain to save the child? Absolutely not, replied the count with the firmness worthy of a better use. We do not know God's ways, so who is to say that the child is more valuable than the bandit? All we know is that "thou shalt not kill," and this is what we must follow if we want to live moral lives:

Every lay person reading the gospel knows deep down that, according to this teaching, one cannot, on whatever pretext, not for vengeance, not for self-defense, not for saving another, do violence to his neighbor; and therefore, if he wants to remain a Christian, he has one of two choices: either to change his whole life, that is now based on coercion, i.e. doing violence to his neighbor, or somehow hide from himself that this is what Christ's teaching demands. And that is how people accept so easily the false teaching of the church, replacing the essence of Christianity with various dogmas.

(*The Way of Life*)

It was the same moral and theological confusion that led Tolstoy to his rejection of the state. However, the count was wrong in his assessment of that institution. Though some states are evil, and all can perpetrate the odd evil deed, the state is not evil in itself. Compared to the chaotic existence where *homo homine lupus est*, something that would inevitably result from Tolstoy's anarchism if it were allowed to triumph in this life, the state—almost any state—is, relatively speaking, a force for good. (Compare, for example, the excesses of even the ghastly state of Saddam Hussein with the carnage that followed its demise.) But a religious ideal demands absolute perfection, and there Tolstoy was right. Where he went wrong was in denying the innate imperfection of man, which makes the state necessary in this world, and the state's coercive violence inherent.

Assuming, as he does, that man is either perfect or at least perfectible is the first step on the road toward political anarchism. Tolstoy was naturally attracted to that doctrine and indeed to its leading practitioners. Having befriended Pierre-Joseph Proudhon, he based his view of economics on the latter's illiterate dogma "property is theft."

Also, he was friendly with Pyotr Kropotkin and even edited one of his books.

In his propaganda of anarchism Tolstoy, as was his wont, invoked Christianity, specifically the Sermon on the Mount. But the Sermon does not reject the state with its laws—it simply ignores it by never leaving the higher plane. Using the Sermon, as Tolstoy does, to justify anarchism is a gross swindle: he tries to pull the Sermon down to earth, ignoring that Christ himself moderated his ethics when applying it to temporal existence. The same swindle was to lead youthful intellectuals in the 1960s to insist that Christianity was in its essence the same as socialism. But for the Incarnation, the Resurrection, and Christ's kingdom that is not of this world, so it might be. As it is, Christianity is the exact opposite of socialism (and Tolstoyism). Its soul strives to soar upward, whereas socialism is soulless—it is chained to the earth, and its materialistic tethers cannot be slipped by definition.

That Christianity condones the state in earthly life follows not only from Christ's words about rendering unto Caesar that which is Caesar's. In his epistles, St Paul several times refers to the state as a divinely ordained tool of the good (for example, in Rom. 13:1). Thus even martyrs dying for their faith never rejected the rule of law the way the anarchists do. In this case Tolstoy would have done better had he read, or else paid attention to, Kant's later works, not just the two *Critiques*. There the same Enlightenment philosopher, who just like Tolstoy rejected the formalism of church dogma, extolled the virtue of the rule of law and tripartite division of power, both despicable to Tolstoy.

The only problem with anarchism, or for that matter with communism, that Tolstoy ever acknowledged was its violent component. "The great thinker" never explained how the state could be wiped out without violence, but then he never really cared about the practical nuts and bolts. Those who did even a little, such as again Soloviov, instantly saw that, once the talk stopped and action began, the violent men would take over as surely as night follows day. Peaceful anarchy, to Soloviov, was merely a masked transition to an anarchy far from peaceful.

That view was richly vindicated by latter-day Tolstoyans, such as Gandhi or King, whose non-violent diatribes inspired violent men. In spite of being eloquently implored to "learn, baby, learn," King's grateful listeners still chose to "burn, baby, burn." And Gandhi in his *For Pacifists* practically admitted that his non-resistance was merely resistance by other means: "My non-resistance is active resistance in a different plane. Non-resistance to evil does not mean absence of any resistance whatsoever but it means not resisting evil with evil, but with good. Resistance, therefore, is transferred to a higher and absolutely effective plane." Allow me to translate from the Tolstoyan-Gandhian: the non-violent sage does the talking; his violent minions do the killing. But for the time being, Tolstoy could indulge his little fantasies in *The Way of Life*:

Anarchists are right in everything: in rejecting everything that exists [*sic!*] and in asserting that, given the existing morals, nothing can be worse than governmental coercion. But they are grossly mistaken when thinking that anarchy can only be brought about by a revolution. Anarchy can only be brought about by more and more people appearing who wouldn't need the power of government's protection, and more and more people who would be ashamed to exercise this power.

Denouncing revolutions is good, we are all in agreement on that. But does "rejecting everything that exists" sound practical? Or moral? Or indeed sane? No more than his next pearl in *The Way of Life*: "Anarchy doesn't mean the absence of all institutions, but only of those that make people obey by force. One would think that a society of creatures endowed with reason couldn't, or wouldn't, have been organized in any other way." All government institutions collectively "make people obey by force." If they were unable to do so, they would be impotent and therefore useless. As such, they would soon become extinct. For, if a state cannot force its more recalcitrant subjects to fall in line, it will itself fall to the first revolution worthy of the name. Russia went on to prove this in short order.

Toward the end of his life, Tolstoy, along with most literate Russians, sensed that a revolution was in the air. And while he ostensibly deplored such upheavals, one can detect in him more sympathy for the bomb-throwing revolutionaries than for their victims. The latter, when all is said and done, have only themselves to blame:

The cruelty of all revolutions only results from the cruelty of the rulers. Revolutionaries are good students. Innocent people could never have got the monstrous idea that some people can, and have the right to, run other people's lives by force if everyone in power, all rulers hadn't taught it

(*I Cannot Remain Silent*).

"The cruelty of the rulers" in Russia resulted in about 1,800 death sentences during the entire nineteenth century, most of them for murder. In 1909 the total number of prisoners in Russia was 181,000, including offenders in all categories. In per capita terms that is not particularly oppressive even by the liberal standards of today's United States.

In the entire reign of Alexander II (1855–81), there was only one execution (Dmitry Karakozov, for an attempt on the tsar's life[5]). In the following 27 years, when guns and bombs emerged as acceptable tools of political debate, 141 were put to death: an average of less than six a year. The first year after the bloody 1905–06 upheaval saw 1,139 executions, a record at the time. This number then rose to almost 5,000 in 1908–10, but fell sharply to 73 in 1911 and 126 in 1912. This was the notorious White Terror that made the world shudder and Tolstoy fire off his article *I Cannot Remain Silent*.

Thus the whole of the White Terror fell far short of one month of the Red Terror after 1917. "The cruelty of the revolutionaries" then resulted in almost *2 million* judicial executions in just the first five years of the Soviet regime, plus untold and uncounted millions of extrajudicial ones, most of them for no wrong-doing other than belonging to a wrong class.

Melgunov's harrowing book *The Red Terror*, published in the West while Lenin was still alive, documents thousands of instances of such niceties as skinning people alive, rolling them around in nail-studded barrels, driving nails into people's skulls, quartering, burning alive, crucifying priests, stuffing officers alive into locomotive furnaces, pouring molten pitch or liquefied lead down people's throats. On these bases one is tempted to think that the revolutionaries had learned what they knew about violence from a teacher other than just the Russian jurisprudence of the nineteenth century.

It is of some interest that most of the same Westerners who had routinely written petitions on behalf of condemned Russian revolutionaries (Gerhart Hauptmann in Germany, Anatole France and Romain Rolland in France, Bernard Shaw and Wickham Steed in England, George Brandes in Denmark, Maurice Maeterlinck in Belgium, et al.) later either denied the Red Terror or saw nothing wrong with it. They were all Tolstoy's followers and admirers.

3

Tolstoy's odd idea of moral equivalence reached its risible peak in his celebrated article *I Cannot Remain Silent* (1908), the Russian answer to Zola's *J'accuse*. What brought on that self-confessed bout of uncontainable logorrhea was the government's attempt to stem the tide of revolutionary terrorism. In response to the brushfire of peasant revolts and the brutal murders of 1,600-odd officials, including members of the royal family, Stolypin's government had begun to carry out death sentences. Tolstoy had felt no urge to expand on the subject during the former phase; it was only the government's belated response that broke through the gossamer lid of his silence.

Tolstoy wrote the article in the form of an open letter to the government. First he described with meticulous attention to detail the mechanics of a hanging, which sensitive people would have found revolting. He then explained that nothing at all justified such cruelty, and certainly not revolutionary murders. Even though Tolstoy ostensibly deplored both types of violence, implicitly he found the revolutionaries easier to forgive: "Thus, if there is a difference between you and them, it is only that you want everything to remain as it was and is, while they want a change."

There is hardly a political villain in history who could not be exculpated using the same argument. And hardly a revolution about which the same thing cannot be said, which was proved by Tolstoy's idol Kant, who wrote about the then ongoing French revolution that, for all its lamentable violence, it finds in the heart of all observers the kind of sympathy that borders on enthusiasm.[6] This gives us an idea of how Tolstoy might have responded to the Russian revolution, had he lived so long. While deploring its violence, he probably would have welcomed it on balance.

Also, the revolutionary murderers were brave youths after all, and that almost justified them:

If there is a difference between you and them, it is by no means in your favor but in theirs. Their mitigating circumstances, first, are that they commit their villainies under the conditions of greater personal danger than those you have; and risk, danger justify a lot in the eyes of impetuous youth.

Using this logic, we must exonerate suicide bombers altogether. After all, they accept not just danger but certain death.

In addition, most of them were young, which Tolstoy regarded as a good excuse: "Second, most of them are very young people who are prone to errors of judgment, whereas you are mostly mature, old.... Third...no matter how nasty their murders, they are still not so coldly-systematically cruel as yours." Most of today's suicide bombers are not exactly old-age pensioners either.

We know now that when the impetuous youngsters took over Russia, they murdered millions in short order with the kind of "coldly systematic" savagery that any Romanov, with the possible exception of Peter I, would have envied. So where was Tolstoy's much-vaunted understanding of human nature when his people needed it? Where was his ability to think prophetically, for which he is so unjustly famous?— Buried under the weight of visceral nihilism, which he tried to conceal behind a wall of righteous wrath.

In general, Tolstoy's understanding of human nature seems to have been totally used up by his art (not an unusual situation with artists). There was nothing left for day-to-day life. For example, he said several times that, though both Chekhov and Gorky were his friends, he really preferred the latter. Leaving aside the comparative value of the two men as writers (they simply cannot be mentioned in the same breath), Gorky later distinguished himself by becoming Stalin's poodle, barking his support for concentration camps, slave labor, and mass shootings ("If the enemy doesn't surrender, he is to be destroyed," was the great Tolstoyan's comment on one of the show trials). But even in Tolstoy's lifetime, Gorky was Lenin's agent. Not only did he glorify revolutionary movements in his works, such as *Storm Petrel*, but he also was one of the most effective fund-raisers the bolsheviks had. To that end Tolstoy's bosom friend often used his mistress, whom he shared for a while with the millionaire Savva Morozov. Gorky's activities were well known at the time, and Tolstoy had to be aware of them. So this friendship says a lot about the moral standards of the great moralist.

4

Tolstoy's crepuscular thinking on the subject of the state comes from the same source as his pseudo-Christian morality. He was ignorant of the metaphysical essence of Christianity, the person of Christ, which is neither entirely expressed nor entirely expressible in his sayings. Sound metaphysics would have helped him realize that the kingdom of God is a mystical order, whereas the state is a natural one. "Thy kingdom come" expresses the ultimate ideal of Christianity: it thus means not just the end of the state but also the end of the world. The state will only disappear when the world does.

The state cannot destroy evil—it merely tries to contain it. The two desiderata are entirely different, which is why neither Testament ever treats the state with Tolstoyan maximalism. For example, God tells Samuel that a kingdom on earth is one in which God cannot be king.[7] He then blesses Samuel to become king—because man is imperfect. And in the New Testament, it is Satan, not God, who is the prince of this world (John 14:30).

Christ clearly separates the state from the kingdom of God: "My kingdom is not of this world" (John 18:36). That he divides the realms of God and the state is also evident from his answer to a provocative question from a few Pharisees in a crowd of listeners:

Tell us therefore, What thinkest thou? Is it lawful to give tribute unto Caesar, or not? But Jesus perceived their wickedness, and said, Why tempt ye me, *ye* hypocrites? Shew me the tribute money. And they brought him a penny. And he saith unto them, Whose *is* the image and superscription? They say unto him, Caesar's. Then saith he unto them, Render therefore unto Caesar the things which are Caesar's; and unto God the things which are God's.

(Matt. 22:17–21)

Thus, when Tolstoy states that it is sin for a Christian to pay taxes, he accuses Christ himself. That is an aggressively nihilist sentiment, much as one wishes at times that our tax authorities were to adopt Tolstoy's position. In Tolstoy's writings such thinly veiled attacks on Christ always exist side by side with his open harangues against institutional religion.

Nor did Christ, unlike Tolstoy, believe that Christianity is incompatible with military service. For Tolstoy, this was an article of faith: "It should not be allowed that a man, true Christian, should be a member of a society that has an army and military institutions." But in fact, Jesus himself was a member of just such a society during his life on earth. Moreover, when he had received the Capernaum centurion and heard him out, Jesus did not demand that the officer give up the service as being contrary to his faith—even though one did not get to command a company in a Roman legion without being an expert killer.

Rather than waxing indignant, Christ was effusive in his praise of the officer's faith: "When Jesus heard *it*, he marveled, and said to them that followed, Verily I say unto you, I have not found so great faith, no, not in Israel" (Matt. 8:10). But of course that episode also involves the miracle of healing, so Tolstoy felt justified as ignoring it.

Unlike him, Christianity does not reject the state as such. On the contrary, it values it—not as part of God's kingdom but as part of a historical process leading up to it. For, if someone wants human life to become paradise at some point, he ought to condone any force, even if it is extremely violent, preventing it from turning into hell in the meantime. Going back to the ladder metaphor, if we saw off every step but the top one, we will never get to the top.

Only God can be everything—but this does not mean that man should be nothing. Extremists like Tolstoy, who want to be more Christian than Christ, tout the slogan "all or nothing" and therefore despise anything that only has relative value, including the state. However, the absolute demand to be as perfect as the heavenly father is dangerously utopian unless accompanied by appreciation of every incremental improvement.

Stark, unrelenting maximalism is not only ungodly—it is also inhuman. Thus it is doubly anti-Christian. One should never forget that it was exactly the same spirit that was expressed both through acknowledging chastity as the ultimate virtue and through the blessing of the wedding at Cana. Jesus is capable of saying that a man not ready to reject his mother and father is not worthy of him—and then blessing the family in the same breath.

With his strident sermons of the last things, Tolstoy ignores that the state's first purpose is not to be wholly or even partially absolute. It is to lay the groundwork for the triumph of the absolute. To achieve that, the state must eradicate those manifestations of evil that can be eradicated by force. But in *The Way of Life*, among many other works, Tolstoy rejects any coercive action out of hand: "Coercion produces only an approximation of justice, but it takes people further away from the possibility of living justly without coercion." And, "Why is Christianity so corrupt, why have the morals fallen so low? One reason: belief that violence is a good way of running life."

Many critics of Tolstoy have argued rightly that in real life any society would perish if it did not defend itself against internal and external enemies. That much is obvious. But few have seen that Tolstoy, with his inimitable sleight of hand, transferred the commandments addressed to the individual onto the whole society. Granted, they do overlap somewhat—but not completely.

One cannot deny that the more citizens there are who actively seek moral self-improvement, the better the society will be. But neither can one deny that, in a modern kaleidoscopic society of all comers and all sorts, the proportion of such virtuous individuals is unlikely ever to be high enough to obviate the need for the state with its coercive laws.

It is also clear that the personal morality of a saint, something Tolstoy thinks ought to be community property, inevitably runs ahead of social ethics, which have to follow more primitive laws. The two are reflected in the two Testaments, which is why both are essential parts of the Christian canon. The Old Testament mostly, though not exclusively, codifies this world; the New Testament mostly, though not exclusively, paves the way to the next. That is why an ethic based on "an eye for an eye" is as valid as one based on loving one's enemies. The two are simply meant for different purposes—they are complementary parts of the same revelation.

Our day-to-day world is governed by legal principles that go back to the Old Testament. An individual guided by the New Testament can forgive the evil done to him, but society has to function according to the laws of justice. The victim's mother may, for example, forgive the murderer—but the state does not have this option: it has to prosecute the evil-doer to protect the community at large.[8] That is why the death penalty was never regarded as cruel and unusual punishment in the ultimate moral code of our civilization, the Scripture.

When society and community were more than just figures of PC speech, the moral validity of the death penalty was not in doubt. It was understood that murder sent shock waves throughout the community, and the amplitude of those destructive waves could be attenuated only by a punishment commensurate with the crime. Without it, the agitated community would run the risk of never recovering its irenic order. But Tolstoy did not care about his community or order therein. All that concerned him were his threadbare abstractions.

Even as the Old Testament largely prefigured the New, the laws of the ancient Hebrews were designed to retain the social and moral cohesion in this world so that people could prepare for the next. Thus, the biblical "an eye for an eye, a tooth for a tooth" is the practical law of social organization, while Christ's "turning the other cheek" is the heavenly ideal toward which to strive. Tolstoy consistently mixed the two up, thus proving that the Oblonsky household was not the only place where confusion reigned.

5

In this context Tolstoy quotes Mohammed, one of his favorite sources: "God honors the most him who forgives an evil done him, especially if the evil-doer is in his power."[9] Even Islam came in handy when the Count felt the urge to score moral points off Christianity.

Naturally, as Tolstoy abhors the state, he vehemently rejects the coercive arm of the state, its justice. I have said enough about the faulty premises from which he proceeds not to have to repeat the same arguments. So perhaps it is best to let "the great thinker" dig his own juridical hole and sink into it all by himself, with only my brief comments accompanying his disappearance.

"If I can force someone to do what I consider to be good," he writes, "then someone else can force me to do what he considers to be good—even if what he and I consider to be good is mutually exclusive." But that is precisely why the mediation of the state is necessary. The state is based on certain presuppositions of what is good. If these are clearly communicated, widely shared, and vigorously enforced, no misunderstanding is likely to arise.

And he continues in the same vein, "Forcing people to do what I consider to be good is the best way of making them detest what I consider to be good." This ignores the obvious fact that people who commit vile acts usually do so because they detest any decent perception of the good to begin with. So there is no danger of making them detest it even more.

"Punishment never achieves the purpose for which it is permitted." That depends on what we regard as the purpose of punishment. Some will see it as simple retributive justice, as Kant did. Others will emphasize its deterrent utility. Still others will feel that punishment, in addition to its obvious utility in isolating criminals from their potential victims, has a great symbolic value. It asserts the moral superiority of good over evil, thereby restoring the social serenity upset by the wicked deed. These are a few of the purposes that punishment can achieve quite successfully. Some will even suggest that it can serve the purpose of rehabilitating the criminal, although this has to come low down the list.

What it neither can nor is designed to achieve is the elimination of evil and the moral regeneration of mankind. Yet it is precisely this purpose that Tolstoy attributes to the state the better to hate it. "The superstition that punishment can eliminate evil is particularly harmful because as a result those who punish do evil believing that it's not only permitted but morally useful." And, "Punishment, or threat of punishment, can scare a man, keep him from evil for a while, but not improve him in any way." Most will argue that keeping a recidivist thug "from evil for a while" is worth having—whereas improving him is a task for the church, not for the state.

Tolstoy's fellow reformers did not share his view of punishment. For example, Luther divided the world into the religious and secular realms and argued that the Sermon on the Mount only applied to the spiritual one. In the temporal world, the balance between faith and duty to the community forces believers to compromise. Thus a judge, as a servant of the public, should follow his secular obligations to sentence a vile murderer to death, if such a verdict is appropriate. But, as a servant of God, he ought to mourn the fate of the criminal and pray for his soul. Tolstoy had heard all the arguments in favor of punishment before he rejected them:

Many years ago people began to understand the discordance between punishment and the higher properties of man's soul, so they went about making up all kinds of theories that could justify this base, beastly urge. Some say punishment deters, some that it rehabilitates, some that it's necessary for justice, as if without judges God wouldn't be able to bring justice to the world. But all these theories are empty words because they are rooted only in evil feelings: vengeance, fear, egoism, hatred. They come up with a lot of ideas but can't bring themselves to doing the only right thing, namely: to do nothing, leaving the sinner to repent or not, to improve or not; while the people who come up with those ideas, and those who apply them in practice, should leave others alone and concentrate on living the virtuous life themselves.

Every word of his own in this tirade is false, while most of the ideas Tolstoy ascribes to his opponents are correct. For example, the deterrent value of punishment: this has been demonstrated empirically throughout the world. It is no doubt counterintuitive, not to mention empirically unsustainable, to aver that the death penalty does not deter murderers. But even if we go against both intuition and evidence, there is still no denying that the death penalty deters the punished criminal from murdering again. That is no mean achievement. After all, in the 40 years after the abolition of the death penalty in Britain, more people were murdered by recidivists who had already served time for one murder than had been executed in the 40 years before the abolition. So never mind the human quality of the victims involved—even the quantitative argument supports the death penalty. As to doing nothing, there is a good aphorism usually, if perhaps erroneously, attributed to Burke: "All that is necessary for the triumph of evil is that good men do nothing." Or else that they follow Tolstoy's bright ideas.

But even such utilitarian arguments would make no impression on him. The man had tunnel vision, with no light at the end.

Only those completely drugged by lust for power can seriously believe that people's lives can be improved by punishment. It only takes abandoning the superstition that punishment improves people to see clearly that changes in people's lives can only be caused by inner changes in their souls, and not from evil they do to others.

But we already have abandoned that superstition. The only lives that can and should be improved by punishment are those of the good people outside prisons, not those of the bad people inside. And that happens to be the whole idea.

They say that, when God wishes to punish people, he deprives them of their minds. If that is true, Tolstoy's punishment was severe, with no tariffs applied. To wit: "Most of people's misfortunes are caused by sinful people thinking they have the right to punish." Tell that to the wife of a murder victim. Or to a pensioner robbed of his life's savings. Or to a woman raped and beaten within an inch of her life. No doubt they will all agree.

When Tolstoy was on a moral rampage, evidence fled for its life. "Punishing a man for his evil deed is the same as heating a fire. Any evil-doer is already punished by lack of peace and pangs of conscience. And if he feels no pangs of conscience, then any punishment imposed by others can only enrage, not improve, him." A good friend of mine, a prison doctor, swears he has not in his long career seen many evil-doers tossing and turning in their bunks all night because of their restless conscience. Most do not have those pangs, and if they are enraged they are better off in prison, not to mention that society is better off.

But Tolstoy is relentless:

We don't, and cannot, know what common good is, but we are certain that this common good can only be achieved if everyone obeyed not the law given by people but that eternal law of virtue that is revealed to each both in human wisdom and in his own heart.

But we can and do know what common good is. Having tested our prejudices against centuries of experience, which Tolstoy dismissed out of hand, has taught us that.

And unfortunately, contrary to what Aristotle, Kant, and Tolstoy preached, experience does not confirm that God's moral law lives in every soul. Though it is revealed by God, some people remain deaf to such revelations. Consequently, they are contemptuous of human laws that are, at their best, derived from God's. Bending such outcasts to the common will, by force if necessary, is the only way for a community to stay above the water, using the state as its life belt.

"It's much more natural," according to Tolstoy, "to imagine a society governed by reasonable, beneficial and universally acknowledged rules than a society in which today's people live, obeying state laws passed by no one knows whom." If he was unaware of the origin of state laws, then such ignorance could have been corrected by a visit to a library. And if it is so natural to imagine a perfect society in no need of a state, then how is it that in the 5,000 years of known history people have not got around to creating one? Yet again, "the great thinker" fails to bring his awesome intellect to bear on a vital issue.

6

As if to prove that his violent propaganda of non-violence had nothing to do with Christianity, Tolstoy applied it to animals as well, so as to justify his vegetarianism. "The same spiritual substance lives not only in all people but also in everything living," he writes in *The Way of Life*.

Since when? Certainly not since Genesis 1:28 drew a line in the sand between man and beast. And certainly not since Jesus, who ate paschal lamb (washing it down it with wine—another taboo for our hero[10]) and in general gave no indication whatsoever that he either was a vegetarian himself or thought that others should be. The Scripture says this in as many words: "The Son of man came eating and drinking, and they say, Behold a man gluttonous and a winebibber..." (Matt. 11:19).

In addition, according to any monotheistic religion, man and animals do not share "the same spiritual substance." Man, after all, was created in the image and likeness of God, whereas the Bible states unequivocally that animals were created only to serve man. And those possessors of "the same spiritual substance" that are equipped to do so will tear a man apart limb from limb should he look the other way. So where in the Scripture did Tolstoy read about vegetarianism as a moral commandment?

The answer is, he did not read it in the Bible. He read it in our hearts: *"Thou shalt not kill* refers not to man only, but to everything living. This commandment had been written in man's heart before it was written on the tablets."[11]

That would make the sixth commandment inexplicably different from the other nine. But in fact it is not. All ten of the commandments had to be written on the tablets precisely because they were not written in the hearts of men. All ten establish the unbreakable rules governing man's relationship either with God or with other people. And if Tolstoy just this once chose to invoke the Old Testament, which on other occasions he rejected with contempt, he ought to have reminded himself that animal sacrifice had been an essential ritual of Judaism from Abraham until the destruction of the Temple. And it was God himself who explained to Abraham, not in so many words, the ethical difference between human and animal sacrifice.

Sanctimonious, anthropomorphic worship of animals usually pre-supposes dislike of people. By implicitly or, as in Tolstoy's case, vociferously equalizing in status man and beast, a vegetarian robs man of his dignity. God says we cannot kill other people because they are our equals. Replace "other people" in this sentence with "animals," and we have deprived man not only of his link with God but also of his humanity.

As to the Kantian idea of this or any other moral imperative being written in our hearts, nothing in either Testament—or in everyday life—shows that to be the case. On the contrary, throughout the Bible people are shown to be weak creatures who can only become morally strong by suffering and lifelong exertion. Tolstoy ought to have read the Book of Job before reading *The Critique of Practical* (or, for that matter, *Pure*) *Reason*.

If God had wanted us to be vegetarian, he would not have made us omnivorous. Some of his creatures are herbivorous, some are car-nivorous, and man is both. None of the creatures other than man can choose which it wants to be. People have that ability, but they are bet-ter off not exercising it, so as not to throw half of what God kindly gave us to eat back into his face. And certainly, those who choose to do so anyway have no claim to any moral ascendancy.

For example, St Paul categorically, not to say imperatively, denies that vegetarianism occupies a higher moral ground than meat eating. For him, one's diet is strictly a matter of personal choice, with neither option having a particular moral content: "Let not him that eateth despise him that eateth not; and let not him which eateth not judge him that eateth: for God hath received him" (Rom. 14:3).

However, some saints, notably St Augustine, did become vege-tarians as part of their overall asceticism. In general, early Christians overstressed asceticism partly because they were locked in a struggle for survival against pagans and had to counterbalance their deifica-tion of the flesh. Hence the extreme asceticism of some Fathers of the Church, such as Tertullian, Origen, and Augustine. But this is the ground we have already covered from various angles: the practices of the greatest saints in history are not something even they themselves expected most people to follow. The saints were in direct contact with God and but half a step removed from his kingdom. Those who can-not, as Tolstoy could not, even approach the spiritual or intellectual heights reached by St Augustine ought not to single out his asceti-cism, the least consequential part of his heritage. Let us start with *The City of God*, shall we? Just replacing our Sunday roast with tofu is the easy way, the holier-than-thou way of a sentimental moralizer, not the compulsory moral choice of a Christian.

Tolstoy's vegetarianism, like all other chapters of his ascetic canon, was seemingly moral but at heart nihilistic, part of his blanket denial, more in word than in deed, of all normal life. His rejection of wine and tobacco fell into the same category. "No one," he wrote in *The Way of Life*, "has ever drunk or smoked himself to a point where he would do a good deed: work, think through a problem, care for the sick, pray to God. But most evil deeds are done in a state of drunkenness."

Here Tolstoy deploys his usual tactic: putting into the mouths of his imaginary adversaries words that his real opponents never uttered. One cannot think offhand of many people who regard their drinking and smoking as intermediate steps on the road to moral perfection. Most of us drink and smoke for the innocent pleasure of it, which is devoid of any moral value, negative or positive. Doing either thing to excess is not good for our health, but we can remain at our normal moral level while enjoying a cigarette or a glass of wine.

But for Tolstoy everything had to be morally charged, and he would ignore any evidence to the contrary. For example, there is absolutely no evidence that most evil deeds are done "in a state of drunkenness," not even in Russia. Nor are the most evil of men necessarily hedonistic drinkers and smokers. Hitler, for instance, was a vegetarian who neither drank nor smoked. His fellow mass murderer Lenin did not smoke and rarely drank. Stalin puffed on his pipe but drank moderately. Mao was no binge drinker. Bin Laden probably does not plan his murders in the middle of a bender. On the other hand, Churchill smoked like a chimney and drank like a beached sailor, and yet one does not usually think of him as an evil man.

St Francis stands apart from other great Christians in his attitude to fauna. He preached to animals and called them "brother" and "sister," which is why most painters starting with Giotto depicted him surrounded by every manner of beast. Yet throughout the Middle Ages—at the height of Christianity—this sort of thing was frowned upon as borderline heretical. In fact, only the saint's worldwide popularity saved him from a direct charge and subsequent punishment, the fate that befell many of his followers. However, in spite of his eerie anthropomorphism, St Francis was not a vegetarian. So even regarding animals as man's relations in God does not necessarily preclude having some protein in our diet.

Here too Tolstoy likes to paint or at least hint at the graphic details of a practice he finds objectionable. "If only all people who eat animals had to kill them themselves, the greater half of mankind would reject meat," he writes in *The Way of Life*. If we ignore the mathematical impossibility of one half being greater than the other, that very well may be. Similarly, if most people had to dispose of their own sewage, our cities would probably stink to high heaven even more than they do already: we are a lazy and squeamish bunch.

On the other hand, the same *noble sauvage* Rousseau and Tolstoy held up as a shining example to us all both killed and consumed his own meat, as do today's hunters. And throughout history, all serious thinkers regardless of their philosophical leaning, from Aristotle to Descartes to Kant, regarded animals as more or less inanimate creatures to which ethical consideration did not apply. So the count's conjecture had no grounding either in experience or in philosophy. It was as unfounded as it was ideologically driven.

It was, however, an ideology that played into the frenzied sentimentality with which modern, post-Christian people were replacing faith. In their faithless minds, protestations of equal love for all living things somehow took the hard edge off their absence of love for God. It gave them a chance to flirt with something super-personal without ascending to anything supernatural.

At the same time, vegetarianism, with its subcontinental implications, was like a vector pointing toward Oriental agnosticism. As such, it was a religious surrogate, an ersatz faith for the faithless. The only thing missing in vegetarianism until Tolstoy's propaganda of it had been social respectability. Herbivorous extremism had been regarded as either a psychological quirk or else some biochemical eating disorder.

Tolstoy, by throwing the weight of his popular persona behind the vegetarian cause, made it fashionable. Today, up to one-third of all pupils in Britain's top public schools cringe at the thought of eating meat. Alas, given the standards of education even at our best schools, most of them probably would not be able to place Tolstoy's name. That is a shame. One would cherish the sight of those pimply youths saying a prayer to the patron saint of vegetarianism before tucking into their soya cutlets.

7

But let us suppose we have managed, non-violently to be sure, to get rid of the state with its coercive laws. (The natural question is "How?," but posing such questions to Tolstoy would have been both tactless and pointless.) We now love one another ecstatically, equally and ideally, with nary a dirty thought among us. We eat nothing but carrot patties, drink nothing but celery juice, and—with ever-growing justification—see animals as our spiritual brethren (though we may still be allowed to wear leather shoes, for Tolstoy forgot to get around to castigating that outrage). And we have reconciled ourselves to the end of the world that logically has to follow a few decades of such sexless existence accompanied by unbalanced nutrition. But how do we keep the body and soul together while Tolstoy still allows us to?

Actually, I am being slightly disingenuous here: the good count had developed his prescriptions for the good life a few years before he began to agitate for total celibacy. But apart from that, his meticulously numbered prescriptions are exactly what we would expect to come down, in *The Way of Life*, from the towering height of his intellect:

All that is required for happiness is, first, a link between man and nature, i.e. living under the skies, in the open air, in the sunlight, in communion with the earth, plants, animals; second, free, loving labor—physical labor that gives good appetite and deep, relaxing sleep; third, family; fourth, free, loving contacts with all kinds of people of the world; fifth, health and painless death.

Happiness as seen by pantheists; harmony as prescribed by Rousseau.

Worshipping nature and proclaiming the *noble sauvage* as the ideal human type was the pet idea of the Romantic age inaugurated by Rousseau, one of the two men Tolstoy ever admitted to having worshipped, Jesus being the other. Rousseau thus found himself in most congenial company at the far recesses of Tolstoy's mind. But Jesus never suggested that the moral ideal toward which to strive is best personified by an unkempt gentleman joyously tossing his hirsute female on the grass in the spirit of unbridled joy. Rousseau, however, did.

In reality the *sauvage* never was *noble*. He himself resembled Hobbes's definition of his life: nasty, brutish, and short. Archaeological evidence abundantly confirms the *sauvage* part, whereas nobility is nowhere in evidence. What is in evidence is plenty of busted skulls and mangled bones, with the implements that inflicted the busting and mangling strewn about nearby. In short, prehistoric man, even though he could draw better than most Turner Prize winners, was no better than us. Nothing suggests that primitive life had the serene, bucolic quality of Rousseau's imagination. Of course Jean-Jacques was the precursor of our Leo, so he only invoked the *sauvage* to attack Western civilization, not for any of his intrinsic goodness. Tolstoy chose his teachers wisely.

As to the neo-pagan, pre-Platonic adoration of nature, at the time this aberration was—and still is, come to think of it—widespread as an expression of the Romantic ideal. Like all such ideas, this one came from the fantasies of the predominantly urban intelligentsia, or else the semi-urban gentry, both types insulated from nature by a thick layer of peasants. These, on the other hand, did find themselves face to face with nature, and they did not like it one bit.

In real life, peasants in general, and particularly Russian peasants, tended to regard nature as an enemy, not a friend. Nature killed them with epidemics, hurricanes, wild beasts, snakes, and insects. It starved them to death when no rain came for months. It also killed them when too much rain poured down, drowning their crops. Nature left them, in central Russia, only four months in which to feed themselves for the whole year. The rest of the time their fields and meadows were swept by blizzards and covered with ten feet of merciless white stuff—sorry: of gloriously gleaming, joyously sparkling, exuberantly crunching snow.

It is only during those four months that Russian peasants spent much time out in the open—doing so the rest of the time might have been moral but, in minus-forty frosts, it would also have been short-lived. The remaining eight months they lounged on top of their gigantic stucco hearths, drinking moonshine and beating their wives.[12]

As to physical labor, the count, needless to say, never experienced the horrors of real poverty. That is why he never found himself in a situation where his manual work was solely responsible for keeping himself and his family alive. Physical labor was for him what jogging is for a modern man: trying to get healthier physically by clocking up miles, and better morally by punishing himself for all the excesses of his working life. The ideology came on top of that, as it always did with our hero.

"Without manual labor," he wrote in *The Way of Life*, "neither a healthy body nor a healthy mind can exist." However, the average life expectancy of the Russian men involved in physical labor is in the low fifties now, and it must have been lower then. As to such toil being a *sine qua non* of a healthy mind, most of the great philosophers and scientists in history somehow managed to get by without it. But then Tolstoy did not always take the trouble of thinking before talking. He did not feel he had to; the count knew he could do or say nothing wrong anyway.

His own peasants could not suppress contemptuous smiles when watching their master push a plow, split logs, or carry buckets of water. One can understand them: they could not live his life of luxury, but at least they had their own life, their own space, to use modern jargon. It was this space that they saw Tolstoy invade so tastelessly, denying them even the exclusivity of their lowly station. And the count's friends chuckled at his social transvestism and role playing, quipping "Your Highness, the plow is served," but only behind his back. They knew His Highness's explosive temper only too well—the great proponent of non-violence could have killed for a joke like that.

In short, there is no evidence now, and there certainly was none in Tolstoy's time, that back-breaking physical slog makes people better either physically, morally, or intellectually. There is every evidence to the contrary. Physically, the health of Russian peasants was—and still is—shockingly bad. Intellectually, that social group has only made a trivial contribution as compared to other classes. And morally, apart from the moonshine and wife-beating aspects of it, throughout history the moment the Russian peasant felt the government's hand slacken on his shoulder, he would instantly set to "letting the red cockerel out."

In the poetic Russian phrase this meant burning to cinders everything they could, but especially baronial manors and houses of the more industrious peasants. In *A Course in Russian History*, Klyuchevsky vividly describes this method of redistributing wealth by leveling down (the only direction in which it is ever possible to level by whatever method): "Brave people often resorted to a particular way of benefiting at someone else's expense: they set rich people's houses on fire, ran to the blaze pretending to want to help and then stole as much as they could."

Murdering landowners they did not like was also the peasants' favorite pastime. When Dostoyevsky's father, for example, took his eyes off the ball for a brief moment, one of the saintly *muzhiks* promptly stuck an axe into his head (which tragic event did not prevent the orphaned Dostoyevsky from glorifying the common folk). "The Russian rebellion, senseless and merciless," vividly described by Pushkin and unleashed by the bolsheviks, sent millions of eager peasants on a war of all against all—for, though their orders came from above, it was mostly the erstwhile peasants who murdered, raped, robbed, and tortured tens of millions of innocent victims.[13] And it took them not years but days to turn into cannibalistic beasts,[14] which suggests that the beast had lurked not far beneath the surface.

When talking about economic matters, Tolstoy reduced them all to slogans, half communist, half anarchist, with no serious thought anywhere to be seen. At the crux of it was his overall doctrine of self-simplification as a guide to self-salvation. In this he made his usual error of ignoring the Christian balance between the two planes, physical and metaphysical, which reflects the two natures of Christ: God and man. When Christ talks about living like fowls in the sky, with no care for tomorrow, he stays in God's plane, ignoring the needs of everyday life. Francis of Assisi is one example of a saint who in his life, and not just in his sermons, embodied the Gospel commandment of freedom from labor and property. Compared to his life, Tolstoy's pet idea of creating colonies where people would live by agricultural labor sounds positively materialistic.

But side by side with a call for fowl-like and flower-like existence, the New Testament contains a direct endorsement of work, reflected in the Lord's Prayer ("Give us this day our daily bread"). Christ the carpenter also talks about "the laborer worthy of his hire" (Luke 10:7), and St Paul the tent maker states categorically that "if any would not work, neither shall he eat" (2 Thess. 3:10). The New Testament may occasionally be simple but it is never simplistic—which Tolstoy tended either to forget or to ignore.

An essential part of his self-simplification was his denying the validity of intellectual work—in fact renouncing the intellect as such, except naturally his own. Along with that came Tolstoy's rejection of the products of intellectual labor, be that culture, medicine, or science. Yet again one detects the religious aroma of the Indian subcontinent, with nary a whiff of Christian incense in the pungent air redolent of curry spices.

Tolstoy's frequent references to the Gospel as a source of his call for mental simplicity miss the mark by a mile. Jesus says to his disciples, "Behold, I send you forth as sheep in the midst of wolves: be ye therefore wise as serpents, and harmless as doves" (Matt. 10:16). St Paul echoes the same theme: "Brethren, be not children in understanding: howbeit in malice be children, but in understanding be men" (1 Cor. 14:20).

Simple, dove-like morality thus does not presuppose a simple mind. It not only allows but indeed demands serpent-like wisdom. Put in a different way, the child-like simplicity of the Gospels only has a metaphysical, not empirical meaning. This simplicity is the innocent purity of God's children. They can then build on it the sage complexity gravitating toward the highest wisdom—the Sophia that is central to Christianity, and especially to Orthodoxy.

When Tolstoy enlarged upon economics, another subject in which he had acquired instant expertise, his views—though he had arrived at them via a different route—were not a far cry from Lenin's, with a bit of Proudhon mixed in. In his key work on the subject *So What Is to Be Done?*[15] (which would strike any infidel as economically illiterate), Tolstoy declares that the whole idea of the poor and the oppressed being compensated in heaven is nothing but a ruse the rulers developed to boss the ruled. He thereby dismisses the very Sermon on the Mount he professed to love. In passing he takes a predictable swipe at those political economists who disagree with him, accusing them of "stupidity" and "bad faith."

The pamphlet became an instant hit with the extreme Left. In his article on Tolstoy, G.V. Plekhanov, the most influential Russian Marxist before Lenin, remarked rightly that "Tolstoy in his teaching on property ends up by adopting the socialist point of view.... The proletariat mainly cherishes Tolstoy as the author of these remarkable pages." The proletariat would have been better off just concentrating on *War and Peace*. In any case, it must not have read "these remarkable pages" very closely, for otherwise it would have noticed that, had Tolstoy had his way, all proletarians would have been forced to go back to the land.

For, in the name of the *sancta simplicitas* that was firing his imagination at the time, Tolstoy preached a bucolic life of manual labor in agricultural communes. It is hard to argue with him: life would indeed be simpler if all people stayed in the country tilling the land, producing just enough to keep body and soul together. The problem with such simplicity is that it cannot work in the modern world: the simple people would simply starve.

Russia has proved this empirically throughout her history and especially in the nineteenth century when about 80 percent of her arable land was in the hands of peasant communes. These were not just communal but largely communistic in that their main objective was not higher productivity but the economic leveling so dear to Tolstoy's heart. Wealth there was distributed not from the less efficient to the more efficient, but in the opposite direction. Also, from the reign of Peter I onward, it was the commune as a whole and not individual peasants who were taxed. Thus it did not pay for any peasant to work harder and do better than others. Those who did so anyway, often were beaten up or even killed, with their houses burnt down. That taught them not to set an example others might have found hard to follow.[16]

The incentive not to go bust was weak, for it was possible to survive in Russia handsomely without working. While all Western countries had strict laws against vagrancy, in Russia vagrants and beggars were protected by law. For example, in 1809 Alexander I announced severe punishments not for vagrants but for those who failed to look after them. Predictably, toward the end of the nineteenth century the country was inundated with beggars, and about 80 percent of them were professionals, whose income often far exceeded that of a qualified worker.

Any student of economics will know that such an institutionalized lack of incentives, especially in the harsh climate of central Russia, was a recipe for low yields. So it should come as no surprise that in 1898 a German peasant obtained, from the same-sized plot in similar climatic conditions, 2.5 times more grain than did his Russian colleague. Murderous famines were by no means a rarity. There were 120 of them recorded between 1024 and 1854—which is one every 7.5 years. And later in the nineteenth century famines took tens of thousands of lives, especially in the Volga region.[17] That area was plagued by droughts and subsequent famines throughout its history, with the sole exception of the 15 years during which Stalin allowed ethnic Germans to have their own "republic" there. Suddenly the province began to produce record crops of grains, vegetables, and fruit. This suggests that Russia never had many economic ills that would not have been immediately cured if more Germans, or other Westerners, had settled there.

The obvious link between industry and wealth did not pass unnoticed in the Bible: "He becometh poor that dealeth with a slack hand: but the hand of the diligent maketh rich" (Prov. 10:4). But Tolstoy's analysis of the situation was different, much closer to *Das Kapital* than either to the Bible or to *The Wealth of Nations*. According to him, it was not economic leveling that was to blame; the culprit was not enough leveling.

And then of course let us not forget the blood-sucking exploiters of the toiling masses: "If a peasant has no land, horse or plow . . . that means that someone drove him off the land and either took away or cheated him out of his plow, cart, horse." Lenin could have happily signed his name under that statement. Of course another explanation of that unfortunate situation could have been that the peasant had sold "his plow, cart, horse" for vodka—or simply let them come to ruin by neglect. In fact we have just seen that what made the peasant so deprived was mostly his own indolence, either created or promoted by proto-communism.

Well, we may have seen it, but the (instantly) great economist of the Russian land did not. His solution to the economic ills of the peasantry was akin to his idea of salvation: self-sufficiency. As he put it tersely, "all I need is what I can make myself: my plow, my samovar, my water, my clothes."

Splendid idea. But is one permitted to ask where the steel for the plow and the copper for the samovar were going to come from?

Assuming, of course, that there were no mines, smelters, and steel mills at Yasnaya Poliana? If there were none, then the metals would have had to come from somewhere else. But with everyone sowing and reaping, there would have been no one left to mine the ore, produce the metals, and transport them to Tolstoy's forge.

Moreover, those facilities are expensive to build and maintain. The money would have had to come from somewhere, a financial institution of one type or another. That meant some people would have had to wield an abacus, not a plow. Some others would have had to make the abacus (not to mention the machinery for the steel mills) and build the office for those blood-sucking leeches to work in and the furniture for them to sit on. As those abacus jockeys would have been unable to make their own clothes, we would have needed a few textile mills, which in turn would have required some machinery, which in turn...well, you get the picture. By this crude route we arrive at the need for division of labor and at least some kind of post-cave economics.

But even such an economics primer was beyond Tolstoy, partly because he did not really care what would have happened to the people had his ideas been acted upon. As was his habit, he started out by talking about the plight of the poor, but then somehow forgot them and focused yet again on how he could become morally pure by liberating himself from his privilege and ceasing to take part in evil. As long as he was blessed, he did not mind if the poor were damned.

Step by step, Tolstoy came to share the ideas of Henry George, the American economist who claimed that private ownership of land was the root of all economic evil. In fact, Prince Nekhliudov, Tolstoy's protagonist in his weakest novel *Resurrection*, explains George's theories more lucidly than George ever did himself. But then he was not a writer of genius, while Nekhliudov was the mouthpiece of one.

Tolstoy himself tried many agricultural experiments, similar to those attempted by Lyovin in *Anna Karenina*. Having run into the stone wall of the peasants' indifference and, often, hostility, they all failed miserably. Tolstoy's sacred cows thus slaughtered, he had to look for scapegoats. Like Caesar's wife, he himself was above suspicion; so he had to blame the peasants' "savagery" and "stupidity" for the collapse of his agricultural schemes. In general, his peasants tended to have their fake halos ripped off their heads and stamped into the dirt whenever they disagreed with the great agrarian of the Russian land.

These breathtaking economic ideas came to Tolstoy early in life (no late bloomer, he) and stayed with him until his death. All he did was dress them up in the Russian folk garb. Thus his diary entry of August

18, 1865: "Russia's task in world history is to bring to the world the new idea of order relative to landed property." And, "Russian people reject landed property.... This is not daydreaming but a fact, reflected in peasant and Cossack communes. This idea has a future. It is the only possible basis for a Russian revolution. This won't be a revolution against the tsar and despotism, but against landed property."

His crystal ball was in working order. The idea did have a future, and the bolsheviks did use Tolstoyan slogans to trick the masses. The masses first welcomed "the new idea of landed property" and then were killed by it—in millions, and this time not just in the Volga region. And, on Lenin's direct orders, the Cossacks were practically liquidated as a group, in spite of their erstwhile communes.

Yet again we see that, though Tolstoy might have disliked the communists' propaganda of violence, he shared most of their other ideas. "If one man owns too much," he writes for instance, "then many others don't have the necessities." This is Marxist zero-sum economics at its crudest. The assumption is that an economy is like a pie whose size never changes: if some greedy glutton grabs a big piece, then there will be little left for everyone else. But modern Western and Western-like economies prove that the amount of wealth is never constant. New wealth can be created. Whole new industries, such as our modern high-tech, can appear out of nowhere. The task for a successful economy is thus to bake a large economic pie, not to make sure that everyone would get an equal slice of a small one.

And most people who "own too much" create wealth not only for themselves but also for others, which explains the high standards of living in the West. There was plenty of evidence to that effect at the time as well, but Tolstoy did not want to know. He had it all figured out, with a little help from his friends Pierre-Joseph Proudhon and Henry George: Any property is theft (Proudhon), and especially landed property (George). To give credit where it is due, Tolstoy is generous with his attributions in *The Way of Life*:

A man can acquire wealth only in three ways: by physical labor, begging or theft. Laborers get so little precisely because beggars and thieves get too much. (After Henry George)

And,

All rich people who don't labor themselves but live off the labor of others—whatever they call themselves—if they don't labor themselves, they take away the fruits of other people's labor; all such people are robbers. (After Proudhon)

And then from Tolstoy's own unattributed heart, in the convoluted prose of a man whose emotions outpace his brain, comes a detailed explanation, starting with the recapitulation of the opening theme: "People can feed themselves in only three ways: by robbery, begging or manual labor."

Those chaps with cups, sitting at street corners, are not even aware that they represent one of only three possible models of wealth generation. But one cannot help noticing that left outside of this tripartite economy are teachers, doctors, scientists, priests, writers, entrepreneurs, musicians, artists, engineers. None of them are either manual laborers or beggars. So they must be thieves.

But do let us allow the great economist to explain his explanation in the next paragraph:

It's easy to tell those who feed themselves by labor; just as noticeable are those who feed themselves by begging; only robbers aren't recognizable at once, because there are two kinds: one are simple robbers, those who rob by taking people's possessions by force or by theft. These are known to all, they themselves know they are robbers and thieves; they are caught and punished. The other kind of robbers are those who don't consider themselves to be robbers, those who are not caught and punished, but who, by the methods allowed by the government, rob working people by taking away the fruits of their labor.

Thus the professionals I mentioned earlier are not just thieves, but stealthy ones too.

Tolstoy frequently relied on Henry George to add his usual hysterical overtones to an idea that was fundamentally unsound to begin with: "All wealth is sinful and evil. But there is no wealth more sinful and evil than that based on landed property. What is called the *right* to landed ownership has deprived half the people on the globe from their legal and natural inheritance." And my particular favorite: "He who possesses more land than he needs to feed himself and his family isn't just partly but wholly to blame for the poverty, calamities and corruption suffered by working people."

Out of curiosity, exactly how is a Scottish laird wholly responsible for the plight of the poor in the East End of London? Tolstoy's economic analysis is so false that one feels, to quote him himself, "almost embarrassed to argue against it." Suffice it to say that it runs contrary not only to any sensible economic theory but also to any evidence before our very eyes.

With his heart bleeding for the poor, Tolstoy tried some well-publicized philanthropy and, to his credit, made an important contribution to the relief of the 1890 famine in the Volga region, where the Germans had not yet settled in sufficient numbers to preclude such calamities. But, as was usually the case with him, he soon lost interest and in fact made numerous sweeping statements against philanthropy as an institution. Tolstoy condemned it as a symptom of "the willingness of the rich to do everything for the poor except to get off their backs."

Someone must have forgotten to tell this to the authors of the Bible: "Thou shalt open thine hand wide unto thy brother, to thy poor, and to thy needy, in thy land" (Deut. 15:11). And someone had forgotten to tell this to the Morozovs, the Tretiakovs, the Zimins, the Mamontovs, the Shchukins, and numerous other rich families who at that time were endowing museums, supporting the arts, founding schools and hospitals, financing public works, and building free housing for the poor on a scale unmatched anywhere else in Europe. Philanthropy at that time acted the way social welfare does now, as insurance against failing too badly. Except that philanthropy did it better.

Naturally, Tolstoy claimed he based his economic ideas on the Bible, and not without some, albeit facile, justification. For, if along with Tolstoy we ignore the higher, heavenly layer of the Christian attitude to wealth, then Christianity may sound downright socialist:

Then said Jesus unto his disciples, Verily I say unto you, that a rich man shall hardly enter into the kingdom of heaven. And again I say unto you, It is easier for a camel to go through the eye of a needle, than for a rich man to enter into the kingdom of God

(Matt. 19:23–24).

So what should the rich do with their money? Why, give it away of course: "...go and sell that thou hast, and give it to the poor" (Matt. 19:21). Unlike Tolstoy, the apostles practiced what they preached: "And all that believed were together, and had all their things common; And sold their possessions and goods, and parted them to all men, as every man had need" (Acts 2:44–45). "To each according to his needs," along with all of Tolstoyan economics, grew straight out of this passage, appropriately perverted.

The apostles were not wealthy, and surely they realized that spreading their meager possessions among the needy hardly amounted to responsible economic policy. By redistributing their wealth they were seeking self-purification. But the subversive potential of such acts, when misinterpreted by people who are not normally driven by high urges, is obvious. Since then we have had ample opportunity to observe what happens to communistic ideas whose full potential is realized.

Jesus, when he shifted his prophesies from the heavenly to the earthly plane, had no illusions about the coming of an egalitarian bliss: "For ye have the poor always with you" (Matt. 26:11) Incidentally, as if to refute Tolstoy's assertion that Christ rejected everything in Judaism, he repeated there, almost word for word, a similar thought from the Old Testament: "For the poor shall never cease out of the land" (Deut. 15:11)

Like Jesus himself, the more subtle Christian souls had no problems finding a nuanced compromise between heavenly dicta and everyday life. Thus, for example, comments Aquinas:

The perfection of the Christian life does not consist essentially in voluntary poverty, though that is a tool of perfection in life. There is not necessarily greater perfection where there is greater poverty; and indeed the highest perfection is sometimes wedded to great wealth.

Tolstoy probably never read, and certainly never quoted, *Summa Theologiae*. He cherished his own ideas, however ill-conceived. But amazingly, he was unsound not only when expounding upon subjects about which he knew next to nothing. He also managed to remain unsound when talking about the subject about which he knew next to everything: art.

8

When Nabokov, already a famous writer, first applied for an academic post at Cornell University, he was turned down. "You wouldn't hire an elephant to teach zoology," remarked the head of the Russian Department, dismissing his colleagues' entreaties.[18] True, with notable exceptions, of whom Nabokov was one, there does not seem to exist an automatic link between the talent for creating art and the ability to comment on it.

Probably that is because analytical writing on any subject ought to be a cold-blooded rational exercise, while creativity is not always, and never merely, rational. Many serious artists writing about their art realize that, no matter how comprehensively they cover the intellectual part of what they do, something critical will remain unsaid. So they either do not bother to talk about their art at all, or else resort to variously witty and frivolous generalities.

For instance, if you look at Glenn Gould and Sviatoslav Richter, two of the greatest post-Romantic pianists, you will agree that they are best listened to, not read. Most of Richter's pronouncements on music spanned the full range from the banal to the vulgar. And Gould, though a good writer, clearly reserved his more penetrating insights for the keyboard of his Steinway, not of his typewriter. Conversely, pianists like Alfred Brendel and Charles Rosen, while not fit to turn the score pages for the other two, write about music with lucid and penetrating brilliance.

By the same token, some great writers also happen to be great analysts of literature and some do not. Among Russian poets, Mandelstam and Brodsky were examples of the former; Pushkin and Lermontov, of the latter. But by and large whenever a serious artist delivers himself of a silly or inconsequential pronouncement on his craft, it is because he does not care to talk, not because he does not know what to say. He is a creator, not a pontificator.

Tolstoy stands apart from others in that he insisted on being both. And even as his art was at odds with his religion and philosophy, so was it at odds with his theories of aesthetics. For literature neither tolerates nor forgives tendentious generalities. It is all based on concrete existential images. In fact, unlike philosophy, literature is by its nature existential. Therefore, when philosophy adopts existentialism, it commits theft which seldom goes unpunished. Conversely, when art abandons its existentialism for sententious rationalism, it treads on alien soil.

Hence the conflict that Tolstoy experienced between his sublime art and his puny religion, along with the moral philosophy that came out of it. His religion was rationalistic and impersonal. Because of this it could not be reconciled with his art that is infinitely richer mystically than his denatured faith. Thus, when Andrei Bolkonsky in *War and Peace* thinks of death looking at a craggy, moribund oak, we sense artistic truth in that scene. Many of us have experienced such mystical moments consciously or unconsciously. So we are thankful to the great writer for capturing the instant, thus revealing something we may not have realized about ourselves. However, when exactly the same sentiment, generalized and intellectualized, appears in a philosophical work to suggest that man is but an extension of nature, then what was artistic truth becomes pantheistic falsehood, and a trite one at that.

When Tolstoy introduced long, tedious asides into the finely balanced narrative of his novels, he often upset the artistic balance and only his irrepressible genius enabled him to get back on track. But when he left the world of existential images altogether, his writing became nothing but one long, tedious aside. There was no salvation in craft, no beautiful descriptions of sunsets or battles, childbirth, or death. There were no probing looks into man's heart behind which he could hide his suspect philosophy.

Tolstoy's problem was not unique. Many artists find it hard to reconcile their religion with creativity. That is partly why all the greatest composers after Haydn (such as Mozart, Beethoven, Schubert, Schumann, Chopin, Brahms, and Tchaikovsky) eventually distanced themselves from the religion in which they had been raised. Part of the reason was, of course, the general humanization of life: music along with Western culture in general began to edge away from its source, Christianity. Witness, for example, Bach, who was already seen as an anachronism in the middle of the eighteenth century because he had never severed his religious roots. But the Zeitgeist was not the whole story. For regardless of the cultural climate, many an artist can create freely only when his religious consciousness is suppressed. The moment it comes to life, it may curtail his expressive freedom, forcing him to choose one or the other.

It is on rare occasions that the two do not clash, instead joining harmoniously into a free union. When that happens, art is sanctified by a religious ideal, which enables it to reach out for greater heights even on its own terrain—as shown by Bach or, closer to Tolstoy's field, Dante, or, closer still, Dostoyevsky. These artists found a way of blending their art with religion. Dostoyevsky, for example, did not need long asides to convey a religious message—it was woven into his narrative and dialogue as an organic part of his protagonists' self-expression. He took the aesthetic route to God, and it turned out to be a two-way street in that God then helped his art.

But Russia's two greatest prose artists, Gogol and Tolstoy, were not so fortunate. When they became preoccupied with religion, they found no way of fusing it with their art without compromising both. As a result, they renounced all art as being sinful. It did not matter that Gogol's religion was Christianity and Tolstoy's was, well, whatever it was that month. As neither writer was able to use his art to uphold an ideal, they both decried it as upholding idolatry.

Gogol burnt his manuscript of the second volume of *Dead Souls* and instead produced the pious but otherwise weak tract *Selected Excerpts from Correspondence with Friends*. Effectively he murdered the artist within himself, a calumny that Tolstoy also attempted, though with less success. In that, he was like a man who tries to shoot himself but only manages to graze his forehead.

The trigger was pulled shortly after he wrote *Anna Karenina*, in 1878, when Tolstoy repudiated writing fiction as hubristic, sinful, and covetous. The philosophizing in which he had indulged on the margins of his sublime *War and Peace* now shunted his art aside and stepped forward. Tolstoy began to express himself in a genre for which, as we have seen, he lacked true religious inspiration, philosophical rigor, and indeed intellect. By trying to become more than an artist, he only succeeded in becoming less than an artist. By trying to be a philosopher to end all philosophy, the great writer could not even reach the level of an earnest assistant professor at a provincial university.

We also ought to remember that, while many artists cannot reconcile their work with their faith, many religions are in their turn suspicious of art. Early Christianity and Judaism, with their ban on graven images, shared this attitude to a large extent. For example, Clement of Alexandria wrote that art contravened not so much the second commandment as the eighth: by displaying creativity, man was stealing God's prerogative. In other words, pre-Christian and early Christian monotheism frowned upon not just pictorial or sculptural representations of God but on artistic creativity as such. It was only when Christianity produced its own aesthetics by incorporating its Hellenistic cultural precursors that art was accepted as a possible medium for communicating religious truth. But Tolstoy was unable to do this in his novels, and characteristically he could not blame himself for that failure. The fault had to lie with art *qua* art, not himself.

In *What Is Art?*[19] he expanded on his rejection of art, using it as just one aspect of his overall nihilism. Art to him became one of many cultural lies perpetrated by he was not quite sure whom: "All that we call culture: our arts and sciences...are an attempt to cheat the moral, innate needs of man; all that we call hygiene and medicine are an attempt to cheat the innate, physical needs of human nature." "The innate needs of man" must have included artistic expression from the time man was created, as shown by those magnificent drawings in the caves of Santander. And if "the innate physical nature" of man presupposes painful death at an early age, then we ought to thank medicine for cheating it. Any way we look at it, rejecting all human activity outside digging potatoes as unnatural simply does not add up either intellectually or morally.

Tolstoy's hostility to culture was more than just about culture. It was part of his rejection of history as a sum total of people's deeds, and also of his religious egotism springing from his rejection of the church. The only reality for him was individuals acting individually, and he acknowledged no unity among them, either historical or mystical. Such views make it impossible to accept culture, or indeed economics and statecraft, which represent a collective effort of generations.

Tolstoy did not even attempt to solve the problem, possibly because he did not recognize it as such. Instead he hacked through the Gordian knot by rejecting culture in its broadest sense and, more narrowly, art. This is straight nihilism characteristic of the Russian intelligentsia at that time. Much as Tolstoy despised that group, he shared this trait with it.

So what specific problems did Tolstoy have with art? Which of his expectations had art failed to fulfill? His answers to these questions, though strewn about many of his works, including *Anna Karenina*, are most comprehensively expressed in his essay *What Is Art?* Apart from some perceptive comments on the principles of writing one would expect from Tolstoy, this work is yet another chapter in his saga of moralizing populism.

Just like his populism and his moralizing, it has only negative value—the essay provides the blueprint for the cultural catastrophe to come in our own time. Everything unobjectionable in the philosophy of *What Is Art?* is not so much truth as truism (e.g. "art is an organ of human life, transmitting man's reasonable perception into feeling"). But most of the book is an ideological sermon that contradicts every word Tolstoy produced as an artist, not to mention common sense.

"Art is not a handicraft," he defines with his usual imprecision, "it is the transmission of the feeling the artist has experienced." So is gossip. So is a chat at a cocktail party. So is practically any communication between people. What turns such things into art is precisely the "handicraft," understood broadly as ability to sculpt the right form for conveying the right content. Defining art so as to include practically everything, as Tolstoy does here, is tantamount to saying that it does not exist as an autonomous entity. But a brief look at, say, his *Hadji Murat* shows that art does exist. Therefore his definition is meaningless and self-refuting.

However, Tolstoy persisted with his syllogisms, each failing either by its weak premises or *non sequitur* conclusions. The gist of many of them is the same: either art is universally accessible or it is not. If art is important, then it is universally accessible. Therefore, if it appeals only to an educated elite or specialized taste, art is not important. Thus most great art is not art.

"Good art," claims Tolstoy, "always pleases everyone." Replacing "everyone" with "precious few" will get us much closer to the truth. Good art—as opposed to popular rubbish—always has been created for few by fewer. And from Plato onward, aesthetic philosophers have always distinguished between high art and low. By Tolstoy's criterion *Jesus Christ Superstar* that pleases millions is better art than *St Matthew's Passion* which at best pleases thousands. But do let us allow the great aesthetic philosopher to expand on his aphorism:

The very best art meets these conditions:

- It uses pictures, sounds, or designs understood by everyone or, in the case of prose and poetry, is understandable to any speaker of a language in which it's expressed.
- Audience response does not depend on knowledge of art (it appeals not just to an elite class).
- It is sincere, and the artist is compelled by inner need to express this particular emotion.

The third condition, sincerity, is the most important of the three. "It is always complied with in peasant art, and this explains why such art always acts so powerfully; but it is a condition almost entirely absent from our upper-class art, which is always produced by artists animated by personal aims of covetousness or vanity."

Tolstoy does not specify what he means by peasant art, but contextually it has to be his beloved village songs, the Russian aesthetic answer to Morris dancing. In their normal context they "act so powerfully" only on people devoid of any comprehension of music, especially if the listeners are generously lubricated with moonshine. As to "upper-class" art (Brahms? Rembrandt? Tolstoy himself?) lacking sincerity, no comment is necessary—apart from bemoaning yet again the destructive effect of ideology even on the kind of minds that ought to know better.

It is undoubtedly true that peasant ditties are sincere, but alas that is all they are. They seldom have any poetic or musical value, and at best can only act as raw material for real composers, most of whom would quote from them occasionally. Tchaikovsky, for example, used many folk tunes in his music; so did Chopin; so did Bartok; and Stravinsky's *Petrushka* is based on one folk song. But that "upper-class" artists can make use of such ditties does not make them art by themselves. Similarly, some vegetables hanging off a string only become devotional art in the hands of a great painter like Sanchez Cotán. By themselves they are ratatouille ingredients.

As to the motivation of artists, one finds it hard to believe that Mozart, Shakespeare, and Leonardo were spurred on exclusively by "covetousness or vanity," even if those motives were present some-where. Neither was Tolstoy, for all his seemingly self-lacerating but in fact self-serving confessions. The count is yet again talking non-sense here. Yet this is not the same kind of nonsense as, say, Glenn Gould saying with a straight face that he considered Orlando Gibbons the best composer ever. Gould simply was in the mood for facetious paradoxes, while Tolstoy was preaching his ideology in all earnestness.

As he was throughout the essay: "To say that a work of art is good but incomprehensible to most people is the same as saying of some kind of food that it is very good but that most people can't eat it." In England, potato crisps and pork scratchings are enjoyed by more people than fresh fish, but that does not necessarily make those better food. Then again, Tolstoy does not need us to contradict him. He is perfectly capable of doing so himself: "Art is a human activity which has as its purpose the transmission to others of the highest and best feelings to which men have risen."

If you juxtapose his two statements in the previous paragraph, you will have to infer that all people are equally capable of appreciating "the highest and best feelings to which men have risen." But that is wishful thinking, and not of a particularly clever or observant variety. Even grammatically, the highest and best are superlatives. What makes them so is precisely that they are "incomprehensible to most people." Otherwise they would be commonplace, not superlative.

The belief that good art must be accessible equally to all is patently false. It is so far from truth as to be its exact opposite—and, what is more, Tolstoy knew it. So he himself did not in this instance practice the sincerity he preached. When he was creating his own art, it was beyond the reach of about 80 percent of Russians who were illiter-ate at the time (even though they were "speakers of the language"). Moreover, since much of the dialogue and many of the asides in *War and Peace* were written in French, that narrowed the group of poten-tial Russian readers even further. Thus we can arrive at the minimum theoretical precondition: to gain access to a work of literature, the per-son must be able to read the language in which the work is produced. Tolstoy himself acknowledged this in a later letter when he identified his target readership as the literate peasant. To qualify as literate in contemporaneous Russia, an individual only had to be able to read ABC texts and sign his name.

But of course even the ability to do so is insufficient to the task of reading, say, *War and Peace*. It takes more than basic literacy to work one's way through a 1,500-page book. It takes some experience of reading long books, which is to say training. This can be acquired through formal education or simply by reading copiously for many years, or usually by a combination of the two. To spend years reading books upon books of gradually increasing complexity, one has to have a strong interest in that sort of thing, which is a form of intellectual ability and predisposition. One should also have the imaginative ability to translate the graphic symbols of words on paper into the physical reality of the people and situations described—and that requires at least some training of the mind and senses.

If we agree with Tolstoy that art is a form of communication, then to some extent it has to be a dialogue between the author and the audience. But no meaningful dialogue is possible without at least approximate parity between the two sides. For before a written word, sound, or image can produce the effect the author desires, it has to be refracted through the prism of the recipient's mind and senses. That is why the closer the reader is to the author's world, the more successful will the author be in conveying his feelings and thoughts. And conversely, a Shakespeare sonnet will not move an habitual consumer of rap. (As an experiment, I once played a Bach cantata to some youngsters who only ever listened to pop. They were physically unable to listen, and one of them—a well-brought-up girl in her mid-twenties—walked out of the room after 30 seconds with a pained expression on her face.)

In short, even such an inherently semantic art as prose fiction[20] is accessible only to a minority whose size varies from one time to the next, and from one place to another, but never so as to become the majority. If we step away from straightforward verbal semantics toward the more complex and less concrete means of expression, such as those found in music, then the minority narrows much further. But the basic requirement remains: to understand any art, one has to have thorough command of the language in which it is expressed.

As this language becomes more esoteric and subtle, it takes more time and effort to master. In parallel with learning the language, the audience must also work on honing their aesthetic sense to make it adequate to the form of a great work—and on deepening their souls to make them adequate to its content. Both tasks are demanding, and the greater the art the more demanding they get. Thus, the better the art, the narrower the group that can appreciate it. Just compare the popular appeal of a Strauss waltz to that of, say, the *Diabelli* variations.

To find a way around this obvious fact, one has to redefine great art. Tolstoy, realizing that he is about to paint himself into yet another corner, comes up with the concept of "universal art" that "expresses simple and accessible positive feelings" and that is "found in all arts, but most of all in music. Simple and comprehensible melodies fall into this category." Thus, if Tolstoy were alive today, in order to be consistent he would have to agree with a modern barbarian who believes that the "simple and comprehensible melodies" of the Beatles represent the apex of musical attainment these days, even if their equals Bach and Beethoven may have done so in the distant past.

Tolstoy then goes on to say that "religious art does not express the doctrines of any organized religion or cult. It expresses an understanding of the meaning of life which . . . is connected to the message of love of God and of one's neighbor."

But apart from putting the word "love" into a song, how can a musical piece convey "the message of love of God and of one's neighbor?" Is it not a bit too specific to function as musical content in an instrumental work? Can any music other than a vocal piece actually be religious then? The answer does not lie close to the surface; to find it we would have to delve deeper.

We may have to touch upon the divine origin of beauty and harmony, which makes any great piece, even if ostensibly secular, sound like a work of religious art. We may opine that in great music—or in any great art—the form and content are always in perfect harmony, and the more devout of us may suggest that this parallels the duality of Christ. At a weak moment we may even appeal to the Greco-Romans who ascribed divine characteristics to the perfection of form. ("Music is the moral law," according to Plato.) Whichever way we go, we shall soon realize that we have embarked on a long, winding road. Eventually it may or may not take us to a plausible theory of aesthetics, but finding out one way or the other will take time. However, Tolstoy was a man in a hurry.

Even though art had existed at least since those Santander drawings, until he got around to it no one had been able to understand what art was. Generally, it took Tolstoy about a fortnight's study of a new subject to arrive at that type of conclusion. Since art was what he had been doing all his life, and with glorious success, it would have been a miracle to expect any other view. So:

Art is not, as the metaphysicians say, the manifestation of some mysterious idea of beauty or God; it is not, as the aesthetical physiologists[21] say, a game in which man lets off his excess of stored-up energy; it is not the outward expression of man's emotions; it is not the production of pleasing objects; and, above all, it is not pleasure;[22] but it is a means of union among men, joining them together in the same feelings, and indispensable for life and the progress toward the well-being of individuals and of mankind.

In that way, having sorted out all those ignoramuses, and explained what art is not, Tolstoy then redefined what art is. But his definition defines nothing; it is but a slogan to be screamed off a soapbox, not the thought of a serious thinker. "Union among men?" "Indispensable for life and the progress toward the well-being of individuals and of humanity?" Lenin and Trotsky must have learned their way with words from Tolstoy.

Anyway, if art is so indispensable, then how come Tolstoy ended up rejecting it? And by the sound of it he was not the only one:

Some teachers of mankind—Plato in his *Republic* and people such as the primitive Christians, the strict Mohammedans and the Buddhists—have gone so far as to repudiate all art.... Evidently such people were wrong in repudiating all art, for they denied the undeniable—one of the indispensable means of communication, without which mankind could not exist. But not less wrong are the people of civilized European society of our class and day who favor any art if it but serves beauty, i.e., gives people pleasure.

Let us see if we can figure this out. Art is only acceptable if it neither serves beauty nor gives pleasure (village songs obviously fall into that category). The moment it begins to commit those outrages, it ought to be repudiated, but not until then. In any event, according to Tolstoy, art cannot be defined philosophically as an activity that produces beauty. Beauty, he says, cannot be described objectively, and therefore cannot be used as a criterion to define what is, or is not, art.

That statement invalidates in one broad stroke the very idea of aesthetic philosophy as a science. After all, in order to qualify as such, a science must have a definable object of study. Yet one could suggest that Tolstoy's inability to define beauty does not mean that it is indefinable. To him "objective" had the same meaning as "empirical," and it goes without saying that beauty cannot be defined in strictly empirical terms. But this does not mean that it does not exist objectively. Here one has to side with the logic of a US federal judge who, when pressed by his opponents to define pornography, said, "I can't define it, but when I see it I know it."

Of course, one can never remove some subjective criteria from deciding what is or is not art. It is just that some such criteria are more valid than others. One would be more prepared, say, to accept a strong opinion on musical ensembles from the members of the Borodin Quartet than from the Spice Girls. And, at the risk of incurring Tolstoy's posthumous wrath, one would be inclined to favor Leonardo's concept of beauty over that of a chap who flogs pictures of white swans embroidered on black velvet. In other words, real art is not, and can never be, egalitarian. If we try to make it so, it stops being art.

Leveling, be it aesthetic, economic, or social, can only be vectored downward. Mindless (or else subversive) do-gooders take their cue from Tolstoy to claim that, by making art equally accessible to all, all will be elevated to the perch of high art. The actual result will always be the lowering of art to the crudest human level. Today, we have ample proof of this simple truth. Not only is the artistic scene dominated by activities that have nothing to do with art, but even traditional arts have been cheapened by mass accessibility. When artistic issues are decided by majority vote, expressed through cash, the tastes of the majority rule. These never have been refined, and now less so than ever. The direct result of mass accessibility then is not only a dearth of any new art worthy of the name, but also the vulgarization of the great art already in the public domain.

This situation is not unprecedented in history. In fact it is a time-honored symptom of a dying civilization. "Thus our once silent audiences have found a voice, in the conviction that they understand what is good and bad in art; the old 'sovereignty of the best' in that sphere has given way to an evil 'sovereignty of the audience'." This was not written by one of today's cultural conservatives fighting a losing rearguard battle. The author of that lament was Plato in his *Republic*, yet again confirming the validity of the *plus ça change* view of history.

Tolstoy, on the other hand, did all he could to bring about exactly such a demise. As he has done in his pronouncements from the time of his bare post-pubescence, Tolstoy in *What Is Art?* and his other works, including *Anna Karenina*, simply ignores the ability and the purpose of art to express its content through form and beauty. Instead, he defines it strictly in terms of its ability to communicate concepts of morality. For Tolstoy, all aesthetic values are shaped by his moral values, which are in their turn based on his patchwork religion without God.

Let us remind ourselves that his religious teaching was a clash of the two main constituents of his soul: mysticism and nihilism. The latter always emerged victorious, as it did in Tolstoy's wholesale rejection of culture. Now, are these failings indigenously his own or do they to some extent reflect the peculiarities of the Russian national character? That is the subject of the next chapter.

CHAPTER 11

TOLSTOY AS A RUSSIAN

[Russia] is a riddle, wrapped in a mystery, inside an enigma . . .

Winston Churchill

1

At this point, I must emulate Tolstoy and indulge in a few longish historical asides. These are not justified, as in his case, by an urgent desire to communicate an offbeat version of history. I simply believe that not only do figures of Tolstoy's magnitude make history, but history also makes them. And as history is irrevocably linked to the backdrops against which it unfolds, most such figures can only be properly understood in their national context.

Tolstoy was a historical phenomenon not only because he was a writer of genius but also because he was a larger-than-life reflection of the Russian character, itself a reflection of a millennium of Russian history. It was not only the Russian revolution that he was a mirror of, to borrow Lenin's phrase; it was Russia herself. As the mirror was both concave and convex, the traits it reflected appeared magnified, big enough for all to see. In that way Tolstoy was not so much a mirror as a caricature of Russia. And like all good caricatures he succeeded in drawing our attention to some salient features by exaggerating them to grotesque proportions.

For example, the Russians are known for at best lukewarm affection for foreigners. At its extreme end this feeling can become downright xenophobia, dialectically co-existing with exaggerated admiration for

Westerners. As Tolstoy loved his extreme ends, one cannot help detecting a certain xenophobic bias in his hatred of all institutions, both sacral and secular. Though he professes to detest the state as such, when he gets down to specifics one realizes that it is the Western state—and its elements in Russia—that he mostly abhors. Nor was it just the Western-like state that he disliked, it was also what he saw as Western-like traits. While Tolstoy was less obsessive, or rather less overt, in his attacks on Western formalism, legalism, and mercantilism than were the Slavophiles and Dostoyevsky, he did launch such attacks with tedious regularity.

His letters in particular are full of broad swipes at the West. Here, for example, he writes to his son in 1894: "In Paris it is the same slavery as one you will exploit by receiving 500 rubles from Russia; it is the same, but it's hidden." Rather well hidden, may one add: France at that time was one of the freest nations on earth.

Or, in the same vein: "Some family of a *rentier*... want to give a moral upbringing to their children. But that is as impossible as teaching children a foreign language without speaking it yourself." Or, in a letter to his daughter Maria, "This European life is very clean materially but terribly dirty spiritually." Presumably, Russia was by contrast an exemplar of spiritual cleanliness, a claim that was difficult to support even then, never mind a few years later. Throughout it is hard not to discern a certain pattern there into which Tolstoy fits in spite of his individualism. This is worth exploring in some detail, starting with the pronouncement of another great Russian man of letters.

"One cannot fathom Russia with the mind," writes F.F. Tyutchev, he of the glorious poetic trio of Russia's Golden Age (Pushkin and Lermontov being the other two), "all common yardsticks are deceiving. We are a very special kind; so Russia's there to believe in." If we shift this stanza from the language of poetry, made somewhat less poetic by my translation, into the sober tongue of everyday life, we shall uncover the underlying layers, as implied by Tyutchev:

Russia is defined by her irrational, mystical aspect. Any rational criterion applicable to understanding any other land is here useless as the Russians are unlike anyone else. Moreover, Russia's irrational aspect is not just mystical but God-like. After all, to most other nations only God is to be taken purely on faith. Others may issue the battle cry of "God and country," but they tend to know where one ends and the other begins. To Russians, at least to those who share Tyutchev's point of view, the demarcation line between those is so smudged that to all intents and purposes they are one and the same. In other words, to them Russia is God. As such, it cannot be decorticated, and any attempt to do so will only confuse the issue unless the decorticator establishes his credentials as a believer first.

Was that Tyutchev's artistic license or a deeply felt conviction? The answer is, a bit of both. Actually, with Russian writers, sometimes it is hard to tell the difference. Here is one example: "Rare is the bird able to fly halfway across the Dnieper," observes Gogol, perhaps the greatest artist ever to write Russian prose.

However, that particular turn of his pen lays Gogol open to variously sarcastic questions. Are we to assume that few birds are capable of flying three miles (the Dnieper is about six miles across at its widest point, the delta)? Even though we happen to know that such a paltry range is not beyond the stamina of even a lowly sparrow, and that many birds happily migrate thousands of miles? And what happens to those that do manage to huff and puff their way to the middle of the river and then have no strength left to reach either bank? Do they drop stone-like into the water and drown? If they are so feeble, why not choose a narrower spot anywhere else along the 1,300-mile length of the Dnieper, where they would only have to struggle with a few hundred yards? And how observant an artist is Gogol anyway?

These are the kind of questions Mark Twain once asked of another writer (in *Fenimore Cooper's Literary Offences*), which enabled him to have good knockabout fun at the latter's expense.[1] But outside the genre of humorous magazine piece, such questions will not be asked, at least not by wise readers. They know that a work of art is not created to provide factual information on the topography of a country any more than it is supposed to elucidate her socioeconomic conditions.

The Dnieper Gogol describes is not the picturesque waterway meandering at the foot of Kiev. Neither is it the historic divide between the Russified east and the Polonized west of the country. Nor is it the river in which Russia was baptized. Gogol's Dnieper does not exist as a physical entity at all. It only flows within the confines of the unreal reality of the artist's world, wholly imaginary and so much more palpable for it.

If a writer of genius tells us that the Dnieper is improbably wide, we believe him because he has allowed us to peek into the world of his creation and we accept its reality on his own terms. In doing so, we put on hold our own idea of reality according to which any self-respecting bird can fly across any river without working up a sweat. Like Euclid's parallels, the two worlds never meet. Like Lobachevsky's parallels, they could meet but choose not to.

Now let us look at a passage written by another great writer, our hero. He describes the aristocratic girl Natasha Rostova listening to some folk music played by her family's serfs. When dared to join in the folk dance, Natasha,

setting her arms akimbo, also made a motion with her shoulders and struck an attitude. Where, how, and when had this young countess, educated by an émigrée French governess, imbibed from the Russian air she breathed that spirit, and obtained that manner which the *pas de châle* would, one would have supposed, long ago have effaced?

Shall we give the same latitude to Tolstoy as we have given Gogol and assume that we are being offered temporary lodgings in an imaginary world? Surely Tolstoy must have realized that Natasha would not have had to imbibe anything from the Russian air to be able to improvise a passable imitation of a peasant dance. Children are good at mimicry, which is why they pick up foreign languages more easily than most adults. By doing "the right thing with such precision" Natasha was indeed expressing herself in a foreign body language, and she was good at it partly because she was a trained dancer. Gavottes and mazurkas provide excellent training for any choreographic self-expression, much as the knowledge of several foreign languages makes it easier to learn others. Surely the unreality of the dancing episode must be obvious to anyone, not just to a great writer known for his power of observation?

Let us just say it must have been obvious to some. Compare, for example, how another writer, Alexander Griboyedov, describes in *A Trip to the Country* a similar scene taking place at about the same time. Here peasants, watched by the author and other noblemen, are singing a folk song at the outskirts of a village. He comments:

Leaning against a tree, I accidentally diverted my eye to the listeners-observers themselves, that corrupted class of semi-Europeans to which I myself belong. Everything they were hearing and seeing seemed absurd to them: to their hearts those sounds were meaningless, to their eyes those costumes looked odd. By what black magic have we become strangers among our own people?. . . If perchance a foreigner had landed in our midst, surely he would have concluded that, considering the sharp divergence of our mores, the masters and the peasants came from different tribes not yet intermingled in their manners and customs.

In this instance, Griboyedov is merely writing a travel sketch, which is why his world and his readers' both begin and end on the same plane. Thus, far from suggesting that all Russians have a metaphysical bond impervious to class, upbringing, or even the language they speak, he correctly identifies, and is horrified by, the underlying problem of Russia: people like him regarded 90 percent of the country's population as a race apart, a feeling that was richly and often violently reciprocated. For Griboyedov and his friends a trip to the country was a trip abroad.

Are we then to assume that, in a similar genre, Tolstoy would not have insisted on the metaphysical Russian air from which a thoroughly Westernized, French-speaking child could "imbibe" her folk spirit? And had he really believed what he was saying, could he not have found a better illustration of that substance than a girl being able to "strike an attitude"?

We could assume this, but we would be wrong. For not only in all his writing, but also in his private life Tolstoy stuck to the ideas behind his observation. In his estate he sought to help his peasants realize the potential of their incomparable souls, all to no avail. The count's attempts to educate his serfs ran into the stone wall of their indifference and, often, hostility. His agricultural experiments all failed. And his risible pretensions at somehow having been transformed into a peasant himself, complete with an unkempt beard, bast shoes, and a plow, only succeeded in confusing his serfs and amusing his friends. Undaunted, Tolstoy even managed to ascribe the guiding force of a mysteriously acquired folk soul to Alexander I, who, mostly German by blood and French by upbringing,[2] only ever saw Russian peasants toting muskets in palace parades.

Was this Tolstoy's flight of fancy, an artist's attempt to step back from reality so as to see it more clearly? Indeed, Tolstoy's magic art, like Gogol's, did not always live on the same plane as the drab reality of life. Gogol's artistic equal, he too created a dimension that soared above the world. But in his case this was not the only dimension. There was another in which Tolstoy's prose also existed, and one that was alien to Gogol, at least for as long as he remained an artist: ideological bias. It was that extra dimension that sometimes distorted all others. Failure to realize this has led astray even some competent commentators, who were tricked into accepting Tolstoy's bias at face value.

There is a mystery to the glorification of the Russian people, so widespread among the intelligentsia. Actually, the mystery starts with the very words "Russian people." For, as one wades through yards of books by Russian writers, one realizes that they apply the term only to the poorest and least educated tiers of the population. Such exclusivity is unique: teachers, doctors, and—God forbid—even landowners are not denied their nationality, say, in England or France. The implication is that, since education in Russia always has been Western, the educated classes have been tainted to a point where they no longer qualify as the Russian people. In other words, by deifying the peasant Tolstoy and his colleagues were demonizing the West.

Characteristically, Russian literature—whether produced by "Slavophiles" or "Westernizers"—includes not a single sympathetic portrayal of a Westerner, at least none that I can recall. Tolstoy is no exception. He lampoons every foreigner to cross his pages, including Joseph de Maistre who provided the blueprint for Tolstoy's concept of history (the difference was that de Maistre's historical determinism came from his belief in divine providence, not in some unidentified historical forces). For instance, Tolstoy falsely described all Prussian officers fighting the Russian corner in 1812 as bunglers and nincompoops. This took much fancy footwork, since that group included such respected warriors as Stein, Bennigsen, and Clausewitz. But then Tolstoy even managed to describe Napoleon as a military nonentity.

On the other hand, Tolstoy extolled the unremarkable Gen. Dokhturov and especially the senile Field-Marshal Kutuzov, the Commander-in-Chief of the Russian forces. In the eyes of serious military historians, the latter fought a do-nothing campaign of staggering incompetence which could easily have ended in catastrophe. As it was, Kutuzov lost the only major battle of the war, surrendering Moscow as a result. Later he missed the easiest of chances to finish off the French army in full flight, capturing Napoleon and ending the war a couple of years sooner. However Tolstoy, ever the dialectician, argues that even the battle of Borodino was actually a Russian victory because Napoleon lost the war in the end. That is akin to saying that the French defeated the Nazis in 1940 because de Gaulle triumphantly entered Paris in 1944.

But facts did not matter to Tolstoy. What mattered was that Dokhturov and Kutuzov were ethnic Russians, a group only sparingly represented in the Russian officer corps. Therefore, as descendants of the ancient Rus, they were supposed to be in touch with the mysterious forces governing matters martial without any contribution from any human agency.

Those who did not share that God-like ethnicity, even if born in the Russian Empire, were portrayed as either brave but obtuse (such as the Georgian Gen. Bagration, respected even by Napoleon) or chronically indecisive (such as Gen. Barclay de Tolly, a Russian of Scottish descent). Alas, Tolstoy's desperate search for folk goodness resident in the breasts of simon-pure Russian commanders was never likely to be richly rewarded. All 1812 officers came from noble families, and many such families were of Tartar, Mordovian, Lithuanian, German, Georgian, Scandinavian, or other non-Slavic origin.

Yet Tolstoy's version of the 1812 war has become canonized in history books. Any Russian schoolchild will tell you that Kutuzov was a giant among pygmies, and Borodino was a Russian victory. Similarly, most commentators, both in Russia and—amazingly—in the West, accept Tolstoy's idealized portrayal of "Russian people" as real. The angelic Tushins and Karatayevs are seen as typical run-of-the-mill Russians, not figments of Tolstoy's imagination. Incidentally, Gogol, unimpeded by ideology, was unable to come up with a single positive Russian protagonist much as he tried. Unwilling to smear his artistic lens with Vaseline, he kept laughing through tears and finally gave up literature. No such problems for Tolstoy: he had no shortage of either Vaseline or rosy filters.

It is true that in 1812 Russia was saved not only by minus-forty temperatures, for which Napoleon's army (just as Hitler's in the next century) was ill-prepared, but also by large-scale partisan warfare. But this was not quite the spontaneous expression of the folk spirit that Tolstoy describes. The idea for it had come from some aristocratic cavalry officers, such as Denis Davydov (appearing as Denisov in *War and Peace*) and Alexander Figner (Tolstoy does not make much of him, possibly on account of his foreign-sounding name). And they were the ones who ran it, using regular cavalry units as the core of partisan forces.

Having at first fought their proposals tooth and nail, the omniscient Kutuzov reluctantly sanctioned guerrilla action behind enemy lines. Perhaps he was persuaded by the success of such warfare in Spain. Or, more likely, he felt sleepy, as he did most of the time, and could not be bothered to argue any longer. Indeed, Tolstoy lovingly describes how Kutuzov slept through the military council at Fili, at which the momentous decision to surrender Moscow was taken. In some quarters such somnolence could have been regarded as criminal negligence, but, as far as Tolstoy was concerned, Kutuzov could do no wrong.

According to Tolstoy, the field-marshal did not need to follow the proceedings because he, as a true Russian, had his finger on the pulse of the unidentified secular forces that govern wars. Thus the 1812 war began not because Napoleon had global ambitions and the Russians refused to compromise—and definitely not because of any personal animosity between Napoleon and Alexander. The reason for the war was that the 600,000 men making up the French army suddenly had felt the urge to march eastward so as to kill large numbers of Russians.

The urge was so strong that Tolstoy insists they would have done so with or without Napoleon. The pull of historical forces was all it took.

One wonders how Tolstoy envisaged those forces actually working in practice. How did they exert their sway on a Jean-Pierre Dubois of Macon? Let us see. Perhaps Jean-Pierre woke up one morning, had his coffee, and was about to go out to clip his vines. But suddenly he was overcome by an irresistible urge to kill many faraway people about whom he knew little and cared even less. He was no longer his own master: an invisible hand grabbed him by the collar and dragged him to the local recruitment office.

And while that eerie thing happened to Jean-Pierre, it was also happening, presumably by osmosis, to hundreds of thousands of others all at the same time. Napoleon's ambitions, France's aspirations, her recent revolutionary upheavals, Alexander's policy, stubborn and vacillating at the same time—none of those had anything to do with it. The force was running amok, and so were Tolstoy's gnostic fantasies.

2

The glorification of the Russian spirit as a way of demonizing the West has a long history in Russia, going back to the founding of the Russian state. Animosity toward that state, typified by Tolstoy, originated at the same time—and it is still going strong.

Contrary to Tolstoy's view, held before he became an anarchist, the Russian state did not come to life so as to embody the divine spirit of Holy Russia. Attractive though it may be to some, this version of history does not tally with known facts. These point more toward the view that the Russian state never was, and still is not, a national state in the sense in which the term is understood in the West. Rather, it was conceived, has usually behaved, and has been perceived by its people as an occupying power, alien to the nation it rules.

The Russians respond to the state not as its citizens, but as its slaves whose attitude to their master more closely resembles fear and hatred than respect and love. The expression of these feelings has only ever been contained by the masters' brutality. When the rulers were powerful and cruel, the people would be browbeaten into the kind of meek submission that outsiders so mistakenly associate with fatalism and Christian resignation. When the masters tried to treat people in a more humane fashion, the latter would take it as a sign of weakness and pounce in that "senseless and merciless" way so poetically described by Pushkin.

The people and their sovereigns never had a truce, much less peace. The balance of power in the war between them periodically swung from one end to the other, with initiative passing between the two sides. Rulers like Ivan IV (the Terrible) and Peter I (the Great) kept the power firmly in their hands by treating the people with the savagery that was only to be outdone by the bolsheviks. The people responded with smoldering hatred but outward docility, which was misconstrued by many foreigners as a national Russian trait.

Other rulers, such as "False" Dmitry, Peter III, Alexander II, and Nicholas II, were somewhat influenced by Western liberalism and Christian morality. They strove to soften the inhuman treatment traditionally meted out by other tsars. That let the initiative slip away, and each of the would-be liberators was—respectively—ripped to pieces, strangled, torn in half by a bomb, and riddled with bullets together with his whole family.

The same tendency is observable in literature. Books and articles attacking the state only began to appear during the comparatively liberal reign of Catherine II. The tide of anti-government literature was temporarily stemmed by her stricter son Paul I, only to come back in force in a more permissive nineteenth century. In that way Tolstoy was a creature not only of his place but also of his time.

But even in the absence of incendiary pamphlets, resentment always seethed under the surface. The ongoing conflict between the people and their rulers predates the Romanovs and will doubtless outlive the current KGB dynasty. It goes back to the very birth of the Russian state precipitated by the arrival of the Vikings in the mid-ninth century. The word "arrival," rather than "conquest" (normally used to describe Nordic expansion in other parts of Europe), is important here. For, according to the *Primary Chronicle*[3] and the historiography based on it, the Vikings did not actually conquer Russia. They were humbly asked to take over by the natives who were desperate for some order. "Large and rich is our land," the ancient Slav "woodsmen" are supposed to have pleaded, "but there is no order. Come and rule over us and bring order to us."

Whence the proto-Russians acquired this urgent desire for order never has been made clear. Let us just say that among the many talents the Russians possess, a quest for order never has been the most prominent. But even discounting national characteristics, it is psychologically unlikely that any tribe would politely ask aliens known mostly for marauding to come and rule over them, with all the unpredictable hardships that such a development would entail.

One cannot recall a single other example of such a request being addressed to the Vikings, who were not at that time known for their organizational ability. Their better-known talents were expressed through fearless raids both at sea and on land. And, whatever the *Primary Chronicle* claims, it was these talents that enabled them to take over Russia.[4] However, once they did take over, the Scandinavians refused to assimilate, continuing for centuries to behave like invaders. Perhaps they did so because the locals did not have a rich culture to charm the Vikings into civilized behavior, as they were later charmed by the Moorish grandeur of Sicily. Or else the Slav "woodsmen" did not possess any ready-made institutions that the Vikings could comfortably fit into, as the Normans did in England. Or perhaps the "woodsmen" were more freedom-loving than other conquered tribes.

Indeed, rather than begging uncouth outlanders to come and bring order, the locals were prepared to fight to preserve their simple tribal liberties. Alas, they were no match for the professional, battle-hardened warriors that the Vikings were. The "woodsmen" were routed, and the "Varangian"[5] Rurik dynasty was ensconced until the sixteenth century.

Official history describes the early Scandinavian chieftains as Russian princes, something they emphatically were not and something their descendants did not become until centuries later. What they were at the time was a band of foreign invaders, which was brilliantly pointed out by the satirist A.K. Tolstoy (our hero's relation) in his versified parody of Karamzin's *The History of the Russian State*: "And then the Prince was Igor, with Oleg in the van. *Das war ein grosser krieger* and very clever man." Even though Oleg spoke Swedish and not German, the point was well taken.

The history of Russia's baptism is also full of myths. Some of them deliberately mask the real story, which had much to do with anti-Western sentiments. According to the most persistent myth, Prince Vladimir at first struggled with the choice of Western or Byzantine Christianity, Islam, or Judaism. Finally he did settle upon the Eastern confession of Christianity—but not for the reasons outlined in the *Primary Chronicle*, allegedly written by the monk Nestor. For example, Vladimir is unlikely to have rejected Islam just because he found the Muslim injunction against alcohol hard to reconcile with the Russians' propensity for drunkenness ("Drinking is the joy of Rus," Vladimir is reputed to have said). More likely, he rejected Islam because he did not see the Muslims as promising strategic allies.

And the story of Vladimir's rejection of the Jewish missionaries is clearly Nestor's invention. According to him, the Jews told Vladimir,

"Our land has been handed over to the Christians," to which Vladimir replied that this pointed at the superiority of Christianity. In actuality, Palestine belonged to Muslims at the time, a fact no doubt known to Vladimir. He may have toyed with the idea of converting to Judaism as he was aware that the Khazar Qaghanate, whose rulers had done so, had become powerful and prosperous. However, Vladimir also remembered that his father had wiped the Khazars off the face of the earth, and the Qaghanate no longer was a geopolitical player.[6] Vladimir, ever the realist, could see no immediate gain in adopting Judaism.

His grounds for rejecting the German Catholic missionaries were more complex—and more crucial to our story. According to the *Chronicle*, Vladimir's decision mostly had to do with his respect for the memory of his predecessors: "Go whence you came, for it was our fathers who rejected this," he is claimed to have said. It is true that Bishop Adalbert had arrived in Kiev in the mid-tenth century with the mission of baptizing Princess Olga and all her subjects. The bishop had failed, but not, according to the *Chronicle*, "for any lack of industry on his part."

However, filial deference to his mother could not have been the deciding factor in Vladimir's choice. Nor could he possibly have doubted that an alliance with the Catholic West would bring long-term strategic benefits. Though the triumph of the West over Byzantium was still two centuries away, the former was in the ascendancy, and Vladimir must have sensed that. And yet he rejected the Western religion with as much vehemence as his descendants continued to reject it centuries later.

The reason was primarily the ethos of Western Christianity, which already, less than 50 years after the split with Byzantium, was acquiring a different character. Western religion was inspiring a statehood in which the relationship between the sovereign and the people was based on inchoate liberties. That was something princes from further east were finding hard to accept, and Vladimir was no exception. As he represented an occupying power, the prince knew that, given breathing space, the people might well begin to get ideas beyond their station. That was the nature of the fundamental problems he had with Western Christianity and by extension with the West itself. In time those problems became an essential fiber in the fabric of the Russian psyche.

Throughout Russia's early history, Scandinavian princes were fighting one another, much as the English did during the Wars of the Roses. The difference was that the rulers were also fighting the ruled, setting a pattern that made it forever impossible to have any government by consensus in Russia. There was no consensus. There was a war of all against all, and it took its heavy toll. In fact, when in the fourteenth century Tamerlaine came up to the borders of Russia, he realized that the country had been so thoroughly devastated that it had nothing left worth taking. The great conqueror shrugged his shoulders and did not bother to conquer.

Ivan IV ("the Terrible"), the last tsar in the Scandinavian dynasty, began his reign in 1533 by issuing a direct declaration of war on his people. "From time immemorial, the Russian people have been rebellious towards our ancestors . . . [They wanted] to wipe out our whole dynasty . . . and, had God not protected us, would have murdered us together with our children." Implicitly, that was not a situation Ivan was prepared to tolerate for much longer. This he proved by leading a punitive military campaign against his own people.

Nothing was left to chance: no more knee-jerk responses. To begin with, Ivan created the first organ of institutional oppression in Russia: *oprichnina*, the precursor of the KGB. Then he struck out in the northwesterly direction, systematically sacking every Russian town in his path, presaging Sherman's "scorched-land" strategy of three centuries later. The pro-Western Hanseatic city of Novgorod was sacked, and its clergy, aristocracy, and merchants were all murdered in the imaginative ways Ivan favored. No one was allowed to lean toward the West and get away with it.

Thus Tolstoy's hostility to the West with all its history, culture, and institutions was not his exclusive property. It went back to the very roots of Russian nationhood. However, Russia would occasionally make some concessions to things Western. For example, in the century preceding Tolstoy's, the Romanov tsars, while remaining hostile to the spiritual foundations of the West, had realized Russia still needed the material goods the West produced. This resulted in an enforced Westernization of the upper classes, creating a mostly Francophone elite and further deepening the gulf separating the peasant population from its rulers.

3

For all her borrowing of Western culture, the country became more self-isolated and self-conscious. Officially, Russia's borders no longer just separated her from other countries—they separated good from evil. Therefore they were vigilantly patrolled to keep outsiders out and, more important, insiders in. The only question was how to use some elements of Western evil to promote the Russian good.

That was the nature of the intellectual battles between the Slavophiles and Westernizers that raged in the nineteenth century, defining the terms of intellectual discourse until the present day. These were not clashes between those who wanted Russia to become part of the West and those who did not. The argument was about the tactics, not the objective. The objective for both sides always was to take over the degenerate West so as to lead it to the moral purity for which Russia was so widely famous (but only within Russia). It is just that the Westernizers believed in beating the West at its own game, while the Slavophiles maintained that an indigenous Russian way would work better.

Both parties came from the educated, mostly aristocratic elite. The peasants did not take part in the argument, especially since most of it was conducted in French. They were too busy trying to stay alive, a task in which they succeeded only with variable success. While the Francophone intelligentsia were debating *liberté, egalité, fraternité*, peasants were being sold like cattle (often away from their families), lost at cards, beaten to death, conscripted for 25 years. Though their legal status was technically different from that of the slaves in the American South, in reality this was a distinction without a difference. Actually there was one difference: in America, black slaves were not regarded as Americans. But in Russia the slaves were the same Russian Christians as their masters, which affected both groups in unique ways, few of them ennobling.

The serfs stole their masters blind, burnt their property, or even, given the slightest chance, killed them. When opportunities arose, they would wage full-fledged wars against the government, such as those led by Bolotnikov, Razin, and Pugachev. At the same time, some landowners, a vociferous and ever-growing minority, began to ask themselves how they could reconcile their religion and culture with slavery by any other name.

Step by step, a specifically Russian type evolved: the repentant aristocrat, typified by Tolstoy. Few actually went so far as to renounce their privilege: their living was derived from landed property with its peasant "souls." However, the more eloquent of them could chat about liberation with multilingual ease, talk being cheaper than self-pauperization. Fuelled by shame and repentance, they were assigning to Russian peasants superior spiritual qualities bordering on saintliness. While the ruble value of a peasant was lower than that of a horse, his spiritual value was declared to be higher than that of any Westerner.

Eventually, as often happens, talk led to action. Propaganda against serfdom led to its formal abolition in 1861, but in practice little changed. Peasants remained chained to the land by rents and taxes as securely as before they had been attached to it by law. This gave rise to the populist movement of the 1860s, out of which eventually came most of the revolutionary parties. The literature of that time became one contiguous protest. This could be expressed in purely social terms (Chernyshevsky, Pisarev) or in more spiritual and religious ways (Dostoyevsky, Aksakov). Tolstoy's populism tried to embrace both strains, but the strains were there to begin with. The "us" were desperately trying to become like "them," and before long no one was sure who the "us" and "them" were.

Yet the aristocrats were aware of how tenuous their hold on power was. "In Russia, noblemen are only those I talk to, and then only for as long as I'm talking to them," pronounced Paul I. He was right in general principle though not in every detail, which some noblemen proved by strangling him in 1801. But getting rid of the man did not get rid of the arrangement. In relation to the sovereign, the Russian aristocracy remained the most powerless in Europe—even as it was the most powerful in relation to everyone else. That may have contributed to their desire to identify themselves with the peasants, which tendency Tolstoy pushed to such a risible extreme. They felt kinship: the noblemen related to the tsar the way the peasants related to the noblemen.

Any view of the peasant that did not present him as a saintly figure became socially and intellectually unacceptable. In Russia at that time it was no more possible to suggest that perhaps not all peasants were angels than it is to advocate the abolition of welfare in today's Europe. People of any other country only had their national character; the Russian peasant had a soul. Those noblemen who did not share such views, and there were some, preferred to steer clear of the subject on pain of ostracism. Saying at a fashionable gathering that perhaps prudence was a better guide to reform than passion was tantamount to admitting association with the secret police. And that organization was increasingly seen as a greater danger than any bomb-thrower. No self-respecting *intellighent*[7] would shake the hand of a police officer. The police and the state they protected had become the enemy even for the people who more or less were the state.

Thus Tolstoy's passionate championing of the peasantry and equally passionate assault on the state were not so much heroic as conformist. Whenever a popular figure refused to indulge in such sycophantic populist sermons, he became the focus of public hatred—and often a target for nihilist assault. For, once populism became the only socially acceptable ideology, its banners drew the kind of human flotsam that always drifts to nihilistic causes.

4

Over the centuries, the unique nature of the Russians' interaction with the state had drip-fed nihilism and anarchism into the nation's bloodstream—so Tolstoy was not unique in that respect either. And in its unwitting promotion of amorphous nihilism, the state was assisted in no small measure by the geography of the country. For even that aspect of Russia lacked clear-cut form.

Russia always has been sparsely populated, and her borders have been ill-defined. In her early expansion she seldom had to trample over rival states. There was none to the immediate east or north of her, while her borders in the other two directions, especially to the west, always had two-way fluidity. Also, there always existed large spaces in Russia that remained barely settled. (The population density of Siberia is only about 1/12th of Britain's even today.)

That is partly why the Russians, unlike, for instance, the crowded Dutch, never have felt the need to mold rigid forms into which their self-expression could flow. Naturally hostile to the state, they were ever prepared either to fight it or to escape, especially since there never was a dearth of places to escape to. Therefore the Russians seldom feel the need to improve the state or any public institutions. If they cannot destroy them, they are more inclined to run away. In fact Russians tend to be averse to any disciplined form that might contain their fluid content, which is why all those democracies and free markets are unlikely to succeed there even if they are ever tried for real.

According to the philosopher Nikolai Lossky, this disdain for form even penetrated the Russians' gene pool, having produced so many ill-defined, amorphous facial features clearly different, say, from the chiseled North European profile. Lossky observes that many Russians show a certain lack of straight lines in their faces. It is as if, having drawn a sketch of their features, God then went over it, smudging every line with his thumb. His observation may be too sweeping, but it certainly is evident that the Russians' amorphousness extends to the way they treat every public institution, from justice to religion.

Traditional Russian lawlessness is well publicized, mostly in the context of the state being bound by few legal constraints. It is less commented upon that not only do Russian rulers seldom obey their own laws, but they do not even insist that the ruled do—for as long as they do not mind being ruled. Thus it is not just her governments but Russia herself that historically has been lawless. Nor do the people define liberty in any legal terms. The old Russian word for freedom, *volia*, is etymologically related to "will," which stands to reason. Freedom to a Russian means being able to do as he wills, not obeying just laws that protect his liberties.

Many ascribe this tendency to the Asian part of the Russian character. However, lawlessness in Russia is markedly different from that in the traditional Eastern tyrannies. There the populace was expected to follow every letter of the law, even if the despots themselves ignored its very spirit. But in Russia lawlessness functioned at all levels. At the top the arbitrary will of the tsar was the only law, and he could punish anyone with utmost cruelty for the slightest infraction. At the same time, he could let anyone get away with murder if such was his wish. For example, Paul I once promoted an officer who had had a trader hanged for having refused to sell hay for his company's horses. On another day, the same officer could have been chastised.

The way public servants were reimbursed did not do much to strengthen the sense of legality. In the nineteenth century both the army and bureaucracy were expected to live off the fat of the land. Following the Napoleonic wars, Alexander I was reluctant to embark on wholesale demobilization, fearing its destructive social consequences. (A century later Nicholas II was not so sage.) Instead the huge army was quartered in "military settlements" all over the country, where the soldiers did some perfunctory agricultural work and much whole-hearted robbery. "The army quartered all over the country behaved in Russia as if it was a conquered country," comments Tolstoy's contemporary, the historian Klyuchevsky. The corrupting effect on both the oppressors and the oppressed was predictable.

In the same vein, government administrators, especially in the provinces, were paid derisory salaries, well below sustenance level. They were expected to make up for it by pilfering and bribes, and did so with quite some élan.[8] Once, for example, an inspector general came to audit a wealthy government contractor. Choosing not to wait for any embarrassing discoveries, the contractor took the general aside and whispered, "I'll give Your Excellency three thousand, and no one will be any the wiser." "Give me five thousand," replied His Excellency, "and tell anybody you want."

This live-and-let-live attitude extended to the peasants who could not survive without stealing from their masters with the latter's acquiescence. If peasants overstepped the sensible limits, they were occasionally caught and tried. When that happened, magistrates often gave them the choice: "We have many laws, each one harsher than the other. So do you wish to be tried according to the law or according to my conscience?" Few perpetrators chose the former. They knew that the magistrate, a local landowner, had nothing to gain and much to lose by sending them off to penal servitude for 10 years. It suited his "conscience" much more to keep them in place, where they would continue to grease the wheels of the local economy. So they would take some corporal punishment and crawl back to their huts to recover.

As a millennium of lawlessness was bound to leave a lasting imprint, many Russians felt about law enforcement as Tolstoy did, and they still do. However, few have gone to the same nihilistic lengths in their pronouncements. In Tolstoy's time most iconoclasts did not generalize to the point of rejecting state justice in principle—it was only the Russian state that had in their eyes forfeited the right to judge and punish. But since the Russian state was the only one they knew, it is safe to say that Tolstoy's feelings were similar to those of most Russians.

5

Nor was his hostility to the church uniquely his own. Many Russians had serious problems with formal religion, and the part that especially bothered them was the adjective, not the noun. Exceptionally superstitious, they would take on any faith with alacrity, especially if it pandered to their characteristic mysticism. Yet the faith most of them espoused was Christian, after a fashion.

Peter attached the church to the state by abolishing the office of patriarch and replacing it with the Holy Synod. Thus the church got to be led de facto by lay officials, which undermined its authority. By rendering unto Caesar things that were God's, Procurators of the Holy Synod inherited the hatred traditionally directed at government officials. Even the outstanding men among them, such as Tolstoy's nemesis Pobedonostsev, became odious figures in the eyes of many and easy targets for the kind of sniping Tolstoy favored.

Religion, with its rigid dogma and rituals, was another popular target. For, as I argued in an earlier chapter, abstract mysticism does not a religion make. It even has little to do with faith, though it may sometimes act as a step toward it. Many Russians, with their disdain for form, felt suffocated within traditional creeds and tried to break away in all sorts of directions. That is why heresies and schisms abounded.

Even though the great schism of the seventeenth century came from above, not below, the same cannot be said for the many mini-schisms reflecting a certain religious polyvalence typical of the Russians—and magnified to grotesque extremes in Tolstoy. Communism too is a sort of perverse religion, which may explain why the Russians initially took to it like a duck takes to water—until the bird discovers, too late, that the liquid is actually hot, sputtering oil.

The deep attachment to the church that the Russians allegedly have always felt is a Slavophile myth. In fact, Tolstoyan anticlericalism became so popular precisely because it was viscerally Russian. Even if the Russians ever had had any affection for the church, it took them, in round numbers, minutes to abandon it in 1917. Though some were trying to protect their priests (much as some Germans hid Jews during the war), many more of the recently pious Christians instantly converted to Cheka thugs, happily torturing priests to death, destroying the relics of Orthodox saints, and plundering church valuables.

Such outbreaks of anti-church violence are not unique to Russia— the English had a good go in the seventeenth century, the French in the eighteenth, and even the devout Spanish in the twentieth. But in those countries, these were temporary aberrations, never duplicated before or since. They cannot be plausibly explained by the innate traits of national character. In Russia, however, that is a credible explanation.

The recurrent extremism of anticlerical outbursts there reflected Russian all-or-nothing maximalism, another trait to which Tolstoy could not claim exclusive rights. Even the Orthodox religion goes to such extremes as having up to 200 fasting days a year, with each lengthy, emaciating fast followed by the kind of gargantuan meals that would kill lesser men. And the pendulum of the Russian psyche can as easily swing to one extreme as the other. The philosopher Karsavin pointed out that, if a Russian doubts the absolute ideal, he can become completely bestial and indifferent to everything, capable of shifting from extreme obedience to the most uncontrollable, limitless rebellion.

Latent paganism always acted as a milder form of protest against religious formalism, which Tolstoy so ably translated into protest against religion as such. That is why pagan practices never really went out of fashion, and even these days Russian peasants jump over fires on high holidays. This, however, is innocuous stuff. More sinister are some of the 500-odd sects, Christian in word but pagan in deed, that the Russians have spawned.

This tendency towards sectarianism had been until the Reformation much more prominent in the Eastern than Western confession. It was, after all, Greek Orthodoxy that produced the iconoclastic Bogumil sect (later converted to Islam, it was the precursor of the Cathars), not to mention the actual Iconoclasm.

Sects always have thrived in Russia, many of them practicing hideous rites. For example, the Emasculators would castrate themselves so as not to be distracted from God by impure thoughts—the end Tolstoy tried to achieve by less drastic means, but then with notably less success. Another sect, the Flagellants, would gather together in windowless barns lit by a few candles. There they would chant what today would be called religious rap, while flogging one another into an open-mouthed, eye-popping frenzy so as to exorcise evil spirits. Thus purified, they would then blow out the candles and, in pitch darkness, throw themselves into indiscriminate group sex with invisible partners, often including their own next of kin.

When the best-known Flagellant, Grigory Rasputin, brought his amorous training and alleged healing powers to Petersburg, he was an instant hit with the ladies of the court. His bed became the purgatory they sought, his pagan chants an expression of religiosity those professed Christians had been sorely missing.

In time, Rasputin acquired an inordinate influence over the royal family. Especially falling under his sway was Tsarina Alexandra, Queen Victoria's granddaughter, who by then had rubbed herself clean of any vestiges of the Lutheran princess she once had been. Required by law to convert, she had embraced the Russian religion with neophyte zeal, regrettably also inheriting the Russian propensity for sectarian neo-paganism.

These days, when many Russians go to church with the same pious expressions that in the recent past they reserved for party rallies, they take to sectarianism as readily as ever. Protestant sects, such as Adventism and Pentecostalism, made instant headway in post-perestroika Russia, drawing millions of adherents. To outside observers this may seem like an awakening of the religious feeling dormant during the 74 years of bolshevism. In fact, this is a reflection of traditional Russian paganism that could never fully reconcile itself with what Tolstoy called "church Christianity" (as if there can be any other).

The count was never reluctant to throw his considerable weight behind any odious sect that was persecuted in Russia. The fervor he brought to the task was directly proportionate to how heretical the sect was. In particular, he was in sympathy with those groups that shared many of his pet beliefs, such as pacifism, clean living, vegetarianism, and rejection of the most fundamental Christian tenets.

Among them were the Molokans (so called because they drank milk, *moloko* in Russian, on fasting days) and the "spirit-wrestling" Dukhobors, similar to the Quakers. Tolstoy exchanged dozens of mutually admiring letters with the leader of the Molokans. And when the government took exception to the Dukhobors' refusal to serve in the armed forces, he helped them migrate to West Canada. There they still worship him as a demigod, with the accent on "demi" barely audible.

While the face value of sectarianism may have been mock-Christian anti-dogmatism, the flipside was neo-pagan amorphousness. That quality Tolstoy shared and extolled—which is amazing in an artist for whom perfection of form was essential. Perhaps Tolstoy felt that the more amorphous he was in religion, the less of an artist, and by implication the more of a seer, would he be perceived to be.

6

Tolstoy's anarchistic pronouncements on property are also deeply rooted in the Russian consciousness. As many writers[9] over the last couple of centuries have shown, this is fundamentally different from Western attitudes, especially in Protestant countries. If Calvinists regard wealth as God's earthly reward for righteousness, the Russians are conditioned to regard it as ill-gotten gains. Whereas most Westerners feel proud of pursuing wealth openly, a Russian is more likely to feel embarrassed.

To most Russians money is *ipso facto* dirty, something to get rid of as quickly as possible and then wash one's hands afterward. The idea of financial prudence is despicable to them—it is regarded as an alien characteristic, something Western, or, even worse, Jewish. Thus Russians love to mock the Western concept of not being able to afford something. "I can't afford" to a Russian means not having the where-withal to pay for it. If the money is physically there, he will spend it with scant regard for tomorrow. And he will despise a middle-class Westerner who claims he cannot afford, say, a £500 bottle of wine. "Don't you have five hundred pounds in the bank?" a Russian would ask with contempt.

If a Russian comes into some money, he often does not know what to do with it. Many Western readers, for example, think that Nastasia Filipovna tossing a small fortune into the fireplace was Dostoyevsky's way of showing histrionic neurosis. In fact, he was describing a quintessential Russian scene. Likewise, Tolstoy in his youth was behaving as a typical Russian when trying to stake his whole estate on a single hand of cards. Had he lost, his family would have been impoverished, but only a covetous Westerner or, perish the thought, a Jew would worry about such trivialities.

By displaying disregard for money, Russians implicitly assert their superiority over the West. In Tolstoy's time, rich merchants would publicly burn stacks of banknotes, light their cigars with 100-ruble notes, bust up restaurants all over Europe and then pay ten times the value of the broken furniture, tip large amounts for the privilege of smearing mustard over a waiter's face, maintain crowds of distant relations and unnecessary staff, donate huge sums they could not afford to all sorts of causes. Some of those were revolutionary, and millionaires would joyously finance the very parties that were doctrinally committed to the mass cull of millionaires (Savva Morozov, Gorky's mark, was the best-known example—and victim—of this propensity). But it was not just revolutionaries who treated the rich with antipathy in Tolstoy's time. That attitude cut across the entire spectrum of the Russian psyche.

It is still observable today in the behavior of the so-called "new Russians." Having come into unlikely fortunes overnight, they act in the way of the Western *nouveaux riches*—times a thousand. It is if they are competing with one another in who can get rid of his money in the fastest and most tasteless way. Vulgar ostentation is their way of showing the West how to live—and telling their impoverished countrymen that, though the parvenus have committed the un-Russian act of becoming rich, they remain Russian in the way they dispose of money. Their spending millions on gilded monuments to bad taste is implicit propaganda of Russian spirituality—they know their possessions are vulgar (some of them do, at any rate). But they scream their contempt for material possessions even as they are enjoying them. The lower their outward taste sinks, they seem to suggest, the higher do their souls soar.

This is a form of gnosticism, implied possession of unique and secret knowledge. Tolstoy had that weakness in spades, and he indulged in it so freely because he knew he was thereby catering to the Russians' self-image. He was articulating their feelings, those they may not even have suspected they had. His pronouncements on economics, which to any literate Westerner would have sounded nonsensical (such as that landed property is solely responsible for all economic ills), sounded prophetic to his countrymen.

The Russians' minds did not get involved in all this. They responded to such drivel not rationally but viscerally—much in the same way as they responded to Tolstoy's novels. And at that level it made sense to them. Tolstoy's economics, and his thought in general, appealed to them not as philosophy, but more in the way art appeals. It circumvented reason and touched the innermost chords deep inside them.

Shortly after Tolstoy's death, the Russians would pay dearly for their economic gnosticism. The bolsheviks put two and two together, knowing their countrymen would accept that this made five. Lenin and his men had learned—partly from the people's response to Tolstoy's similar ideas—that the clarion call of economic nihilism would be answered at the grass roots. So it was, until the bolsheviks sprayed the grass roots with herbicide.

Such neo-gnosticism is one reason for the bizarre behavior of the moneyed Russians. Another reason is more obvious: for long stretches of Russian history there were practically no rich people outside the court. Therefore there exists no culture of dealing with money.

Most wealth in the country was in the hands of the aristocrats who had received it courtesy of the tsar. (Witness the fact that the word *dacha* is a cognate of the Russian word for "give." That stands to reason: country houses were given, not earned.) Catherine II, for example, would reward her more ardent lovers with estates the likes of which few European landowners had ever seen. Such long-standing paramours as her morganatic (and secret) husband Potemkin would receive whole provinces. In the same late eighteenth century, the country only had a few hundred wealthy non-aristocratic families, and the average Russian spent a paltry 17 kopecks a year on commercial goods (about nine US cents at the time). Only in the nineteenth century did a sizeable number of well-to-do commoners begin to appear, but not even remotely on a Western-like scale.

Thus most of "the Russian people" Tolstoy knew had no tradition of having any property beyond what was necessary to keep them from starving to death. And those who had bucked the trend by acquiring a surplus possessed few opportunities to pass it on to the following generations.

With no concept of primogeniture ever existing, big estates were fractured to a point where they could no longer provide a living. In Tolstoy's will, for example, Yasnaya Poliana was equally divided among his wife and nine surviving children. That made about 400 acres each—another generation, and there would not have been enough left to feed a family in the conditions of central Russia. Mercifully, the bolsheviks prevented such a problem by confiscating the lot in 1918.

While the opportunities to maintain wealth were few, the opportunities to lose it were endless. This left an indelible mark on the psychology of the people. First, one must consider the nature of the wars Russia waged throughout her formative early history. These were different from those fought in the West at the time. Most of the time her adversaries were not hostile states but nomads who had no vested interest in keeping much of even their own male population alive. Only about 20 percent of the men were necessary to look after their horses. The rest could ride them into battle, gaining booty if they won. Thus Russia's enemies could afford to sustain 80 percent casualty rates, which gave them an edge over any agrarian populace.

Even as nomads did not distinguish between their own combatants and civilians, they did not draw that distinction among the people they conquered. All were often slated for destruction. Thus at the time when the Russian state (and mentality) was being formed, the country fought non-stop do-or-die wars it could not afford to lose for fear of extinction. Among other things, that required the maximum straining of the nation's financial resources. For not only were Russian towns and villages regularly plundered, but they also had to pay draconian taxes to keep the war going. In addition, not only would they be bled white by tax collectors, but their own army would rob them blind as it passed through. "I am not sure if the Tartars ever behaved any worse," writes Klyuchevsky.

Another obstacle to wealth generation was fires. In the West people had moved into stone dwellings back in the Middle Ages, but the Russians mostly lived in wooden houses—and in villages they still do. The inevitable result was that, while houses in the West were passed on from generation to generation, often forming the bulk of the families' wealth, Russian houses burnt down *en masse*. In Moscow, only fires claiming the better part of 10,000 houses were even deemed worthy of mention in the papers. The whole city burned down like kindling on many occasions, the last being the French occupation of 1812. (This followed what Tolstoy regarded as a triumph of Russian arms.)

Another wealth-busting factor was something I have mentioned earlier: frequent famines, striking the Russian countryside on average once every 7.5 years. When people were dying of hunger, they begged both their wealthier relations and their landowners for help. This was usually proffered, the result being downward leveling: after a major famine, redistribution of wealth would have left everyone equally poor.

Yet another—and perhaps the most important—factor was the legal status of property, or absence thereof. Wealthy people never were in secure possession of their money. The state could expropriate them for any reason, or none. Rich merchants, for example, had to finance government contracts out of their own pockets. If the government was dissatisfied for whatever reason, or simply did not feel like paying, the merchants would be ruined. And even aristocratic landowners only had what in today's terms could be described as leasehold on their livelihood. The tsar, who would have given them the estates to begin with, was the ultimate freeholder. And what the tsar awarded, he could take away.

No one in Russia had any certainty that tomorrow he would not starve. The Russian folklore reflects both the insecurity and the resulting disdain for acquisition in proverbs like "don't be sure you'll escape prison or beggar's bag," "work isn't a wolf, it won't run away into the forest," "work likes fools," "you won't build a stone house by honest work." The Russian for sacking someone is *uvolit'*, meaning "to set free"; and playing truant is *progulivat'*, which literally means "to have a good time." Countless others proverbs and expressions all preach the same line: money is worthless, working to earn it is useless, and those who do so are either fools or knaves.

Some commentators tend to ascribe contempt for money to the Russians' Christian spirit. Christianity, they say, has laid such deep roots in the Russians' psyche that they reject material wealth even as they sometimes try to acquire it. This does not quite ring true. For Christian asceticism governs not just the disposal of money but also its acquisition. By breaking mirrors in a Paris restaurant and then defecating into the piano, rich Russian merchants were not expressing their religion any more than they had expressed it in having become rich in the first place. True Christianity discourages such displays. One finds it difficult to imagine St Francis, or even St Augustine in his youth, paying king's ransom to a waiter for the privilege of abusing him in public.

What those upstarts were venting was not their Christian spirit but their innate gnosticism. It was because of that trait that most of Russia eagerly saluted when Tolstoy ran economic nihilism up the flagpole. The Russians found it easy to regard property as theft, or the rich as blood-sucking exploiters. And they saw no incongruity in a wealthy landowner decrying landed property. After all, the count repented his wealth and made efforts, however half-hearted, to get rid of it.

The bolsheviks had drunk from the same poisoned emotional brook. Keen students of the Russian national character, they knew how to take advantage of it for their purposes. It goes without saying that Tolstoy would have been aghast had he seen how his economic lessons were put to work, how they had softened the soil for nihilistic saplings, making it ready for irrigation with blood. But regardless of his intentions, his irresponsible ranting acquired a life of its own, and this is one lesson we can learn from Tolstoy. There are also many others.

CHAPTER 12

THE LESSONS OF LEO TOLSTOY

> Then said Jesus, Father, forgive them; for they know not what
> they do.
>
> (Luke 23:34)

All his life, and even in his death, Tolstoy yearned to teach the world
a lesson. That he did, though not in the way he wanted. For the lesson
taught by the count was only negative: what not to think, how not to
live, and which gods not to worship. But such was the scale of his
personality that even his folly soars above the errors of lesser men. So
it is there for all to see and, one hopes, heed. And if we understand his
folly for what it is, we can draw positive lessons even from his negative
sermons.

*Lesson 1: Metaphysics is fundamental to both understanding and
organizing life.* A faulty metaphysical premise invariably throws even
secular ideas out of kilter. If we look deeply enough, we shall realize
that the most spectacular errors mankind ever makes all come from
a metaphysical misunderstanding. In Tolstoy's case, we do not even
have to look hard: every word he ever uttered proves that an initial
metaphysical error can set off a chain reaction of folly.

Metaphysics is the basis of all knowledge of life, for non-believers as
much as the faithful. For, even during its most violent swerves, human
life never skids too far away from human nature. The two are irrevocably linked, and that makes metaphysics a historical science. There have
been many philosophies and creeds (including Tolstoyism) trying to

hide that link behind what they described as historical inevitability. But a closer look through the murky glass of history will always discern human nature shining through. That is why the understanding of it is essential to organizing this life and, if one happens to believe in it, preparing for the next.

But the understanding of anything starts with a satisfactory answer to a question, either overt or implied. Thus it is impossible to understand music without first answering the question, "What is music?" We shall never understand morals unless we answer the question, "What is morality?" And any cohesive understanding of man's nature has to be an answer to the question, "What is man?" Such an answer can only be metaphysical because the question is. That is why even atheists make a metaphysical statement in their very denial of metaphysics.

As I have argued throughout this book, it was a metaphysical blunder that formed the basis of Tolstoy's outlook on life. The more he persisted in it, the wilder did all his ideas sound—the more they lost touch even with the common sense he thought was the highest stage of man's spiritual growth. For common sense can only tell us that, if A equals B, and B equals C, then A equals C. It cannot tell us what the A, B, and C really mean. The simple syllogism can be worked out empirically. The meaning behind it can only be grasped metaphysically.

One can sometimes get away with an empirical miscalculation, but a metaphysical error never goes unpunished. Thus, when Tolstoy, taking his lead from Rousseau, proclaimed that man was good to begin with and could be further perfected by a moral sermon, he was proceeding from a wrong metaphysical premise. That is why every idea that then flowed out of the original error was in itself erroneous.

Lesson 2 (related to Lesson 1): Bad metaphysics can make even an intelligent man sound silly. So what was that fundamental religious error that threw out of joint every idea Tolstoy ever had?

The error was in preaching Christian ethics while rejecting Christian eschatology, which logically led to his denying personal resurrection and therefore life after death. Another logical consequence was Tolstoy's belief that man could bring about the kingdom of God solely by his own efforts. Depending on his mood, God was to him either nature or morality or "desire for universal welfare"—anything but God. In that way Tolstoy established his credentials as an Enlightenment thinker—and ruined his credentials as a thinker.

This could have been an ideal starting point on the road to straightforward atheism, and in a way that would have been preferable. For by honestly admitting his atheism, to himself if no one else, the count would then have been able to operate within a different intellectual system. Within that system—inferior though we may think it is—he could have kept his ideas not far from common sense, and, the bright man that he was, some of them could have been reasonable. He thus could have left the metaphysical realm within which his philosophy sounded like arrant nonsense and entered the safer low ground of materialism tinged with a bit of moralizing.

But Tolstoy did not wish to go there. He felt a mystical longing, a need for God, but this need was not satisfied by Christianity, or for that matter any other known religion. That is why he had to look for a spiritual ideal elsewhere so as to found his own religion "without faith and sacraments." But the ideal did have to be spiritual. As heaven was off limits, life on earth was all that remained as a potential source. Thus, according to his religion, man's life had to be fulfilled "here and now," and the kingdom of God had to be seen as achievable before physical death. That logically led to Tolstoy's rejection of original sin and the ensuing evil that clashes with virtue in everyday life. After all, in order to become morally perfect in his lifetime, man has to be fairly moral to begin with.

A theatrical fall into Rousseau's embrace had to follow. Tolstoy either had to dump his whole religion or to repeat the Enlightenment fallacy of man being both perfect and tautologically perfectible. And it was reason, understood as common sense, that was the tool of self-perfection. People only ever did nasty things because they had not been told what was good. Tolstoy magnanimously took it upon himself to tell them, only to find they were not exactly rapt in attention. And even those who did listen would nod their perfunctory assent and then go on living in their usual sinful way.

But the count was nothing if not stubborn. He persisted in his metaphysical error, trying to build on its basis both a philosophy and a guide to everyday behavior. Yet nothing can be built on rotten foundations. So Tolstoy extolled the virtue of just that: nothing. The count ended up espousing nihilism of the most sweeping kind: he rejected marriage, family, the church, the state, science, art, law, formal education, culture, history, defense of one's own country, any work other than menial agricultural labor—and even decent food and drink. By way of justifying this ghoulish nihilism, he offered increasingly insane prescriptions for daily life. These would have made him a universal laughingstock anywhere but in the febrile intellectual chaos of a moribund, pre-revolutionary Russia.

In the process Tolstoy unwittingly struck a powerful blow for the very Christian metaphysics against which he had fought his whole life. He showed by his own tragic example that wrong metaphysical premises do not just destroy philosophical abstractions. They can destroy life itself.

These days we can see how elevating happiness in this world to a metaphysical status can make life ugly. Someone who dedicates his whole life to pursuing earthly happiness is bound to come a cropper: happiness is a reward for righteousness, not for frantic attempts to fulfill eudemonic aspirations. Someone who denies happiness in this world is more likely to find it than someone who actively seeks it. Nor can happiness be found in the celibate agricultural commune of Tolstoy's fantasy, his rationalistic paradise enveloped in the smokescreen of pseudo-religious verbiage. Happiness is a metaphysical concept—or it is nothing.

Everywhere we look, we can see how ideas similar to Tolstoy's are destroying our society. If there are people who, along with him, believe in the innate goodness of man, then they do not think we need any laws to protect us. All such laws are evil to them because they presuppose the existence of evil-doers who can only be punished, not rehabilitated by a secular sermon. They will see no criminal as being beyond redemption in this life. Hence our laws, which are increasingly skewed to upholding the criminal's "rights"—not to providing justice for his victim and, consequently, society.

If our judges believe, along with Tolstoy, that punishment is *ipso facto* immoral if occasionally necessary, they always will try to keep it down to the barest minimum. And if they believe, as Tolstoy did, that punishment has no deterrent value, they will make it a self-fulfilling prophecy by imposing the kind of derisory punishments that do not indeed deter.

If our teachers believe, as Tolstoy did, that children ought to be given total freedom to do what they like and not to do what they dislike, then their pupils are bound to grow up illiterate and unfit for real life. Hence the educational catastrophe we have suffered in the last 50 years, where ten years of "education" fails to teach many pupils how to read and write. Even more important, children grow up disconnected from their civilization—they no longer perceive it as their own, and they will do nothing to maintain it. On the contrary, as they will be more likely to see Western civilization as alien, they may try to kill it and dance on its grave.

If our governments believe, along with Tolstoy, that all private property is immoral, even if some of it regrettably has to be allowed, then they will feel self-righteous in plundering for their nebulous schemes most of what we earn in the sweat of our brow. Hence the swelling of our governments' coffers. And hence, paradoxically, the uncontrollable growth of the very state Tolstoy abhorred. This is yet another proof of the law of unintended consequences: assailing the state does not mean it will disappear. It only means that the traditional state will be replaced by a modern one, more powerful and less benign.

If we believe, along with Tolstoy, that our religion, and the way of life based on it, is no better than any other and worse than some, then we cannot muster the resolve needed to defend it. And that is precisely what is happening. Like Rome centuries ago, we have lost confidence in the spiritual foundations of our society. We no longer believe in our own goodness. Thus we can fall prey to those who have the resolve to destroy us so as to uphold some inferior creed for which, however, they are prepared to die.

If we believe, along with Tolstoy, that any war—regardless of who wages it and for what cause—is evil, then we are unlikely to be prepared to do battle for our country or civilization. And if nothing is worth either killing or dying for, then nothing is worth living for.

If we believe, along with Tolstoy, that all art must be pitched at the lowest common denominator so as to be equally accessible to everyone, then we shall end up with no art worthy of the name. We shall describe as music any cacophony produced by drugged, tattooed plankton. We shall regard as art dead animals pickled in brine. And what we shall see as literature will in no way resemble *War and Peace* and *Anna Karenina*.

And if we believe, along with Tolstoy, that marriage is by definition immoral, and we ought to remain celibate, then the whole world will come to an end. The end will be not so much physical as social. For, as celibacy runs against the grain of human nature, we shall continue to have sex. But marriage, like all traditional institutions, can die of neglect, and a tendency toward this is already observable. That can be the only real effect of Tolstoyan propaganda, regardless of its intent.

One would think that all such beliefs can only be held by either a stupid or an evil man. However, if we know, as we do in this case, that the man who held them was far from stupid, and arguably not even evil, then we have to look for a different explanation. And there is one: a gross metaphysical blunder at the starting point of all his thinking. This proved to be Tolstoy's undoing, especially since it was exacerbated by the character flaws we discussed earlier.

Lesson 3: Preaching wrong ideas can have fatal consequences not only for the preacher but also for the audience. Man is essentially good—proclaimed the count—therefore he does not need religion. Religion only makes him less good by robbing him of his own sterling resources and replacing them with superstitious lies.

He thus added his booming basso to the shrill choir of falsettos singing the militant hymn of destruction in Russia. At that time, Tolstoy could outshout all Russian Marxists put together. People who had never heard of Lenin would have read much of Tolstoy's prose. So it was mostly his thunderous voice clamoring for the destruction of the church that the Russian people heard. All the bolsheviks had to do was add a few murderous overtones. But, however much he proclaimed his non-violence, violence was always implicit in Tolstoy's sustained attack on all ancient institutions. For a cathedral will not destroy itself; it has to be blown up. If you call for the destruction, you ought to expect the dynamite.

Man is essentially good—proclaimed the count—therefore he does not need the state. If an elderly gentleman said that sort of thing over a cup of tea in a chintzy room somewhere, it would be silly but innocuous. But screaming that drivel off the rooftops in pre-revolutionary Russia was different. It was akin to a German philosopher proclaiming publicly in 1933 that, though obviously they ought not to be mistreated, Jews are essentially alien to Aryan culture. Such empty philosophizing at that time would instantly have been translated into action by people who did not know much philosophy but knew what they hated. That is precisely what happened to Tolstoy's half-baked ideas.

For at the time of his sermon, it was not the state in general that was falling apart. On the contrary, if any political trend can be said to describe modernity, it is its burgeoning statism. What was fighting for survival was not the abstract state but the concrete Russian Empire. And people who proceeded from a sounder metaphysical and philosophical base than Tolstoy knew that, far from perfect though that state was, what would follow it could only be worse.

Again, the bolsheviks had to add but a few touches to Tolstoy's sermon. Lev Nikolayevich is right, they were hissing into the people's ear, you don't need the state. And in due course we shall get rid of it; that's what communism is all about. But first things first, eh, Comrades? Socialism comes before communism. And people's power comes before socialism. The tsar's state stands in the way of people's power. So help us demolish the Russian state to start with, put us in power, and then, cross my heart and hope you die, in a few years we shall see what we can do about the state as such.

Tolstoy has a lot to answer for. But we have to thank him for the lesson though: beware of nihilist demagogues preaching destruction while insisting on their own non-violence. For destruction is always violent. If it was peaceful in intent, it will become murderous in reality. You cannot break eggs without breaking eggs, and never mind the omelet. If you cook it at all, it will come out burnt.

Lesson 4: Morality without eschatology is like a chair without legs. One can find some use for it, but ultimately it will prove uncomfortable. Tolstoy's attempt to replace God with morals sprang from the same metaphysical blunder as all his other ideas.

Morality was no longer seen as a bridge to eternity. As no tomorrow existed, what was utilitarian today was moral. By trying to pursue a moral life, we were no longer trying to imitate God. We were scratching our neighbor's back, hoping he would scratch ours in return. And only Tolstoy's commonsensical reason, higher than which nothing had ever existed, could determine what was utilitarian.

Thus loving not only one's neighbor but even one's enemy stopped being a condition for entry into the heavenly kingdom. It became a quid pro quo prescription for daily life. By loving my enemy, I can shame him into loving me. By offering no violence even to those who eminently deserve it, I shall receive none. And presumably if I do not eat animals, I will not be eaten by them, even though the kind of animals I am ever going to eat are unlikely to pay me back in the same coin anyway.

This approach turns morality into a utilitarian free-for-all. It may also render it inoperable. For different people have different ideas on utility, and those may be mutually exclusive. For example, to some the idea of murdering millions in their own generation for the sake of happiness in the next may sound moral. To some others, it may sound satanic. Who is right? Straight utilitarianism can find equally compelling arguments either way. We know which is right, but we shall not be able to prove it without declaring that human life is sacred. Yet this is an argument that is not only metaphysical but also religious. Human life is only sacred because man was created in the image of God, not because some of us happen to think it ought to be sacred.

The utilitarian argument simply does not add up in morals (or anything else, for that matter). That must be why it appealed to our hero. "The greatest good of the greatest number" was one idea of J.S. Mill that secured him a place in Tolstoy's pantheon. But both good and evil are qualitative, not quantitative concepts. Neither can be a matter of arithmetic; they can only be absolute metaphysical truths. For arithmetic will support the very argument we reject with so much revulsion: why not indeed murder millions if that may deliver the greatest good of billions? When morality is determined by Tolstoyan rationalistic utilitarianism, it runs every risk of becoming very immoral in short order.

Morality can only conquer on earth if it comes from heaven. The face of morality must be turned upward, not downward. The bloody history of the twentieth century was a direct result of the opposite belief, a vivid illustration of what happens when morality is divorced from faith or faith from God. Tolstoy used his nimble mind to concoct this gross philosophical swindle, and he milked his popularity as an artist to spread it around. Thus the non-violent count can be held responsible to a large extent for the violence that followed.

These days we are all Tolstoyans. We are all—well, most of us— ready to accept ersatz morals as real. Somehow, we think it immoral to follow a genderless antecedent with a masculine pronoun. Conversely it is moral to describe a chairman as if he were a piece of furniture. Our cripples are physically challenged. If we are short, we are challenged vertically. Our idiots are merely handicapped, as if they were race horses or golf players. We think women are as fit as men to lead a bayonet charge, and men as good as women at interior decoration—for to think otherwise would be regarded as immoral. We see egalitarianism in everything as the acme of morality, a road to secular salvation. Hidden behind all those puny moralets is the ethical chasm into which we have fallen by stepping over God in search of the good life. It is in the name of such bogus morality that we have destroyed our justice, education, family, language. And what have we replaced them with? Posh and Becks?

That is what happens when Tolstoyan ideas or something similar are repeated long enough and loudly enough. We buy them as real—and sell our souls as redundant in part exchange.

Lesson 5: Relativism is lethal when applied to God's truth. Absolutism is lethal when applied to God's world. Because true morality comes from heaven, it cannot be utilitarian—as all ideals, it can only be absolute. But that does not mean its practical application on earth cannot have some flexibility. It can and always will. Despising, as Tolstoy did, all intermediate steps on the way to absolute good can only lead to the triumph of absolute evil. If, for example, in the name of a moral ideal, killing a vicious burglar and strangling an old woman for her month's pension are both regarded as equally reprehensible murders, then the absolute moral standard is not so much upheld as destroyed.

Any serious attempt to enforce Tolstoyan moral absolutism will lead to the victory of evil in both religion and everyday life. But in his sermons Tolstoy was nothing if not absolutist, and we have seen that he used his extremism as a bludgeon swung at, well, everything. That is the only way absolutism can be used in practical life. On the other hand, relativism is a dread word to Christians. But Tolstoy teaches—in his usual negative way—its secular value in moderate doses. That is a hard lesson for a believer to swallow and digest. But it is essential for a balanced intellectual diet.

We just have to accept that this world will only become perfect when it ends. Until then it will remain flawed, as shall we all. Relativism begins when we acknowledge this and realize that, while even in temporal life evil is still evil and good is still good, there exist a spectrum of gradations in between. As the spectrum moves away from the absolute good, it becomes paler and the colors fade. Unless we are careful, soon they will disappear altogether, and evil will vanquish. What we must try to do is not allow the world to move too far in that direction, and we can only do that by fighting for every reasonable approximation of good—not only its ultimate expression.

In doing so, we must still not take our eyes off the absolute—not forget that in the end we shall be judged by an authority that will not let us cop a plea. So we must strive to prevent our fallible personalities from falling too hard and, to the best of our ability, to keep the world from collapsing too deeply into evil.

If you think that the last two paragraphs are contradictory, they are—but only as much as the dual personality of Christ. He understood and showed in his person something that Tolstoy never could grasp: man cannot live after he dies unless he lives before he dies. By refusing to accept any gradations of good, and insisting in his sermons only on one absolute good or nothing, Tolstoy did much to promote evil in real life. That is the only thing intransigent extremism can achieve—even if we happen to agree with the extreme idea.

Any example from real life can serve as proof. Let us say we are passionate in our defense of free enterprise. We have every reason to feel strongly about it: the prosperity of any society is directly proportionate to the amount of economic liberty and inversely proportionate to government interference. However, if we insist on extreme liberty, with the winners swimming in rivers of milk and honey, while the losers fall on the flinty shore from a great height, we shall create a storm with no safety boats available. The losers will become resentful, the winners decadent, and sooner or later an explosion will ensue. Our extreme economic virtue, along with assorted body parts, will be scattered all over the place, and evil will reign. A country that could have been relatively good will become absolutely evil. Similarly, if we overemphasize state protection for the losers, there will be no winners outside the government and its cronies.

"Ye shall know them by their fruits," says the Scripture (Matt. 7:16), adding in the next verse that "a corrupt tree bringeth forth evil fruit." Absolutism in this world is such a corrupt tree, and Tolstoy was one of its most successful gardeners.

Lesson 6: People who try to fashion their own faith will end up with none. People who want to reinvent God will become their own deity. Many these days are sympathetic to the one-man search for faith, Tolstoy-style. Most of them may not have read much Tolstoy, while some others may be conscious followers. But all those autonomous God-seekers owe a debt to our hero, whether they know it or not.

Faith is an act of submission, not self-assertion. Once a person has undergone the seismic shift from pride to faith, he can no longer regard his relationship with God as unique. God will be personal in that the believer will remain, through prayer and ritual, in one-to-one communion with him. But the believer will also be in communion with others who have undergone a similar shift. Together they will form the only true brotherhood known to man: that of God's children.

But children do not just have a father—they also have other authority figures, such as schools, who help their father take care of them. That is why no true believer can ever reject the church out of principle, though some may reject it out of laziness. A man cannot do so unless he arrogantly believes in his own religious self-sufficiency—unless he rejects the entire collective experience of mankind. But that experience goes back to the people who first received the revelation and then conveyed it to the world. Thus our seeker of spiritual self-sufficiency will inevitably end up denying the revelation and, in due course, any traditional faith. In other words, he has to follow Tolstoy's path. That means he is still governed by pride and nothing else, which can only mean that he has no faith.

What he may have instead is what Tolstoy had in abundance: a vague mystical longing. But pride will not let that feeling leave its physical shell and soar toward heaven. Instead it will continue to circulate within the person's head until before long it will be impossible to tell where one ends and the other begins. For such a person there will be no God but himself, and he will be his own prophet.

In this negative way Tolstoy teaches a valuable lesson to all of us. By his own folly he shows the pitfalls inherent in anticlericalism and what Voegelin called "the privatization of the spirit." One such pitfall is humanism with its concomitant self-deification, the replacement of God with man, which makes metaphysical confusion inevitable. That in turn is bound to lead to the kind of practical mistakes that can make even an intelligent man sound rather less so.

Even as the ultimate pitfall of anticlericalism is atheism, the ultimate pitfall of humanism is inhumanity. For man is not only a physical creature. Reduce God, as Tolstoy did, to the "desire for universal welfare" in this life, and there will not be much life for us to live. We shall be left staring at a gaping spiritual abyss—not unlike one we see closing in on us now.

Lesson 7: The Scripture does not lend itself to simplistic interpretation. Those who insist on biblical literalism either do not understand Christianity or, more likely, really wish to destroy it. You will have to make up your mind on which category Tolstoy belonged to, and I hope this book has been helpful in that regard. Either way, his call for a literal following of some of the Scripture (while ignoring its core) is traceable back to the same metaphysical blunder I mentioned earlier. Tolstoy misconstrued Christian metaphysics—and therefore Christian ethics—by reducing its two planes to one.

One plane, most comprehensibly described in the Old Testament, but also echoed in the New, is virtuous life on earth. The other, revealed in the New Testament, but also prefigured in the Old, deals with life in heaven, outlining the steps leading up to it. Only Christian metaphysics based on the person of Christ has managed to merge the two planes into a unity. This unity is a precarious balance of the human and the godly, the sacred and the profane, the physical and the metaphysical. It enables man to live until he dies, but also after he dies.

Both the founder of Christianity and his disciples understood that it has to exist on two planes if it is to exist at all. Conversely, those who rather hope it will not continue to exist know that, to achieve this end, they must upset the balance. This can be done only by throwing some extra weight either on one end or the other. People who at heart detest Christianity usually try both stratagems at one time or other. Tolstoy was such a man; he attempted to destroy the divine in man by dour rationalism—and the human in him by moralistic literalism. But the count only succeeded in destroying himself, thus teaching us another valuable lesson, which, alas, few of us will ever heed.

A parallel with music could illustrate the point about literalism. By and large, the greater the performer, the more liberties he is likely to take with the text. Mediocrities not blessed with the subtlety required to understand the spirit of the music dutifully stick to the letter of the score. In their deft hands all the notes come across, but little of the music. "Faithfulness to the score" thus becomes the undoing of every-thing sublime. But a great musician can grasp music in its entirety—he hears it as an overall structure containing the underlying spirit. That entitles him to the creative liberty of bringing out those details that best reveal the structure and downplay those that are peripheral. As a result, he will come much closer to the composer's intent than a plodding literalist ever could.

It takes creativity to understand a creator—and the same applies to understanding the Creator even within the narrow limits in which we are ever destined to understand him. As this kind of creativity is the lot of very few, for many centuries the church discouraged unmediated perusal of the Scripture. It knew that not many people possess the cre-ative ability to see the whole for the details. The church was also aware that biblical literalism could easily become an anti-Christian weapon for those who sought such weapons. And Tolstoy proves the church was right to be worried.

His destructive efforts serve to remind us of the pitfalls ever present in attempts to reinterpret the Scripture—even when such attempts are made in good faith. Unless the believer possesses a first-rate philo-sophical ability, he would be better off just reading the Bible the way one listens to music, without trying to rationalize it too much. And if he needs explanations, then 2,000 years' worth of probing metaphys-ical and theological study is always at his disposal—not to mention his church.

Lessons 8: Bad ideas will have bad consequences—and the scale of these is directly proportional to the grandeur of the man enunciating the thoughts. The world began with an idea (God's) and it can end with one (not only God's but, if we are not careful, our own as well). There is an idea behind every significant development in history, both good and bad.

In this life ideas come from people exercising their free will to the best of their ability. The overall course of history is determined by the law of God's design. It can be understood as a temporal pro-cess seeking its timeless fulfillment. But within time, history has no laws—it only has causes. And most of these are the consequences of ideas. Therefore, whenever an influential individual puts an idea to the public, he must exercise responsibility. He must weigh in advance the effect his idea may have on other people. He must be certain that he has considered every aspect and run it through the most rigorous of intellectual tests. He must never forget that, in however small a way, by enunciating a thought he makes history. A thought uttered may not always be a lie, as Tyutchev believed it was. But it always is a deed.

This view of history is at odds with Tolstoy's determinism. He believed that there were no causes in history, only laws. What those laws were he never explained in any detail, preferring instead to make the variously incoherent gnostic noises so beloved of those who have no faith. Since he never mentioned divine providence as a possible law, one must assume that Tolstoy believed in some secular tectonic shifts occurring of their own accord. He refused to see that a powerful personality can coax humanity into diverting the course of history. The count ignored both the creative and destructive potential of ideas.

Self-refutingly, he did hold the view that his own ideas, if no one else's, could have a profound effect on mankind. Tolstoy believed that he could do God's job of laying down the moral law, and forcing people to obey it by the sheer power of his genius. Consequently, the kingdom of God would arrive as bliss in this earthly life. In other words, while he did not believe that the ideas of others could change history, he was sure his own ideas could end it.

But ideas are like musical tones: even the purest of them will have dissonant overtones. In the case of Tolstoy's ideas, only the dissonances proved to be influential. For, as I have argued in this book, there was little positive substance to his thought—little that could pass the most rudimentary of intellectual tests. But the nihilistic overtones bypassed people's minds and wreaked much havoc by their destructive resonances—much in the way of a company of soldiers bringing a bridge down by marching in step.

And that is the last lesson taught by Leo Tolstoy: it is not only ships that can be sunk by loose lips. The century following his death showed the awful potential of ideas, especially those that promise bliss on earth. The echoes of an imploding world are still with us, and all the charges were set off by ideas. Many of them, not the biggest yet not the smallest, came from Leo Tolstoy.

Even though some of us may have thoughts on the subject, we cannot know for sure whether he caused harm wittingly or unwittingly. In either case, we should pray for his soul, hoping that when he faced God he was treated with mercy—something he himself had always denied his opponents.

RUSSIANS, REAL AND FICTIONAL, MENTIONED IN THIS BOOK

Aksakov, Konstantin (1817–60). Slavophile philosopher, served a prison term for criticizing serfdom.

Aksinia. Tolstoy's serf, mistress, mother of one of his illegitimate children.

Alexander I (1777–1825?). Tsar, whose death is still shrouded in mystery.

Alexander II (1818–81). Tsar, murdered by terrorists.

Alexander III (1845–94). Tsar.

Alexandra, Tsarina (1872–1918). Wife of Nicholas II, murdered by the bolsheviks.

Alexei, Prince (1690–1718). Heir to Russian throne, personally tortured and killed by his father, Peter I.

Alyoshka. Tolstoy's serf.

Ambrosius, Elder (1812–91). Chief monk at Optina monastery, one of the prototypes for Elder Zosima in Dostoyevsky's *The Brothers Karamazov*. Thought Tolstoy was "hopeless." Canonized in 1988.

Bagration, Pyotr (1765–1812). 1812 general of Georgian descent.

Bakunin, Mikhail (1814–76). Revolutionary and anarchist.

Barclay de Tolly, Mikhail (1761–1818). 1812 general of Scottish descent.

Behrs, Stepan (1855–1910). Tolstoy's brother-in-law, author of memoirs about him.

Berdiayev, Nikolai (1874–1948). Philosopher, expelled from Russia in 1922.

Bezukhov, Pierre. Character in *War and Peace*. Along with Andrei Bolkonsky, Tolstoy's mouthpiece.

Biryukov, Pavel (1860–1931). Tolstoy's secretary and propagandist.

Blavatsky, Helen (1831–91). Founder of theosophy.

Bogdanov, Alexander (1873–1928). Marxist writer and revolutionary.

Bolkonsky, Prince Andrei. Character in *War and Peace*.

Bolkonsky, Maria. Character in *War and Peace*.

Bolkonsky, old prince. Character in *War and Peace*.

Bolotnikov, Ivan (?–1608). Leader of uprising against Tsar Vasiliy Shuisky. Blinded and drowned.

Borodin, Alexander (1833–87). Composer, member of the "Mighty Handful" group.

Botkin, Vasiliy (1812–69). Writer, aesthete, Tolstoy's one-time friend in Petersburg.

Brodsky, Iosif (1940–96). Poet, sentenced to penal labor, expelled from Russia, winner of Nobel Prize for Literature (1987).

Bulgakov, Mikhail (1881–1940). Novelist, playwright.

Bulgakov, Sergei (1871–1944). Philosopher, theologian, economist. Expelled from Russia in 1922.

Bulgakov, Valentin (1886–1966). Tolstoy's secretary, author of memoirs about him.

Bunin, Ivan (1870–1953). Novelist, first Russian winner of Nobel Prize for Literature (1933). Emigrated from Russia in 1919.

Catherine II (1729–96). Tsarina, wife of Peter III in whose 1762 murder she was implicated. Possibly the greatest monarch in Russian history.

Chaadayev, Pyotr (1794–1856). Philosopher. Declared insane for his work *Philosophical Letters*, critical of Russia. Believed to have converted to Catholicism.

Chekhov, Anton (1860–1904). Short-story writer and playwright, often critical of Tolstoy.

Chernyshevsky, Nikolai (1828–89). Radical socialist writer. Sentenced to "civic execution," imprisonment, and exile.

Chertkov, Vladimir (1854–1936). Tolstoy's secretary and propagandist, accused by Tolstoy's wife of forging his will and having homosexual relations with him.

Danilevsky, Nikolai (1822–85). Slavophile writer, philosopher, naturalist, advocate of pan-Slavism.

Davydov, Denis (1784–1839). Hussar poet, organizer of partisan warfare during 1812 war.

Denisov, Vasiliy. Character in *War and Peace*.

Diaghilev, Sergei (1872–1929). Impresario, publisher, critic, founder of Ballets Russes in Paris.

Dmitry ("False"). Tsar in 1605–06, claimed to be Ivan the Terrible's son. Official history regards him as an impostor, though this is doubted by many historians. Murdered.

Dobrolyubov, Nikolai (1836–61). Influential critic, revolutionary democrat.

Dokhturov, Dmitry (1756–1816). 1812 general extolled by Tolstoy in *War and Peace*.

Dolokhov. Character in *War and Peace*.

Dostoyevsky, Fyodor (1821–81). Novelist.

Drubetskoy, Boris. Character in *War and Peace*.

Druzhinin, Alexander (1824–64). Writer, critic.

Erdenko, Mikhail. Gypsy violinist beloved of Tolstoy.

Fet, Afanasiy (1820–92). Poet, Tolstoy's friend and correspondent until they broke up.

Figner, Alexander (1787–?). Partisan leader during 1812 war.

Florensky, Pavel (1882–1937). Polymath theologian, philosopher, mathematician, electrical engineer, inventor. Shot in Soviet concentration camp.

Frank, Semyon (1877–1950). Philosopher, expelled from Russia in 1922.

Fyodorov, Nikolai (1829–1903). Philosopher.

Gogol, Nikolai (1809–52). Novelist, playwright, short-story writer.

Goldenweiser, Alexander (1875–1961). Pianist, lecturer, Tolstoy's friend and memoirist.

The Gorchakovs. Aristocratic family.

Gorky, Maxim (1868–1936). Novelist, playwright, Tolstoy's friend and memoirist. Probably murdered by Soviet secret police.

Griboyedov, Alexander (1795–1829). Playwright, statesman. Murdered in Persia.

Grigoriev, Apollon (1822–64). Poet, critic.

Grigorovich, Dmitry (1822–89). Writer.

Gurdjiev, George (1866–1949). Mystic, guru.

Hadji Murat (1790–1852). Caucasian resistance leader, one-time collaborator with the Russians, hero of Tolstoy's eponymous novella.

Helen, Princess. Character in *War and Peace*.

Igor, Prince of Chernigov (1152–1202). Scandinavian chieftain, hero of epic poem *The Lay of Igor's Host* and Borodin's eponymous opera.

Igor, Prince of Kiev. Scandinavian ruler of Kievan Rus (912–45).

Ivan Ilyich. Character in Tolstoy's novella *The Death of Ivan Ilyich*, regarded by Nabokov as the best ever written.

Ivan IV "The Terrible" (1530–84). Last tsar in Scandinavian dynasty.

Kandinsky, Vasiliy (1866–1944). Pioneer of avant-garde art.

Karakozov, Dmitry (1840–66). Terrorist, the only man executed in the 26-year reign of Alexander II.

Karamzin, Nikolai (1766–1826). Historian, poet, reformer of the Russian language.

Karatayev, Platon. Charcater in *War and Peace*, mouthpiece of Tolstoyan non-resistance.

Anna Karenina. Heroine of Tolstoy's eponymous novel.

Karsavin, Lev (1882–1952). Philosopher, expelled from Russia in 1922.

Katkov, Mikhail (1818–87). Conservative journalist and publisher.

Klyuchevsky, Vasiliy (1841–1911). Historian.

Korolenko, Vladimir (1853–1921). Liberal writer.

Korsakov, Sergei (1854–1900). First of great Russian neuropsychiatrists.

Kropotkin, Pyotr (1842–1921). "Anarchist prince," major influence on Tolstoy.

Kuragin, Anatol. Character in *War and Peace*.

Kutuzov, Mikhail (1745–1813). 1812 Commander-in-Chief, seen by Tolstoy as expression of Russia's metaphysical essence.

Leontiev, Konstantin (1831–91). Conservative philosopher, critic of Tolstoy.

Lenin, Vladimir (1870–1924). Bolshevik dictator.

Lermontov, Mikhail (1814–41). Poet, regarded by some Russians as second only to Pushkin.

Leskov, Nikolai (1831–95). Writer.

Lobachevsky, Nikolai (1792–1856). Mathematician, developed non-Euclidean geometry.

Lossky, Nikolai (1870–1965). Intuitivist philosopher, expelled from Russia in 1922.

Lunacharsky, Anatoliy (1875–1933). Lenin's Commissar for Enlightenment, wrote brochure on Tolstoy.

Lyovin. Character in *Anna Karenina*, Tolstoy's mouthpiece.

Malevich, Kazimir (1878–1935). Pioneer of abstract art. Banned in Russia under Stalin.

The Mamontovs. Wealthy philanthropists.

Mandelstam, Osip (1891–1938). Poet, died in Soviet concentration camp.

Melgunov, Sergei (1879–1956). Historian, expelled from Russia in 1922. Author of *The Red Terror* (1923), extensive record of bolshevik outrages.

Mendeleyev, Dmitry (1834–1907). Chemist, creator of the periodic table of elements.

Merezhkovsky, Dmitry (1865–1941). Symbolist poet, novelist, philosopher, historian. Nominated for Nobel Prize the same year as Bunin won it.

Meyerhold, Vsevolod (1874–1940). Director, one of the leading figures of modern theater. Executed by Soviets.

Mikhailovsky, Nikolai (1842–1904). Influential populist critic.

The Miloslavskys. Aristocratic family.

Morozov, Savva (1862–1905). Industrialist, philanthropist, patron of Moscow Art Theater. Through Gorky, funded bolsheviks, then was murdered by them in France.

Nabokov, Vladimir (1899–1977). Bilingual Russian-American novelist.

Nagornov. Husband of Tolstoy's niece.

Nastasia Filipovna. Character in Dostoyevsky's novel *The Idiot*.

Prince Nekhliudov. Character in several of Tolstoy's works, including *The Resurrection*.

Nestor. Monk, believed to have written the 1113 Primary Chronicle (*Povest Vremennykh Let*), though some historians dispute his authorship.

Nicholas II (1868–1918). Tsar, murdered by the bolsheviks together with his whole family.

Nekrasov, Nikolai (1821–78). Poet, Tolstoy's first publisher.

Nijinsky, Vaslav (1889–1950). Ballet dancer and choreographer, closely associated with Diaghilev.

Nikitin, Ivan (1824–61). Poet.

Oblonsky, Kitty. Character in *Anna Karenina*.

Oblonsky, Stiva. Character in *Anna Karenina*.

The Obolenskys. Aristocratic family.

Oleg, Prince. Scandinavian ruler of Kievan Rus (882–912), hero of Pushkin's poem.

Olga, Princess (890?–969). After her husband Igor's death, regent of Kievan Rus. First ruler to convert to Christianity, but failed to baptize all of Kiev.

The Ostermans. Aristocratic family.

Ostrovsky, Alexander (1823–86). Playwright.

Paul I (1754–1801). Tsar, murdered in palace coup.

Pavlov, Ivan (1849–1936). Neurophysiologist, discoverer of conditioned reflex.

Pecherin, Vladimir (1807–85). Radical professor of classics, regarded as Russia's first political emigrant (1836). Converted to Catholicism, ended life as monk in Ireland.

Peter I (1672–1725). Tsar, pushed through Westernizing reforms with extreme cruelty.

Peter III (1728–62). Husband and predecessor of Catherine II. Deposed and murdered, probably at her instigation.

Philaret, Metropolitan (1782–1867). Prominent clergyman and theologian.

Plekhanov, Georgiy (1856–1918). Marxist theoretician and revolutionary.

Pobedonostsev, Konstantin (1827–1907). Statesman, Ober-Procurator of the Holy Synod. Admired by Dostoyevsky. Driving force behind Tolstoy's excommunication.

Potemkin, Grigory (1739–91). Statesman, military leader. Favorite, believed to be secret husband, of Catherine II.

Pugachev, Yemelian (1740?–75). Leader of Cossack uprising. Captured and brought to Moscow by General Suvorov. Publicly quartered.

Pushkin, Alexander (1799–1837). Poet, widely regarded as Russia's greatest. Was to Russian language what Shakespeare was to English.

Radishchev, Alexander (1749–1802). Radical writer, imprisoned by Catherine II.

Rasputin, Grigory (1869–1916). Mystic, major influence on Nicholas II and especially his wife. Murdered.

Razin, Stepan "Stenka" (1630–71). Leader of Cossack uprising. Quartered alive in Red Square.

Richter, Sviatoslav (1915–97). Pianist, revered in Russia.

Roerich, Nikolai (1884–1947). Painter, theosophist. Posthumously excommunicated from Russian Orthodox Church in 2007.

The Romanovs (1613–1917). Ruling dynasty.

Rostova, Natasha. Character in *War and Peace*.

Rostov, Nikolai. Character in *War and Peace*.

Rozanov, Vasiliy (1856–1919). Writer, among the most original Russian thinkers. Starved to death under bolsheviks.

The Schukins. Wealthy philanthropists.

Segalin, Grigory. Early twentieth-century psychiatrist, first to analyze Tolstoy's work and personality from clinical point of view.

Shabunin, Vasiliy. Soldier tried and executed in 1866 for striking an officer. Tolstoy acted for his defense, using the trial for airing his opposition to capital punishment.

Shestov, Lev (1866–1938). Existential philosopher, emigrated from Russia in 1921. Analyzed Nietzsche's influence on Tolstoy (and Dostoyevsky).

Soloviov, Vladimir (1853–1900). Philosopher, theologian, critic of Tolstoy's non-resistance. Died a homeless pauper.

Solzhenitsyn, Alexander (1918–2008). Novelist, Nobel Prize winner (1973).

Sonia. Character in *War and Peace*.

Stalin, Iosif (1878–1953). Soviet dictator, died under mysterious circumstances.

Stolypin, Pyotr (1862–1911). Russian Prime Minister (1906–11). Tried to prevent revolution by introducing agrarian reforms. Murdered by terrorists.

Strakhov, Nikolai (1828–96). Philosopher, critic, Tolstoy's friend and correspondent.

Tairov, Alexander (1885–1950). Director, pioneer of modern theater. His Moscow theater was closed down in 1949.

Taneyev, Sergei (1856–1915) Composer, teacher. Friend of the Tolstoys.

Tchaikovsky, Pyotr (1840–93). Composer, critic of Tolstoy's music theories.

Tolstoy, Alexandra A. Tolstoy's aunt (cousin once removed) and love interest.

Tolstoy, Alexandra L. (1894–1979). Tolstoy's youngest daughter, emigrated from Russia in 1929, settled in the United States.

Tolstoy, Alexei K. (1817–75). Novelist, satirical poet, playwright. Tolstoy's distant relation.

Tolstoy, Alexei N. (1883–1945). Soviet novelist, "Red Count," admired by Stalin. Tolstoy's distant relation.

Tolstoy, Dmitry N. (1827–56). Leo's brother.

Tolstoy, Nikolai L. (1874–75). Leo's son.

Tolstoy, Nikolai N. (1823–60). Leo's brother.

Tolstoy, Sergei L. (1863–1947). Leo's son. Author of memoir about his father.

Tolstoy, Sergei N. (1826–1904). Leo's brother.

Tolstoy, Pyotr (1645–1729). First Count Tolstoy; received his title from Peter I for having tricked Prince Alexei back to Russia.

Tolstoy, Sophia Andreyevna (Sonia), née Behrs (1844–1919). Married Tolstoy in 1862.

Tolstoy-Miloslavsky, Nikolai (1935-). British historian, Tolstoy's distant relation.

Stravinsky, Igor (1882–1971). Composer.

The Tretiakovs. Wealthy philanthropists and patrons of art. Pavel Tretiakov (1832–98) endowed the famous Moscow gallery.

The Trubetskoys. Aristocratic family.

Turgenev, Ivan (1818–83). Novelist and playwright. Tolstoy's one-time friend and correspondent.

Tushin. Character in *War and Peace*, paragon of folk virtue.

Tyutchev, Fyodor (1803–73). Poet, commonly regarded, with Pushkin and Lermontov, as one of the best in nineteenth century.

Uspensky, Gleb (1843–1902). Writer.

Uspensky, Pyotr (1978–47). Occult mystic, follower of Gurdjiev.

Utochkin, Sergei (1876–1916). One of the aviation pioneers.

Varia. Tolstoy's niece, his favorite.

Viazemsky, Pyotr (1792–1878). Poet, Pushkin's close friend.

Vladimir, Prince (958–1015). Scandinavian ruler of Kievan Rus, which he baptized in 988.

The Volkonskys. Aristocratic family. Maria Tolstoy, née Volkonsky, was Tolstoy's mother.

Vorontsov, Mikhail (1782–1856). Statesman.

Vronsky, Alexei. Character in *Anna Karenina*. Unwitting agent of Anna's demise.

Yaroslavsky, Yemelian. Head of Lenin's League of the Militant Godless.

Yepishka. Tolstoy's serf.

Yeroshka, Uncle. Character in Tolstoy's novella *The Cossacks*.

Yudina, Maria (1899–1970). Pianist, persecuted under Stalin for her religious views.

The Zimins. Wealthy philanthropists.

APPENDIX 2

WORKS QUOTED OR REFERRED TO IN THIS BOOK

A few general points on the bibliography:

1) A list of all the works that have influenced my lifetime thinking on this subject would be awkwardly long, longer perhaps than the book itself. As that would be impossible to include, I limit myself only to those works whose titles I mention.

2) All biblical quotes come from the Authorized Version (King James Bible).

3) Unless otherwise specified, all Tolstoy's works are quoted from the Russian edition of his complete works (L.N. Tolstoy. *Polnoye Sobraniye Sochineniy*, Khudozhestvennaya Literatura, Moskva 1956–1964). For your convenience, the titles will be first listed in English, with the Russian-language titles and appropriate volumes from that edition added parenthetically.

4) The titles of works by other authors will be given in English, if available in that language, or, if not, in the language in which they were written.

5) *The Way of Life* (*Put Zhizni*) is here disproportionately represented among Tolstoy's quotations. Published posthumously, the book is the summation of his views on every subject he ever touched upon. In most cases, those views never changed throughout his life. When that is the case, he merely repeats the thoughts first communicated in his other works. When the book diverges from Tolstoy's earlier views, it should supersede others, being the last non-fiction work he wrote (or dictated), and therefore the concluding chapter of his canon.

WORKS BY LEO TOLSTOY

The Way of Life (*Put zhizni*, Vol. 45)

A Confession (*Ispoved*, Vol. 23)

The Gospel in Brief (*Kratkoye izlozheniye evangelia*, Vol. 24). I used the complete version of this book, which has never been translated into English (*Chetveroevangileye*, Moscow 2004)

The Death of Ivan Ilyich (*Smert Ivana Ilyicha*, Vol. 26)

Hadji Murat (*Khadji-Myurat*, Vol. 35)

What I Believe (*V chyom moya vera*, Vol. 23)

The Kingdom of God Within You (*Tsartstvo bozhiye vnutri vas*, Vol. 28)

The Critique of Dogmatic Theology (*Issledovaniye dogmaticheskogo bogosloviya*, Vol. 90)

What Is Art? (*Chto takoye iskusstvo?*, Vol. 30)

Response to the Holy Synod (*Otvet na opredeleniye sinoda*, Vol. 34)

War and Peace (*Voina i mir*, Vols 9–16)

Anna Karenina (*Anna Karenina*, Vols 18–20)

The Morning of a Wealthy Landowner (*Utro pomeshchika*, Vol. 4)

Resurrection (*Voskreseniye*, Vols 32, 33)

Childhood (*Detstvo*, Vol. 1)

Boyhood (*Otrochestvo*, Vol. 2)

Youth (*Yunost*, Vol. 2)

The Sebastopol Stories (*Sevastopol v avguste 1855g.*, *Sevastopol v dekabre mesiatse*, *Sevastopol v maye*, Vol. 4)

Lucerne (*Lyutsern*, Vol. 42)

The Romance of a Landowner (*Roman russkogo pomeshchika*, Vol. 3)

Diaries (*Dnevniki*, Vols 48–58, 90)

Letters (*Pisma*. Vols 59–90)

On Life (*O zhizni*, Vol. 26)

The Cossacks (*Kazaki*, Vol. 6)

Three Deaths (*Tri smerti*, Vol. 6)

I Cannot Remain Silent (*Ne mogu molchiat*, Vol. 37)

The Kreutzer Sonata (*Kreitserova sonata*, Vol. 27)

So What Is to Be Done? (*Tak chto zhe nam delat?*, Vol. 25)

WORKS ABOUT TOLSTOY

Behrs, Stepan. *Vospominania o grafe L.N. Tolstom*, Smolensk 1894

Berlin, Isaiah. *The Hedgehog and the Fox*, Weidenfeld and Nicolson 1953

Biryukov, P. *Leo Tolstoy: His Life and Works*, Standard Publications Inc. 2007

Bulgakov, V. *The Last Year of Leo Tolstoy*, Hamish Hamilton 1971

Chertkov, V. *The Last Days of Tolstoy*, Heinemann 1922

Gorky, M. *Reminiscences of Lev Nikolayevich Tolstoy*, B.W. Huebsch, Inc. 1920

Gourfinkel, Nina. *Tolstoï sans Tolstoïsme*, Editions du Seuil 1946

Green, Martin. *Tolstoy and Gandhi, Men of Peace: A Biography*, Basic Books Inc. 1983

Ilyin, V. *Mirovozreniye L'va Tolstogo*, Russki Khristianski Gumanitarnyi Institut 2004

Johnson, Paul. *Intellectuals*, Weidenfeld and Nicolson 1988

Lenin, V. *Articles on Tolstoy*, Fredonia Press 2001

Maude, Aylmer. *The Life of Tolstoy: The First Fifty Years*, Vol. 1, Oxford Paperbacks 1987

Merezhkovsky, D. *Tolstoy i Dostoyevsky*, Respublika 1995

Nabokov, Vladimir. *Lectures on Russian Literature*, Weidenfeld and Nicolson 1982

Plekhanov, G. *Znacheniye tvorchestva L'va Nikolayevicha Tolstova*, Proletariy 1921

Shestov, Lev. *Dostoevsky, Tolstoy and Nietzsche (The Good in the Teaching of Tolstoy and Nietzsche)*, Ohio University Press 1969

Shirer, W. *Love and Hatred: The Tormented Marriage of Leo and Sonya Tolstoy*, Simon and Schuster 2007

Soloviev, V. *A Soloviev Anthology*, Saint Austin Press 2001

Steiner, George. *Tolstoy or Dostoyevsky?*, Yale University Press 1996

Tolstoy A. (Aleksandra Tolstaia). *The Countess Tolstoy's Later Diary 1891–1897*, Kessinger 2008

Tolstoy T. (Tat'ana Tolstaia). *Tolstoy Remembered*, M. Joseph 1977

Tolstoy, N. *The Tolstoys: Twenty-four Generations of Russian History, 1353–1983*, Hamish Hamilton 1983

Tolstoy, S. *Tolstoy Remembered by His Son*, Weidenfeld and Nicolson 1961

Tolstoy, The Diaries of Sophia, Book Sales 1987

Tolstoya, S.A. *Pisma S.A. Tolstoy*, Zapiski 1989

Troyat, Henri. *Tolstoy*, W.H. Allen (Virgin Books) 1968

Weiner, L. *Tolstoy on Education*, The University of Chicago Press 1967

Wilson, A.N. *Tolstoy* (Penguin Classics), Penguin 1989

Yevlakhov, A.M. *Konstitutsionalnyie osobennosti psikhiki L.N. Tolstogo*, Moscow 1995

OTHERS

Aquinas, St Thomas. *Summa Theologiae: A Concise Translation* (ed. McDermott, Timothy), Christian Classics 1991

Aristotle. *Politics*, BiblioBazaar, LLC 2006

Augustine, St. *The City of God* (Penguin Classics), Penguin 2003

Augustine, St. *The Confessions of St. Augustine*, Fleming H. Revell 2005

Boot, Alexander. *How the West Was Lost*, I.B. Tauris 2006

Chesterton, G.K. *Orthodoxy*, Ignatius Press

Collingwood, R.G. *Essays on Metaphysics*, University Press of America 1991

Cooper, Fenimore and Twain, Mark. *The Last of the Mohicans* & *Fenimore Cooper's Literary Offenses*, Wilder Publications 2007

Diagnostic and Statistical Manual of the American Psychiatric Association, The (IV edn)

Dostoyevsky, F. *The Idiot*, Penguin 1973

Dostoyevsky, F. *The Diary of a Writer*, Olympic Marketing Corporation 1979

Dostoyevsky, F. *The Brothers Karamazov*, Dover Publications 2005

Dostoyevsky, F. *The Possessed*, BiblioBazaar, LLC 2006

Dostoyevsky, F. *Crime and Punishment*, Penguin 2007

Gogol, N. *Three Plays*, Methuen Drama (5 Aug 1999)

Gogol, N. *Dead Souls*, Dover Publications 2003

Griboyedov, A. *Polnoe sobranie sochinenii v trekh tomakh*, Notabene 1995

Kant, I. *Critique of Practical Reason, and Other Works on the Theory of Ethics*, Longmans, Green & Co 1954

Kant, I. *"Toward Perpetual Peace" and Other Writings on Politics, Peace, and History (Rethinking the Western Tradition)*, Yale University Press 1991

Kant, I. *The Critique of Pure Reason*, Phoenix 1993

Klyuchevsky, V. *Kurs Russkoi Istoriyi*, Novosibirsk 2000

Knowles, A.V. *Turgenev Letters*, Scribner Book Company 1983

Kothari, M.M. *Critique of Gandhi* (Halo of Divinity Series), Critique 1996

Leontiev, K. *Vostok, Rossiya i slavianstvo*, Moscow 1993

Lermontov, M.S. *A Hero of Our Time* (Penguin Classics), Penguin 2001

Melgunov, S. *Red Terror in Russia*, Hyperion 1975

Muggeridge, Malcolm. *Jesus Rediscovered*, Doubleday 1979

Pipes, Richard. *Russia under the Old Regime*, Penguin 1995

Plato. *The Republic*, Penguin 1974

Prokhorov, A.P. *Russkaya model upravlenia*, Biblioteka Eksperta 2006.

Pushkin, Alexander. *Tales of Belkin and Other Prose Classics* (Penguin Classics), Penguin 1998

Renan, Ernest. *The Life of Jesus*, Promotheus Books 1991

Rousseau, Jean Jacques. *The Confessions of J.J. Rousseau*, The Echo Library 2007

The Russian Primary Chronicle Samuel H. Cross (ed.), Medieval Academy of America 1968

Tertullian. *The Apology*, Kessinger 2004

Trigg, J.W. (ed.). *Origen*, Routledge 1998

Turgenev, I. *Fathers and Sons* (Oxford Paperbacks), Oxford University Press 1998

Turgenev, I. *Literary Reminiscences and Autobiographical Fragments*, Ivan R. Dee 2001

NOTES

1 INTRODUCTION

1. Soloviov, Leontiev, Fyodorov, S. Bulgakov, Shestov, Berdiayev, Florensky, Frank, Lossky, Merezhkovsky, to name a few.
2. Johnson brilliantly described Tolstoy as "God's elder brother." I wish I had thought of it first.
3. By contrast, Dostoyevsky was hardly published in the USSR until Stalin's death in 1953.
4. Alexander Boot, *How the West Was Lost*, I.B. Tauris, 2006.
5. Modern parallels are crying out to be made, but they would be too obvious and much too numerous.
6. I shall be referring to Tolstoy's fiction at times—one cannot help doing that—but only in the context of this book. Otherwise, I shall rely on his non-fiction: *A Confession, What I Believe, The Kingdom of God Within You, The Critique of Dogmatic Theology, What Is Art?, Response to the Holy Synod, Tolstoy's Gospel, The Way of Life*, his diaries, letters, and articles.

2 UNCOVERING THE SECRET

1. Hereinafter the translation of Tolstoy's (and most other Russian) quotes will be my own. I would not mind using received translations, but they are often inaccurate. For example, Tolstoy's promise of founding a "religion without faith and sacraments" often comes across as a "religion without dogma and mysticism," which is not at all the same thing.
2. According to a recent clinical study, 87 percent of all poets suffer from some form of psychopathology; among geniuses this figure has to be even higher.
3. The feminine ending "a" ought to be dropped when rendering a Russian woman's name in English. Thus Mr Putin's poor wife should be Mrs Putin, not Mrs Putina. However, one finds it hard to buck an established tradition. Therefore I shall be referring to Mrs Karenin as Anna Karenina, and the same goes for Natasha Rostova and Tolstoy's other heroines.
4. I shall again bow to tradition and from now on refer to Tolstoy as "Leo" and not "Lev," although it is hard to see why we should anglicize his name (even though he himself did so when writing letters in English). After all,

we do not refer to Gogol as "Nicholas," to Dostoyevsky as "Theodore," or to Turgenev as "John."

3   What Kind of Man Would Take On God?

1. In fact, he was dismissed twice: first from the course in Oriental languages, then, upon re-entering, from the law school.

2. The estate came from the Volkonskys on his mother's side. The paternal estate had been drunk and gambled away by the previous generations of the Tolstoys.

3. Turgenev hated *Lucerne*, describing it as "a mixture of Rousseau, Thackeray and the abridged Orthodox catechism."

4. To Tolstoy's credit, though he disliked Jews, he never quite matched Dostoyevsky's visceral anti-Semitism. To Tolstoy's discredit, he never quite matched Dostoyevsky's metaphysical depth either.

5. Stepan Behrs, '*Vospominania o grafe L.N. Tolstom*,' Smolensk 1894.

6. Tolstoy sometimes uses the words *khristianstvo* (Christianity) and *pravoslaviye* (Russian Orthodoxy) interchangeably, and sometimes he does not. When he does, I shall translate the latter as the former, so as not to confuse the reader into thinking that Tolstoy finds fault only with the Orthodox confession, not Christianity in general.

7. Lyovin, Tolstoy's *alter ego* in *Anna Karenina*, appears under the name of Lenin in an early draft. Considering that the name does not really exist in Russia, and V.I. Ulyanov only adopted it as his *nom de révolution* some 30 years later, this coincidence must mean something, though I am not sure what. However, it is clear that Lenin, though he knew Tolstoy's wavelength was different from his own, sensed it was in the same band.

8. A.M. Yevlakhov. *Konstitutsionalnyie osobennosti psikhiki L. N. Tolstogo.* Moscow 1995. Unless otherwise specified, all quotations in this subsection, including those from Tolstoy, are cited from this book.

9. One way or the other, though Tolstoy was the best writer *in* the Russian language, he was not the best writer *of* the Russian language. That distinction, depending on whom you talk to, belongs to Pushkin, Lermontov, Gogol, or Chekhov. For what it is worth, my vote goes to Gogol.

10. Let us add parenthetically that it is partly Tolstoy's attention to physical details, if sometimes exaggerated, that gives his prose its immense three-dimensional presence.

11. I could quote hundreds of passages like this but shall not, for fear of losing you as a reader.

12. "Gypsies" at that time meant gypsy restaurants with live music on stage and a brothel backstage. As such they were favorite night-time destinations for dissipated youths with a taste for orgies.

13. Fermented mare's milk.

14. The diminutive suffix "ka" is often used in Russian to convey contempt. Landowners always added it to their serfs' names—or, until the late eighteenth century, to their own when addressing the tsar, whose serfs they themselves were deemed to be.
15. Dostoyevsky is another example of this.
16. My feeble attempt to translate the Russian "*Lyova, ryova.*"
17. At one point Tolstoy decided he could uncover the mystery of music by writing down village songs. Only a mocking rebuke by Tchaikovsky, who told him to stop that nonsense and stick to what he knew, made Tolstoy give up that project.
18. Interestingly, it was for taking part in those "monstrosities" that the Tolstoy clan got its title. The diplomat P.A. Tolstoy was thus rewarded for tricking the tsar's son into returning to Russia, which the sensitive youngster, unable to stomach the carnage unleashed by Peter, had fled. Promised safe passage by Tolstoy, young Alexei went back, only to be tortured and then beheaded by the tsar personally. Peter must have believed in the maxim "Spare the axe and spoil the child," as did the first Count Tolstoy.
19. Tolstoy's niece.
20. We shall discuss the philosophical ramifications of this passion later. Kant, another strong influence on Tolstoy, also cherished Rousseau, but he merely kept his portrait in his study.
21. Actually, Utochkin, one of the aviation pioneers in Russia, flew through the air quite well.
22. She probably did not mind the rebuke. Tolstoy's visitors expected to be told off; that was part of the attraction. It is a bit like New Yorkers frequenting bars known for "insult bartenders."
23. A blatant example of the mythology surrounding Tolstoy is the émigré philosopher Vladimir Ilyin writing that the count was blessed with a lifelong happy marriage.
24. My emphasis—this is one of many instances of Tolstoy unwittingly admitting his atheism.
25. Optina *pustyn*, the favorite destination of Russian pilgrims, especially those primarily inclined toward mysticism.
26. Actually, Leontiev was not locked up. He lived in a cottage next door to the monastery.

4 Religion Without Faith, Christianity Without Christ

1. "That is why," quipped Chesterton in his *Orthodoxy*, "so few people ever get there."
2. As we shall discuss later, it is amorphous mysticism, rather than true religiosity, that is a characteristic Russian trait.

5 A CONFESSION THAT WAS NOT QUITE

1. The situation in Europe was somewhat similar and, one suspects, for similar reasons.
2. For an artistic development of this theme, see Dostoyevsky's *Crime and Punishment* and *The Brothers Karamazov*.
3. Strakhov was also close to Tolstoy, but the wealthy count was too preoccupied with the plight of mankind at large to help his friends.
4. False modesty was not among Tolstoy's most salient vices.
5. By varying accounts, between 40 and 60 percent of Russian peasants at that time were Old Believers, which is to say schismatics.
6. Later Tolstoy said that Jesus never "uttered a single word" about personal resurrection. This is the first few of many such words I shall quote.
7. The war was only partly altruistic: Russia was also pursuing her geopolitical objectives in the Balkans.
8. My emphasis—Tolstoy repeats this thought *ad infinitum*, and I love it so much.
9. Of his brother.

6 TOLSTOY'S FAITH, SUCH AS IT WAS

1. It is interesting to see how Tolstoy, who fancied himself as a great religious reformer, did not have much time for other great reformers, such as Luther. Diary entry of March 1884: "What a stupid phenomenon this Luther's Reformation is. Here's the triumph of narrow-minded stupidity." But then we know how Tolstoy felt about rivals.
2. It was Schopenhauer who had shown the way to Tolstoy.
3. Note the detail: "amid the gardens." This one touch makes the whole scene come to life. It also makes us regret that Tolstoy did not stick to what he did best.
4. "Labyrinthine" thinking mentioned by Yevlakhov is evident here.
5. I added the emphasis to remind you of Tolstoy's tendency to repeat the same words within short passages, which Yevlakhov ascribed to his epilepsy.

7 THE GOSPEL ACCORDING TO LEO

1. The church recognizes Paul as an apostle, but it goes without saying that Tolstoy did not.
2. That was about 30 years earlier—another example of Tolstoy's laudable consistency over a lifetime.
3. The complete version I used never has been translated into English.

4. So "understanding" in John refers to Christ after all. What was wrong with the Word then? But then the hullabaloo with Logos unfolded quite some pages earlier. Perhaps Tolstoy forgot what he had written. Or, more likely, "allegedly" is the operative word in the whole passage: as far as Tolstoy was concerned, Jesus revealed anything only allegedly but not really.

5. "Seeming" is the operative word here. Christ was not a dialectician à la Hegel; his contradictions were really not contradictory. They did not just resolve into a unity; they were part of a unity to begin with.

6. Had Tolstoy read the Psalms before claiming that Jesus rejects the Old Testament altogether?

8 DESPERATELY SEEKING GOLGOTHA

1. Quoted from preface to L.N. Tolstoy, *Polnuye sobrania sochineniy*, Moscow 1956.

2. Opinions are divided on whether or not those two actually converted to Catholicism.

3. The church only got around to excommunicating Roerich in 2007, 60 years after his death.

4. Actually, less so. Tolstoy infinitely preferred "the faith of the Brahmins."

5. Mikhail Bulgakov writes about this hilariously in the opening chapter of *Master and Margarita*.

9 SEX, LIES, AND ETHICS

1. We shall discuss Tolstoy's take on nonresistance in a subsequent chapter.

2. Nabokov's wife denied this vehemently against all evidence.

3. The names of many of Tolstoy's protagonists hint at their prototypes. For example, Lyovin in *Anna Karenina* is etymologically related to Lyova, a diminutive of Tolstoy's Christian name.

4. Note his persistent use of pejorative terms ("*devka*" or "*baba*" in Russian) when talking about women. This is widespread among Russian homosexuals, though of course not limited to them.

10 AN IMPRACTICAL IDEA OF A PRACTICAL LIFE

1. Bach may have been one exception, but then he was exceptional in every way.

2. Music is capable of conveying this drama better than any other art, which is why it is the most indigenously Christian, metaphysical art.

3. At the time of this writing, one cannot recall many synagogues or churches in theocratic Mecca or Medina.

4. Soloviov exemplifies the malaise of Russian intellectuals, which is the opposite of the Anglo-Saxon tendency. A deep and original thinker on philosophy and theology, he was much weaker on politics, economics and law. Characteristically, N. Lossky's *History of Russian Philosophy* devotes 57 pages to Soloviov and only two to all the Russian philosophers of law combined.

5. Karakozov, along with Lenin and Tolstoy, was another illustrious alumnus of Kazan University. One wonders what they added to the canteen food there.

6. Obviously, Kant was unfamiliar with the works of either Edmund Burke or Joseph de Maistre, to name just two observers whose hearts were not exactly overfilled with joy.

7. Yet another example of the Old Testament presaging the New. One wonders if Tolstoy ever read the Bible in its entirety.

8. When Alexander III heard of Tolstoy's entreaties that he should forgive his father's murderers, he replied, "I could only forgive an attempt on my own life." Coming as it did from a head of state, that answer was more consistent with Christian ethics than were Tolstoy's animadversions.

9. Unless otherwise specified, all Tolstoy quotations in this subsection are taken from *The Way of Life*.

10. Some Protestant sectarians argue that the wine Jesus drank was non-alcoholic. This goes to show that the freedom of religious self-expression has its downside.

11. Tolstoy here repeats Joseph de Maistre's argument in favor of the Salic law ("it is written in the hearts of Frenchmen"). Isaiah Berlin shows that in *War and Peace* Tolstoy quoted, without attribution, whole pages of de Maistre's articles on history. Obviously, he read his other works with similar attention. De Maistre, who appears in *War and Peace* as a minor character, was a prominent figure in Russia where he lived for years as Sardinian ambassador. He was eventually expelled when the tsar found out that under his ultramontane influence Russian aristocrats had begun to convert to Catholicism *en masse* (as did, for example, Princess Helen in *War and Peace*).

12. In *The Diary of a Writer* Dostoyevsky describes in terrifying detail the characteristic savagery of a peasant taking a belt or a stick to his trussed-up wife, lashing at her, ignoring her pleas for mercy until, pounded into a bloody pulp, she stops pleading or moving. However, according to the writer, this in no way contradicted the brute's inner spirituality, so superior to Western materialistic legalism. Ideology does work in mysterious ways.

13. Then came the collectivization, and it was 10–15 million peasants who got murdered. "What goes around comes around" is an unkind thing to say, but usually true.

14. Ivan Bunin describes this instant conversion with hair-raising pathos in *The Accursed Days*.
15. Unless otherwise stated, Tolstoy's quotes in this subsection come from this work. The title was borrowed from another socialist gospel, the novel by N.G. Chernyshevsky. Later, Lenin chose a version of the same title for his pamphlet on revolutionary tactics. Show me who your friends are...
16. Exactly the same thing later happened to Soviet Stakhanovites. Their record-breaking outputs drove up the production quotas for everybody else, which everybody else hated. The issue was often settled with wrenches and crowbars.
17. Solzhenitsyn wrote in his *Gulag* that "no one in old Russia ever starved to death." That is simply false, not to mention ideologically driven.
18. Nabokov did get the job later.
19. Unless otherwise specified, the quotations in this subsection are taken from that work.
20. Obviously, we are talking about works of art here, not *The Da Vinci Code*.
21. Have you ever met an "aesthetical physiologist"? This job description does not figure prominently in the Appointments pages these days, but perhaps it did in Tolstoy's time.
22. Above all, art *is* a pleasure. If he means that art is not a *frivolous* pleasure, then why not say it? Kant, for example, regarded art as a pleasure of the highest sort, but this came in one of his later works that must have escaped Tolstoy's attention.

11   TOLSTOY AS A RUSSIAN

1. Twain lauded Russian terrorists in *Free Russia*: "If such a government cannot be overthrown otherwise than by dynamite, then thank God for dynamite!" Here is another writer who refused to stick to what he knew best.
2. Alexander spoke French with a better accent than Napoleon, which did not go down well with the latter when the two met trying to avert a war in 1812. Possibly in retaliation the proud Corsican hinted at the role Alexander had played in the murder of his father, after which no reconciliation was possible.
3. *Povest' vremennykh let*, the source of most knowledge about early Russia.
4. The *Chronicle* was written while the Vikings ruled Russia, which must have affected the veracity of this document. That is understandable. Even Shakespeare falsified the War of the Roses by demonizing Richard of York and extolling Henry VII, whose granddaughter was on the throne at the time *Richard III* was written.

5. The word meant "mercenary soldier." Many Varangians' names were later Russified. Thus Ingvar became Igor, Helgi Oleg, and Helga Olga. Actually, Helgi was not even a name but a nickname. It meant "military leader," something the gentleman definitely was, and also "magician," which he probably was not.

6. Arthur Koestler traced the origin of all European Jews back to that event, claiming they were actually the Khazars dispersed by the Russians. This theory is as imaginative as it is imaginary.

7. The word "intelligentsia" was at that time similar to "nihilists" in meaning. In spite of their Latin roots, both words were invented in Russia.

8. Gogol's play *Inspector General* reads like documentary evidence.

9. Richard Pipes covers the property situation in Russia well in his *Russia under the Old Regime*. And one recent book I have drawn on is *Russkaya model upravlenia* by A.P. Prokhorov, Moscow (2006).

INDEX